ICEBOUND *in the* ARCTIC

'A rarity in polar biography: a page-turner'
Arctic Book Review

'Wonderfully detailed and graphic account'
Irish Examiner

'A welcome addition to the polar library'
Sunday Business Post

'[Michael Smith] is consolidating a reputation as champion of those unsung heroes
who deserve greater recognition than history had given them'
Irish Independent

'A riveting read'
Newry Reporter

Michael Smith is an authority on polar exploration who has appeared on TV and radio and lectured extensively. His books include: *An Unsung Hero: Tom Crean; I Am Just Going Outside*, a biography of Captain Oates; *Polar Crusader* about Sir James Wordie; *Tom Crean – An Illustrated Life*, *Great Endeavour – Ireland's Antarctic Explorers*; and *Shackleton: By Endurance We Conquer*. Michael is a former award-winning journalist with *The Guardian* and *The Observer*.

ICEBOUND *in the* ARCTIC

The Mystery of
Captain Francis Crozier
and the Franklin Expedition

Michael Smith

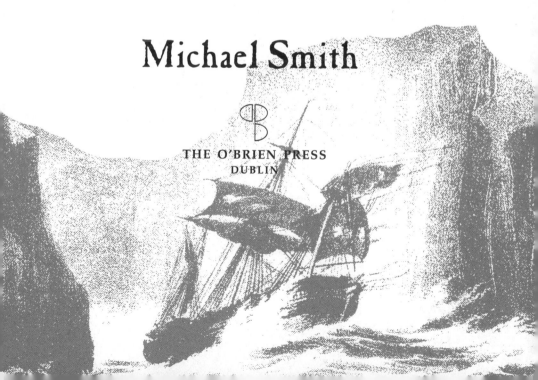

THE O'BRIEN PRESS
DUBLIN

First published as *Captain Francis Crozier: Last Man Standing*
2006 by The Collins Press. Reprinted 2014
This edition published 2021 by The O'Brien Press Ltd,
12 Terenure Road East, Rathgar, D06 HD27, Dublin 6, Ireland.
Tel: +353 1 4923333; Fax: +353 1 4922777
E-mail: books@obrien.ie
Website: www.obrien.ie
The O'Brien Press is a member of Publishing Ireland.

ISBN: 978-1-78849-232-4

9 8 7 6 5 4 3 2 1
24 23 22 21

Front cover: Image of Francis Crozier courtesy of National Maritime Museum, London.
Image of the ship courtesy of Alamy.
Back cover: Image of *Erebus* bell, courtesy of Parks Canada.

Printed and bound in Drukarnia Skleniarz, Poland.
The paper in this book is produced using pulp from managed forests.

Picture credits

The author and publisher thank the following for permission to use photographs and illustrative material:
Alamy pp1, 3, 16, 142, 201, 251, 265; Crozier Family pp170, 252, 266; Institute of Geophysics of the
Czech Academy of Sciences. Photo: Hana Hamplova p260; Getty Images p263; Regina Koellner p272;
National Maritime Museum, London pp8, 155, 177, 186; National Portrait Gallery, London pp39,
212; Parks Canada p283 Royal Geographical Society p44; Royal Society p269; Michael Smith pp2, 183;
Tasmanian Museum & Art Gallery p118. Maps by Michael Murphy, University College Cork.
*If any involuntary infringement of copyright has occurred, sincere apologies are offered, and the owners of such
copyright are requested to contact the publisher.*

Published in
DUBLIN
UNESCO
City of Literature

Dedication

This book is dedicated to those who mean most to me:
Barbara, Daniel, Nathan, Lucy and Zoe.

Acknowledgments

This book could not have been written without the help and support of a large number of people, and I am extremely grateful to all those whose assistance has made it possible to chronicle the life of Francis Rawdon Moira Crozier. Any omissions are unintentional.

Special mention should go first to those members of the Crozier family who gave me valuable support and every encouragement to write this biography. They willingly provided documents and detailed knowledge about the family and its most famous son. I extend my sincere thanks to Carol Crozier, James Crozier and John Crozier for their help and much-appreciated kindness, and to Rodney Freeburn who has been of considerable assistance. In particular, I am deeply indebted to Martin Crozier, who generously and enthusiastically shared his unrivalled knowledge of the Crozier lineage and who was a constant source of assistance. Sincere thanks.

The people of Banbridge – the birthplace of Francis Crozier – are evidently very proud of their close association with such an illustrious figure, and the town's pride was reflected in the warmth of my reception and the support I received during my research. Personal thanks must go to Jason Diamond of Banbridge Genealogy Services, whose help and co-operation have been invaluable. His thoughtful contributions at the outset were very important to my research and I owe him a great deal. Mention must also be made of Evelyn Hanna and the staff of Banbridge Library, who were always helpful and generous with access to the archives and with local knowledge. I also acknowledge the assistance of Lissa O'Malley at Armagh City, Banbridge and Craigavon Borough Council.

I am grateful to Brenda Collins of the Irish Linen Centre and Lisburn Museum and Berni Campbell of Central Library, Letterkenny. I am particularly indebted to the late Shirley Sawtell for her patient endeavours on my behalf in the library of the Scott Polar Research Institute and to Robert Headland, former archivist, for access to the Institute's archives.

I would also like to acknowledge the obliging archivists and other staff at Ballynahinch Library; Berkshire Record Office; British Library; National Archives; Mike Bevan, David Taylor and Barbara Tomlinson and staff at the National Maritime Museum; National Portrait Gallery; Public Record Office Northern Ireland; Mary Chibnall in the library of the Royal Astronomical Society; Julie Carrington and staff at the Royal Geographical Society; Matthew Sheldon, head of research collections at the Royal Naval Museum; Royal Society; Dr Norman Reid, keeper of manuscripts at St Andrew's University; and the Archive Office of Tasmania; Alan Derbyshire at the Victoria &

Albert Museum Conservation Department; Emma Dadson of Harwell Restoration; Zoe Reid, Senior Conservator at the National Archives of Ireland; Paul Cook, Senior Paper Conservator at the Royal Museums Greenwich.

I received valuable assistance from John Hagan, a native of Banbridge now living in Tasmania. He gave me important advice and valued help in researching and understanding the association between Francis Crozier and Tasmania. I must also thank Doris Hagan for her contribution.

Frank Nugent – a member of the first Irish party to sail the North West Passage – was a generous and considerate supporter of this book. I will always be grateful to him for his unselfish assistance and willingness to share his considerable knowledge of Ireland's long involvement in polar exploration.

I must place on record my gratitude to Ryan Harris, Head of Survey for the Underwater Archaeology Team at Parks Canada who generously shared his time and specialist knowledge of the search for *Erebus* and *Terror*. His insight and first-hand experience were hugely important to understanding the modern-day challenge of locating the ships, and I am grateful.

My thanks must also go to Regina Koellner, an enthusiastic and generous supporter of Francis Crozier, who was always ready to help with constructive and valuable suggestions. Crozier himself would have been impressed with her passionate commitment to his story. I am also grateful to Russell Potter, an authority on Arctic exploration, who was generous with his knowledge. I am also indebted for the helpful advice I received from Dr Jim McAdam, David Murphy, Maria Pia Casarini, Louie Emerson and Horace Reid.

Where possible, I have identified all known sources of the material used in this book and provided full accreditation where it can be properly established. I have also made every reasonable effort to trace copyright holders of documents and photographs. Any omissions are unintentional and I would be pleased to correct any errors or oversights.

I owe a special debt of gratitude to Joe O'Farrell, a learned and inquisitive observer of polar history, who generously read the manuscript and provided much thoughtful and constructive advice. Thanks, Joe.

It would not have been possible to write this book without the astute involvement of my two sons, Daniel and Nathan, whose skill and patience in handling my incessant requests for assistance with modern technology has been invaluable. Without their calming influence, this book might well have been written with a quill and ink.

Finally, I must say a huge personal thanks to Barbara, my wife. She was unwaveringly supportive and patient, and these few lines can never fully express my deep gratitude.

Contents

Francis Rawdon Moira Crozier, explorer, sailor and scientist.

Notes

In general, the terminology in use during the nineteenth century is employed in this book and where necessary, the modern version is also included. For example, Van Diemen's Land refers to Tasmania (in use after 1855) and I have generally used Great Fish River or Back's Great Fish River which was in use at the time and is today known as Back River.

The question as to how to refer to the native people of the Canadian Arctic during the age of exploration is difficult. Although the most acceptable term today is 'Inuit', the term 'Eskimo' (or 'Esquimaux') was commonly used during the nineteenth century, when most events in this book took place. For the purposes of this book, I use Inuit and only employ Eskimo where it comes from a direct quotation or reference. Alternatively, significant events in this book occurred around King William Island which is called 'Qikiqtaq' in the Inuktitut language. For simplicity, I refer to King William Island which was in widespread use at the time. No discourtesy is intended.

The punctuation, spelling and grammar used in original quotations are faithfully repeated, however erratic they may be.

Temperatures are shown in Fahrenheit with conversion into Celsius and weights are generally given in imperial measure with approximate metric conversions. Distances are usually given in statute miles with rough conversion to kilometres. Data from the UK National Archives and the Bank of England provide an approximation of the current purchasing power of past monetary values.

Pointing the Way

In April 1848, Captain Francis Crozier, by then in command of the largest expedition ever sent to discover the North West Passage, scribbled a nine-word message on a scrap of paper, signed his name and placed the note in a tin cannister before vanishing into the Arctic wilderness. Crozier's note was discovered eleven years later, and for the next 160 years explorers, scientists and enthusiasts followed the clues he left in an attempt to solve the mystery of what lay behind the biggest disaster in the history of polar exploration.

The most significant breakthrough has come in recent years with the remarkable discovery of the expedition ships, *Erebus* and *Terror*, lying in shallow waters above the Arctic Circle. Crozier did not launch the crusade for clues, but his message sent the crusaders in the right direction.

The precise wording of Crozier's message was: 'And start on tomorrow 26th for Backs Fish River.' Although ambiguous and lacking much detail, the note at least revealed Crozier's intentions and gave generations a clear indication of where to search in the vast, scarcely populated Arctic waste-lands stretching for at least 800,000 square miles (over 2,000,000 square kilometres).

The crucial document, which was found in 1859, was a regulation navy form traditionally left to indicate a vessel's geographic position to those sent in search of a missing ship. Most of the words added to the printed document were written in the margins by the captain of *Erebus*, James Fitzjames, who outlined past events, such as the party's geographical position at the time of abandoning the ships and news of the expedition leader, Sir John Franklin's, death.

Crozier's short message, which is squeezed into a corner of the document and appears almost as an afterthought, is the only surviving written clue to the expedition's plans for escape. Due to the lack of space, he wrote the short message upside down in the corner of the document.

It was a pivotal discovery which sent generations to the barren area along the western and southern coasts of King William Island, leading to a trail of skeletons, scattered debris and ultimately the wrecks of *Erebus* and *Terror*. One authority said it was 'the most evocative document in the long history of Western exploration of the Arctic regions'.

The unfortunate venture is generally known as the Franklin Expedition after Sir John Franklin, who was appointed as leader at the outset. However, Franklin had died a year before Crozier wrote his terse message. While Franklin led his men into the jaws of the ice, the responsibility for leading them out fell into the hands of Captain Crozier.

The search which followed was extraordinary by any standards. The North West Passage expedition initially left London in May 1845 and was last seen on the edge of Baffin Bay in July of the same year, with all 129 on board *Erebus* and *Terror* reportedly in good spirits. The first relief expeditions were sent north in 1848 and over the next few years around forty ships combed the labyrinth of Arctic waterways in a vain attempt to trace the missing men. The official naval search ended in 1854, nine years after the expedition sailed, and the privately financed *Fox* expedition under the leadership of Leopold McClintock discovered the document and Crozier's key message in 1859.

McClintock's return was the signal for the start of an unprecedented quest to uncover what happened to Crozier and his party. Over the next 160 years, at least fifty official and unofficial expeditions ventured into the Arctic, hoping to solve the mystery or to retrieve scattered relics from the snow. The true number of searches is impossible to calculate because so many private groups travelled unannounced to the area. However, more parties went in search of the dead than were ever sent to find the living.

A breakthrough was achieved in 2014 and 2016 when specialist teams found the expedition's ships, *Erebus* and *Terror*, on the sea floor in remote waters above the Arctic Circle. Experts believe the hugely significant discoveries will go a long way towards answering many questions and are eagerly analysing the large variety of objects already retrieved from the depths.

However, locating the ships is only the first stage of a long and complex process. Assorted relics like the ship's bell from *Erebus*, Victorian era scientific instruments and discarded clothing and shoes were the first objects recovered. But the biggest prizes yet to be claimed are the expedition's logbooks, charts and even personal letters which experts believe have survived decades under water and can be safely reclaimed for historians to pore over and analyse. Overall, the full investigation of the secrets kept by *Erebus* and *Terror* will take at least ten years or possibly more.

It will also provide an important opportunity to explore the remarkable story of Captain Crozier, particularly as there was considerably more to Crozier's life than an unrecorded death somewhere in the Arctic.

Crozier was among the most prolific and under-valued explorers of the age. He entered the navy as a child, survived the brutal Napoleonic War and emerged to sail with great distinction on six expeditions to the ice in an outstanding naval career lasting almost forty years. Crozier was deeply involved in the nineteenth century's three great endeavours of maritime discovery – navigating the North West Passage, reaching the North Pole and mapping Antarctica. Only Crozier's great friend, Sir James Clark Ross braved more polar expeditions.

There is a perception that all the great stories from the history of polar exploration involve the outstanding figures of the 'heroic age' of Antarctic discovery in the early twentieth century, such as Roald Amundsen, Tom Crean, Robert Scott and Ernest Shackleton. All are rightly saluted for their memorable exploits, yet to focus entirely on this era would be mistaken. There are other half-forgotten explorers who made history and yet have been neglected by history. Such a man was Francis Rawdon Moira Crozier.

Francis Crozier, who sprang from an old-established Irish family over 200 years ago, was the pioneer whose voyages opened the doors of the Arctic and Antarctic for the more recognised figures who followed in his wake. For example, the destination in *The Worst Journey in the World*, the famous book about a hazardous journey to Cape Crozier during Captain Scott's last expedition in 1911, was discovered by Crozier and Ross in 1841. Other landmarks familiar to readers of Antarctic history – McMurdo Sound, Ross Island, Mount Erebus and the Great Ice Barrier (now Ross Ice Shelf) where Scott died – were discovered and named by Crozier and Ross sixty years before Scott and Shackleton landed on the continent.

As one of the few early explorers to venture into both the Arctic and Antarctic regions, it might be assumed Crozier would be known from pole to pole for his accomplishments. But fame and recognition have eluded him. He was a modest, unassuming man who somehow never strayed into the limelight and received limited reward for his prodigious efforts. He was honest, dependable and without a hint of vanity, although he never rose above the rank of Captain.

Unlike others, Crozier was never asked to write a book about his voyages and adventures in places which others could only dream of visiting. Sadly, he did not live long enough to enjoy a peaceful retirement, writing his memoirs and savouring a little of the limelight. Alone among the era's renowned circle of polar explorers in the first half of the nineteenth century – including Back, Franklin, Parry, Richardson and Ross – Crozier did not receive a knighthood for his great endeavours.

Crozier faded from history in the years after his death. Only the assiduous efforts of a hard core of admirers, particularly around his hometown of Banbridge, County Down, have kept the memory of Francis Crozier alive. The towering Crozier monument in the centre of Banbridge is a permanent reminder of this regard.

I have always nursed a fondness for the unsung hero, the neglected individual whose character and achievements are underestimated or have been overlooked by history. It was this curious fascination that led me to write the first biography of the indestructible Irish polar explorer, Tom Crean. The title, *An Unsung Hero,* seemed singularly appropriate.

Crozier is another unsung hero. He was an exceptional explorer poorly treated by history, who deserves far wider recognition for accomplishments that would have been remarkable in any age of exploration. Helped by the new discovery of *Erebus* and *Terror,* we now have the perfect moment to re-open the file on Crozier.

This is the first comprehensive biography of Crozier and it has a simple aim: to place Francis Rawdon Moira Crozier among those exceptional individuals who shaped Arctic and Antarctic history.

CHAPTER 1

A Bond with History

The long line to Francis Rawdon Moira Crozier can be reliably traced back 600 years and with less certainty by a full 1,000 years. It is appropriate that a man who left such an indelible mark on history should emerge from a distinguished family whose fortunes over the centuries were intertwined with history itself.

Crozier's earliest-known ancestors originated in France and later settled in England. Family members migrated to Ireland in the seventeenth century and created a dynasty of Irish Croziers whose most illustrious son was Francis Crozier.

The clue to his origins comes from the name 'Crozier' itself, which derives from the French word *croise*, meaning crusader. In Old French – in use up to the fourteenth century – the name was written *Crocier*, which is more akin to the present-day English spelling. Over the years, the family name has been variously spelt Croyser, Crozer, Croisier, Crosier and Croysier.

The ancestors of Francis Crozier were of Norman descent and first emerged when they joined the armies of William the Conqueror to invade England in the momentous year of 1066. After they defeated the English at the Battle of Hastings, large swathes of captured lands were given to William's supporters, including Robert le Brus, who was to establish a line of Scottish kings. The Croziers were among the closest allies of le Brus, whose most notable descendant was Robert the Bruce, the Scottish king who triumphed over the English at Bannockburn in 1314.

Members of the Crozier family followed le Brus into newly acquired estates in the north of England and later settled along the notoriously volatile border between England and Scotland in the ancient county of Cumberland (now Cumbria). During the following centuries, generations of Croziers established themselves as landowners in Cumberland and in the fertile valleys alongside the Liddel and Teviot rivers to the south of the old Scottish town of Hawick.

Some Croziers were among the villainous freebooters – called 'moss troopers' – operating along the unruly frontier between England and Scotland, where robbery, kidnap and murder was rife. Sir Walter Scott's classic poem *Rokeby* (1813) refers to an incident where 'a band of moss-troopers of the name Crosier' murdered a well-known landowner in the borders.[1]

Others led a more peaceful existence, notably William Crozier, who was among the band of scholars credited with helping to create Scotland's first university at St Andrew's in 1411. Around this time emerged Nicholas Crozier, the man identified as the founder of the Irish strain of Croziers.

Nicholas moved from the Cumberland town of Cockermouth in the early 1420s to start a new life on farmlands at New Biggin near the small village of Heighington, County Durham. Over the years, the Heighington Croziers put together a sizeable estate of around 1,000 acres and built a fine home named Redworth Hall (a modernised Redworth Hall still stands on the site). It was from these roots set down by Nicholas Crozier in the fifteenth century that the Irish Croziers would emerge around 200 years later.

John Crozier, a seventeenth-century cavalry captain, was the first member of the family to settle in Ireland. He left the Durham estate in the early 1630s as part of Britain's scheme to subdue Ireland through the mass plantation of Protestant settlers from Scotland and England into the province of Ulster, resulting in wholesale land seizures and a seismic shift in power away from the Catholic majority. The reverberations of the plantation are still felt to this day.

Captain Crozier was a member of the troops stationed at Dublin Castle to guard Sir Thomas Wentworth, the newly appointed Lord Deputy of Ireland. Wentworth, a key advisor to King Charles I and a ruthless reformer, was later created Lord Strafford and executed for treason in the sinister political struggles which led to the outbreak of the English Civil War in 1642 and the rise to power of Oliver Cromwell.

Crozier, perhaps sensing the growing political turmoil and impending civil war in England, decided to remain in Ireland with his family and build a new life. His father, Nicholas Crozier, sold parcels of land from the family estate in Durham to pay for his son's new home and within a century the Croziers owned more than 1,000 acres of prime land in the north of Ireland.

The Croziers were part of the large Presbyterian community that settled around the counties of Antrim and Down. They cemented their social status over the years with a succession of well-chosen marriages into other leading northern families, among them the Magills and Johnstons. At this time, a family motto was developed: *Dilengta fortunae matrix*; Hard work is the mother of success.

In 1692, Captain Crozier's youngest son William moved to Gilford, County Down with his three sons, John, Samuel and William. Here, he bought a sizeable estate named Loughans from a local landowner, Sir John Magill. The property was later renamed Stramore ('great valley') and divided in two. The lowland portion, called Lower Stramore, was given to William's second son, Samuel, while John, the eldest son of William Crozier, occupied the upland property to the northwest of Gilford, named Upper Stramore. An adjoining estate – The Parke – was purchased for the youngest son, William.

Among the direct descendants of the Croziers from Upper Stramore was Francis Crozier. Two years after moving to Upper Stramore, John

Crozier married Mary Fraser, a member of the eminent Lovat family, one of Scotland's oldest and wealthiest landowning dynasties. Like the Croziers, the Frasers are originally thought to have come to England with William the Conqueror.

John and Mary had eleven children; their ninth son, George, married Martha Ledlie of Ardboe, County Tyrone in 1742, and was Francis Crozier's grandfather. The union of George and Martha yielded a family of six children.

The youngest son, also named George, married Jane Elliott Graham from Ballymoney Lodge in the small but rapidly developing nearby town of Banbridge, County Down. It was another fruitful marriage and George Crozier and his wife Jane produced a family of thirteen children – seven girls and six boys – including Francis Crozier.[2]

Francis Crozier was born into a prosperous, well-to-do family, led by his astute and enterprising father, George. He was a successful solicitor who manoeuvred the family away from its traditional sphere of property owner-ship and soldiering and built one of Ireland's most successful legal prac-tices. George Crozier was also a man who made the most of high-ranking friends and a generous slice of good fortune.

The key to his commercial success was a close association with the Marquis of Downshire and Lord Moira, the heads of two of the richest and most powerful landowning families in Ireland. George Crozier's legal firm on occasions acted for both Downshire and Moira, links which provided an entrée into the upper reaches of Irish society and, with it, affluence. The bonds were strengthened in later years when George's son Thomas assumed control of the business and became renowned as Downshire's solicitor in Ireland.

The Croziers' association with the Downshire and Moira families went back almost 200 years. The Downshire line in Ireland was established by Moyses Hill, an Elizabethan soldier who came from Devon in 1573. The Hills later acquired estates at Cromlyn – from the Irish *cromghlin* ('crooked

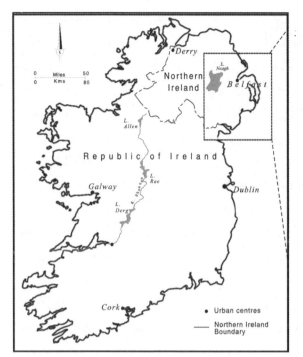

Ireland (indicating Banbridge, County Down).

Banbridge, County Down.

glen') – to the south of Belfast and subsequently became close neighbours of the early Croziers. Wills Hill, the first Marquis of Downshire, built the historic Hillsborough Castle in the 'crooked glen' almost two centuries after the arrival of Moyses Hill.

The Moira dynasty was established by Major George Rawdon, a soldier from Yorkshire who sailed to Ireland in the 1630s with Captain John Crozier and who settled at Moira on Down's border with Antrim, a few miles to the north of the flourishing Crozier estates at Stramore. By the late eighteenth century, George Crozier's circle of friends included Francis Rawdon, the second Earl of Moira, the distinguished soldier and colonial statesman who later became Lord Hastings.

Apart from powerful friends, George Crozier also had abundant good fortune on his side thanks to the rapid emergence of the Irish linen industry and the Industrial Revolution, which brought an explosion of commercial activity around Banbridge in the eighteenth century. Over the space of only a few decades, the once sleepy settlement on the banks of the River Bann – known as Ballyvally until the turn of the eighteenth century – was transformed into a thriving industrial community as local farmers turned to bleaching linen at the numerous falls that punctuate the river.

The gradual introduction of machinery-propelled linen making from a modest cottage industry to a dynamic modern enterprise and by the time of Francis Crozier's childhood in the early 1800s, Banbridge boasted the largest linen market in County Down. Cloth from the town was exported to mills in England, Scotland and even America. The few miles on the River Bann between the small towns of Banbridge and Gilford were a bustling scene of activity which one eyewitness eloquently described as a 'continued theatre of beauty, genius and commerce'.

In 1791, George Crozier took full advantage of his prosperity and position to build a house in the centre of Banbridge. His new home, originally called Avonmore House but subsequently renamed Crozier House, was an impressive Georgian mansion situated opposite the parish church in

The birthplace of Francis Rawdon Moira Crozier in Church Square, Banbridge, County Down. The property, built in 1791, was originally called Avonmore House and became known as Crozier House.

Church Square, Banbridge. Spread over three floors and with an ample basement, the house – it still stands – features above its entrance a lunette decorated with the sleeping Venus and Cupid.

It was at Avonmore House in the early autumn of 1796 that the eleventh child of George and Jane Crozier was born. The precise date of birth is not clear, though it is thought to have been 17 September. The boy, the couple's fifth son, was named Francis Rawdon Moira Crozier after Francis Rawdon, the Earl of Moira.

Little is known about the early life of the young Francis beyond the certainty that it was a privileged upbringing in a typically religious household. He attended Henry Hill School in Banbridge, run by the Presbyterian minister, Reverend Nathaniel Shaw.

However, his birth was followed by a period of upheaval in Ireland with the emergence of the radical Society of United Irishmen, a revolutionary organisation aimed at uniting the Catholic and Protestant communities to overthrow British rule. In the schism which followed George Crozier was forced to steer a delicate path between the Downshires and the Moiras, who took opposite sides in the conflict.

Downshire, the embodiment of the establishment, wrote that George Crozier's family was 'one of only four or five [Presbyterian] families in Banbridge' opposed to the United Irishmen. George Crozier backed the winning side in the dispute. The United Irishmen were roundly defeated and in 1801 Ireland became an integral part of the United Kingdom under the Act of Union – the first time that all parts of the British Isles were subject to single rule.

But despite the outcome, the Crozier family soon began to shift their faith from the traditional Presbyterian roots to the Anglican Church of Ireland. In the following years, family members became ministers in the Church of Ireland.

One indisputable fact about the early life of Francis Crozier is that he enjoyed only a short childhood. In the summer of 1810, at the age of thirteen, Francis was plucked from the cosy security of the family home and sent off to join the Royal Navy. The decision to send young Francis to sea remains a mystery, even though it was customary to dispatch youngsters with sea-going ambitions into the navy as early as ten years of age. Many of those who later earned fame in the polar regions during the nineteenth and twentieth centuries – among them Edward Parry, James Clark Ross and Robert Scott – began their naval careers somewhere in the years between childhood and adolescence.

But the enrolment of Francis in the navy was at odds with the pattern elsewhere in the Crozier family at that time. Although earlier generations of Croziers had served as soldiers, George Crozier appears to have broken the mould by steering his sons towards peaceful occupations in the Church or the world of commerce. Two sons – William and Thomas – followed their father into the legal profession, while Graham, the youngest, became a Church of Ireland vicar.

Francis was the exception and it is unclear why George Crozier allowed his young son to forego his affluent life in Banbridge for the brutal rigours of the Royal Navy, which at the time was deeply embroiled in the bloody Napoleonic Wars with France. The Battle of Trafalgar, the most decisive naval engagement of the war, had been fought only five years before the fresh-faced teenager from Banbridge enlisted, while the Peninsular War, one of the key campaigns, was at that very moment in full swing. More than 90,000 British seamen alone were destined to die in the war which claimed the lives of approximately 5,000,000 combatants and civilians.

So eager was George Crozier to get his son into uniform that he turned to his influential coterie of friends for help. During the early months of 1810, he approached Lord Downshire to pull a few strings at the Admiralty. Downshire contacted Lord Vincent, a well-connected family friend who only a few years earlier held the supreme rank of First Lord of the Admiralty. The seventy-five-year-old grandee, who had over half a century of military campaigns to his name, knew all the right people and shortly afterwards Francis was readily accepted into the navy.[3]

Francis Crozier, still three months short of his fourteenth birthday, made the journey from boyhood to manhood when he travelled south from Banbridge to the port of Cork in the summer of 1810. He formally enlisted on 12 June and his first posting was aboard *Hamadryad*, a 34-gun warship stationed at Cork. It was the beginning of a lifetime of duty and devotion to the Royal Navy.

CHAPTER 2

To the Arctic

The Napoleonic Wars, a defining moment in British history, provided an epic backcloth to the early naval career of the youthful Francis Crozier. The Peninsular War, the long campaign in Spain and Portugal that destroyed the myth of French invincibility, was into its second year when Crozier sailed under Royal Navy colours for the first time. In 1812, less than two years after Crozier's enlistment, Napoleon launched his catastrophic invasion of Russia. The Battle of Waterloo, the final and decisive act of the war, was fought only five years after Crozier enlisted.

The navy was a critical factor in the war, and the defeat of Napoleon provided Britain with a century of virtually unchallenged supremacy on the high seas. When Crozier joined in 1810, the navy commanded an awesome fleet and could muster around 143,000 men. It was the heavy defeats the navy inflicted on Napoleon's fleet and the rigorous naval blockades of French ports, cutting off supplies and destabilising the economy, which proved so important in the ultimate defeat of France.

Crozier's maiden voyage on *Hamadryad* was typical of the era. After escorting merchant vessels across the Atlantic to the Newfoundland Banks, *Hamadryad* returned to Lisbon with fresh troops for the Peninsular campaign. From the outset, Crozier found himself among veterans of the sea.

Sir Thomas Staines, *Hamadryad*'s captain, had lost an arm in battle, and the ship itself, which was originally a Spanish vessel captured off Cadiz in 1804, had a colourful past.

Conditions at sea were in stark contrast to the sheltered, comfortable surroundings of Banbridge. Life afloat in the early nineteenth century was rough, hazardous and enforced by a strict code of discipline that was barbaric by today's standards.

Fortunately, Crozier joined as the navy was making a slow transition from the brutality and primitive conditions of an earlier age to a more humane regime with better pay, food and hygiene. This was due to the new regulations introduced by the Royal Navy as a result of the Admiralty enquiry into the mutinous seizure of Captain William Bligh's *Bounty* in 1789. But navy warships of the time were still invariably dirty and overcrowded and hundreds of men would struggle for space in the dimly lit and smoky recesses below decks. *Hamadryad*, a frigate, accommodated about 200 men.

Punishment was mercilessly severe, although considerably more lenient than in earlier years when miscreants were subjected to keelhauling or had their right hand nailed to the mainmast. Flogging was still commonplace in Crozier's time and offenders in the early nineteenth century could expect at least three dozen or more lashes, depending on the whim of the captain.

Accidents and disease – scurvy, yellow fever and typhus – were a far bigger danger to men than enemy cannon or muskets. Only 6,000 of the 90,000 deaths on navy ships during the war were as a result of enemy action. By contrast, over 70,000 men were lost due to fatal sickness, wounds or mishap.

Despite the hazards, it appears that Crozier made the adjustment to his new life with great aplomb and that he learned fast. He soon picked up the tools of his trade – navigation, mathematics, tidal calculations and general seamanship – which offered the route to advancement and promotion for any would-be officer.

At the end of 1812, the sixteen-year-old Crozier gained his first promotion when he was appointed midshipman, the lowest officer rank. It appears he impressed his senior officers, and Sir Thomas Staines took Crozier with him when he was appointed captain of *Briton* in 1812.

A 44-gun frigate, *Briton* was plunged straight into action, policing the dangerous waters in the Bay of Biscay where French and American ships tried to outrun patrolling British ships and get their precious cargoes into ports such as St Malo and Bordeaux.

In June 1812, the navy was forced to open a new front when America declared war on Britain, a conflict that would last until 1815 and end in stalemate. Crozier was summoned into action when *Briton* was deployed to escort a convoy of 49 merchant ships around the Cape of Good Hope to the East Indies. When one of the merchantmen became disabled during a violent storm, *Briton* ushered the damaged ship into Rio de Janeiro for repairs. At Rio, Captain Staines was ordered to change course to the Pacific and to assist *Phoebe* and *Cherub* in arresting *Essex*, an American frigate harassing British whalers.

The orders meant taking *Briton* alone around Cape Horn against the prevailing strong westerly winds. Rounding the Horn in a sailing vessel is invariably a precarious voyage and Crozier endured a ferocious baptism as *Briton* was assailed by violent storms that incapacitated over 100 crewmen – about half the ship's complement. After a hair-raising trip, *Briton* docked at the Chilean port of Valparaíso in late May 1814, where it was discovered that the *Essex* had already been apprehended.

Briton was now ordered to sail thousands of miles across the Pacific towards the Galapagos Islands and the more remote Marquesas Islands, where Staines was to link up with *Tagus* in pursuit of another American frigate. It was a long, hot voyage across the open expanse of the Pacific and though *Briton* and *Tagus* failed to track down the American frigate, the ships did find signs that the *Essex* had been active in the area before its apprehension.

On Nuku Hiva – one of the largest islands in the Marquesas group – the navy found remnants of a village and fort built by the Americans, who had claimed it for the United States and named it Madison Island after the sitting US President. Staines had other ideas and promptly took formal possession for Britain.

Crozier used his time in the Marquesas to collect specimens of weaponry from the friendly islanders. On his return to Ireland, he presented the collection to the Marquis of Downshire and the weapons were subsequently put on public display at Hillsborough Castle in 1881.

The trip from the Marquesas back to South America in September 1814 was eventful, due to sloppy navigation by the *Briton* and *Tagus*. Navigators miscalculated longitude by a margin of three degrees and came across an unknown island that did not appear on Admiralty charts of the time. Staines moved closer to the heavily wooded coastline and was surprised when four canoes appeared and approached the ship. He was even more surprised when men in the canoes spoke to him in perfect English. He soon discovered that everyone on the remote island spoke English.

The island was Pitcairn and its English-speakers were the direct descendants of the mutineers from Captain William Bligh's *Bounty*. The mutineers and local Tahitians first arrived on the island in 1790 and *Briton* and *Tagus* were only the second outside vessels to reach Pitcairn, an isolated and rugged volcanic spot of barely 2 square miles (3 square kilometres) across.

The little community-in-exile numbered 46 men, women and children when *Briton* and *Tagus* anchored offshore in 1814 and among those greeting the visitors from the Old World was Thursday October Christian, the son of the mutiny leader, Fletcher Christian.

A more noteworthy figure on Pitcairn was John Adams, the last survivor of the original band of mutineers. A stocky and heavily tattooed figure in his early fifties, Adams cheerfully showed the British naval officers around his paradise 'kingdom'. Pride of place was a library of books plundered from *Bounty*, each carefully inscribed with the distinctive signature of Captain Bligh.

When Staines made a tantalising offer to take Adams back to England, the ageing mutineer was sorely tempted. After nearly twenty-five years in hiding, the promise of a return to his homeland was almost irresistible. But his Polynesian wife and family were distraught at the prospect, fearing that Adams would be hanged for his part in the mutiny. Adams – sometimes called Alexander Smith – reluctantly agreed to stay on Pitcairn and he lived the rest of his days in exile. He died in 1829, aged around sixty-five.

Briton and *Tagus* returned to Valparaíso in early 1815, before taking another voyage round Cape Horn. Their arrival in England on 7 July 1815 came just three weeks after Napoleon's defeat at Waterloo, which signalled an end to the Napoleonic Wars.

The following year – 1816 – saw Crozier assigned to the 38-gun frigate *Meander* on guard duty on the River Thames. In 1817, he passed the Admiralty exams for mate and joined *Queen Charlotte*, a first-rate warship of 104 guns patrolling the English Channel. In 1818, at the age of twenty-two, Crozier was posted as mate to *Dotterel* – a 387-ton, 18-gun brig-sloop – where he served for three years.

One of his first missions was to bring urgently required provisions to the isolated South Atlantic island of St Helena, where Napoleon had been exiled after his defeat at Waterloo. Supply ships from Britain had failed to reach the small community and the *Dotterel* formed part of a convoy to bring relief to the islanders.

Crozier's advancement coincided with a period of major upheaval in the navy, which was forced into huge changes when the Napoleonic Wars ended. By a twist of fate, this disruption was to lead Crozier into polar exploration.

The Royal Navy was at that time the world's most powerful fighting machine. But it was an enterprise geared to war and heavily over-provisioned for peace. As the peaceful era of the 1820s approached, the fleet was largely idle and the Admiralty was faced with the major headache of how to deal with thousands of unwanted men.

Managing the ordinary seamen was brutally simple. By 1817, more than 100,000 sailors had been thrown back onto the streets from which most had been press-ganged. But most officers were men of patronage or wealth and not so easily discarded from the payroll. As Joseph Hume, the radical reformer, noted at the time: 'Promotion in the army and navy was reserved for the aristocracy'. Despite the massive overmanning, the number of officers actually rose in the years following the end of the war, though nine in ten were unemployed.

The logjam of superfluous officers was a huge barrier to further advancement, particularly as any new commissions were invariably granted to officers based on their age. Admirals were often still in service at the age of eighty, and some officers spent decades without ever securing a meaningful posting. By the 1820s, the chances of junior officers such as Crozier progressing up the ranks were slim.

Into the post-Napoleonic breach came the unlikely figure of John Barrow, an accomplished civil servant at the Admiralty who proposed a variation on the biblical exhortation to turn 'swords into ploughshares'. Barrow's solution was exploration.

Sensing the urgent need to redirect the navy's efforts, he was to resolutely shape the nation's policy on exploration for the next thirty years and 'fathered' a generation of explorers, including John Franklin, Edward Parry, James Clark Ross, and Francis Crozier.

John Barrow was an *éminence grise* who for over four decades quietly wielded enormous power from his office at the Admiralty. He was the last civil servant to see Nelson alive before Trafalgar in 1805 and it was Barrow's suggestion in 1816 to send Napoleon into exile on St Helena.

Untypical of the elite who ran the country or controlled the military machine, Barrow was propelled to the heart of government by sheer intellect and driving ambition. The son of a poor hill farmer from near the Cumbrian town of Ulverston, he left school at thirteen and continued to study the classics, mathematics and astronomy. By his early twenties

Sir John Barrow, the powerful second secretary of the Admiralty and patriarch of almost thirty years of nineteenth-century Arctic exploration.

Barrow could speak and write Chinese.

In 1804, at the age of forty, Barrow was appointed Second Secretary at the Admiralty, a position he held unbroken for forty-one years. While political power and the elected political post of First Secretary regularly changed hands at elections, Barrow was a permanent feature exercising great authority from behind his desk at the Admiralty. When he finally retired in his early eighties, he took his Admiralty desk as a leaving gift.

Barrow was the embodiment of the wise old adage that 'ministers propose but civil servants dispose'. A stroke of Barrow's pen carried more power than a naval gun battery. His great achievement was to persuade sceptical politicians that exploration would be a worthwhile exercise for the navy, both commercially and scientifically. British authority across the world, he argued, would be further bolstered by gaining footholds in the remaining unexplored regions of the planet. Planting the flag on these blank spots, he postulated, was a solemn national duty.

His words fell on receptive ears in the euphoric atmosphere of the post-Napoleonic years, when the country believed nothing was beyond the capacity of the all-conquering British Empire. The roots of Britain's aggressive imperialism of the nineteenth century can be found in the prevailing mood of invincibility that followed Napoleon's defeat and it was influential men like Barrow who carefully nourished the popular cause of expanding the Empire.

From 1816 until his retirement in 1845, Barrow coolly dispatched a flurry of expedition ships into the unknown to open new territories. His first foray was to send a party into the centre of Africa, but the expedition was a disaster, with only a handful of survivors emerging alive.

Undeterred, Barrow turned to his real obsession – the Arctic. Despite the apparently logical option of opening up the unexplored and undeveloped regions of Africa or Asia, he insisted that the focus of exploration should be the undiscovered North West Passage and the North Pole.

Barrow's intervention signalled a significant change in the motivation for finding the passage or reaching the Pole. Attempts to navigate the

North West Passage going back into the sixteenth century had been driven purely by the huge commercial rewards promised by the opening of lucrative new trade routes to China and India by way of a sea route across today's Arctic Canada.

The high seas of the sixteenth century were heavily dominated by the Portuguese and Spanish fleets, and Britain saw the North West Passage as a means of avoiding enemy ships and to secure access to important markets in the east. The search was given formal authority in 1745 when the government offered a substantial reward of £20,000 (over £2,000,000 in today's terms) for the discovery of a passage.

But the focus had changed a century later in the post-Napoleonic era, with Britain now the most powerful navy in the world and not intimidated by foreign powers. Instead, Barrow wanted to find the North West Passage for the national honour. It was a collective hubris, destined to end in disaster.

At this time, no one had ever stood within 500 miles (800 kilometres) of the North Pole and finding a North West Passage across the top of the American continent had defied generations of explorers – mostly British – for nearly 300 years. But Barrow was aware that the Russians were active in the Bering Strait and he won crucial popular support for his plan by declaring that it would be 'little short of an act of national suicide' if a foreign navy beat Britain to the prize. At Barrow's behest, fresh rewards from the public purse were offered for the first ship to reach the Pacific through Arctic waters.

John Barrow's judgement, however, did not match his passionate ambition and consuming ego. Barrow had made only one brief voyage north and his personal experience was minimal as he drew up bold plans to send a number of ships into Arctic waters. With an implicit belief in the omnipotence of the Royal Navy, he roundly dismissed the knowledge and experience of Arctic whaling captains or the native Inuit population as he aggressively framed his plans.

Typical of Barrow's philosophy was his firm advocacy of the 'Open Polar Sea' theory. According to its proponents, the North Pole was surrounded by ice-free and temperate waters and the only challenge for explorers was to navigate the known ice-belt at lower latitudes before sailing unhindered to the top of the world. Once through the pack ice, they argued, it would be plain sailing to the North Pole. The 'Open Polar Sea' theory was given a boost in 1817 when the highly accomplished whaling captain William Scoresby returned with reports that 18,000 square miles (28,800 square kilometres) of pack ice between the Svalbard archipelago and Greenland had mysteriously disappeared.

Scorseby's reports invigorated Barrow and in 1818 he prepared to send two naval expeditions north. One party was to pick a pathway through the pack ice to the North Pole, while a second was ordered to reverse hundreds of years of failure at a stroke by locating the North West Passage.

The North Pole expedition departed London in April 1818 under the command of Captain David Buchan aboard *Dorothea*, accompanied by his second-in-command, John Franklin, a thirty-two-year-old veteran of Trafalgar, who took charge of *Trent*. Unlike vastly experienced merchant seamen such as Scoresby, none of the ships' officers had ventured into high Arctic waters before. Scoresby's complaint about the 'want of experience in the navigation of icy seas' was contemptuously brushed aside.

The two ships endured appalling weather in the treacherous seas between Svalbard and the east coast of Greenland, and only managed to reach 80° 34' north, near Spitsbergen. *Dorothea* was leaking badly after a bruising encounter with the ice and, in late August, a disappointed Buchan and Franklin turned for home.

The voyage to find the North West Passage was equally unsuccessful, but significantly more controversial. The two ships, *Isabella* and *Alexander*, were dispatched to Baffin Bay in search of an ice-free passage on the western side of the bay that Barrow hoped would be the gateway to the passage itself and the eventual route to the Pacific.

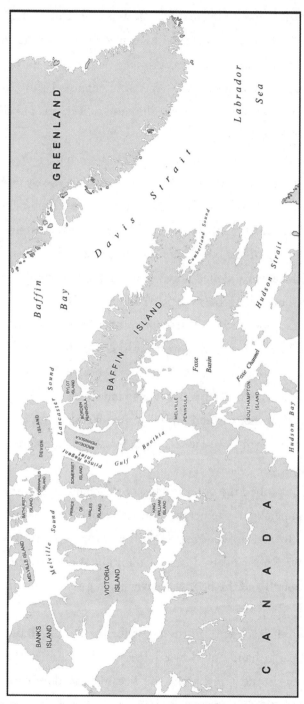

Canadian Arctic.

In command of the 385-ton *Isabella* was John Ross, a highly capable but irascible forty-year-old Scot with an array of war wounds to show for his undoubted bravery under fire. Among the 57 men on board *Isabella* was James Clark Ross, his eighteen-year-old nephew. Lieutenant William Edward Parry, a twenty-seven-year-old naval officer, was placed in charge of the 252-ton *Alexander*.

Isabella and *Alexander* left Britain with *Dorothea* and *Trent*, and the ships separated off Lerwick on 1 May. John Ross took his vessels into the Davis Strait off the west coast of Greenland and entered Baffin Bay. Pushing northwards, the ships battled through thick ice near the entrance to Smith Sound at the top of the bay, where impenetrable pack ice was discovered. Ross immediately abandoned hopes of finding a route to the north.

Turning south along the coast of Ellesmere Island, Ross came to the edge of Jones Sound, which threw up another impassable wall of ice and blocked any hopes of venturing westwards. A little further south, the ships came to the mouth of the more-promising Lancaster Sound.

William Baffin, who discovered the sound in his voyage of 1616, considered it just another bay and turned away, not realising it was, in fact, the opening of the North West Passage. John Ross made the same mistake two centuries later.

Though he probed the outer reaches of the channel for a short while in early September, he was reluctant to press further west and instead turned for home. His return was greeted with a storm of controversy. Barrow never forgave Ross' perceived lack of ambition at not driving deeper into Lancaster Sound and the Scot was never again given command of a Royal Navy ship.

The baton of leadership in the quest for the Arctic Grail now passed into the capable hands of Edward Parry, a determined and ambitious officer. Over the next few years, he became the dominating force in Britain's increasingly energetic attempts to discover the passage. When Barrow – undeterred by the failures of 1818 – calmly dispatched another

Sir Edward Parry, a prolific explorer who recruited Crozier for three of the four Arctic expeditions he commanded.

two expeditions to the Arctic in 1819, Parry was put in charge of the sea-going operation with *Hecla* and *Griper*.

Despite the disappointment of *Trent*, Franklin was ordered to undertake a mammoth overland voyage to trace the coastal outline at the most northern reaches of the Canadian continent. If possible, Franklin was asked to rendezvous with Parry somewhere along the vast coastline.

John Franklin, a portly figure, who first went to sea at the age of twelve, was an unlikely candidate to lead a taxing journey of several thousand miles across barren territory by foot and canoe. He had no experience of trekking or living off the land and was incapable of travelling more than 8 miles (13 kilometres) a day. Seasoned travellers with dogs could move five times as fast in the same conditions, but Franklin never learned how to drive dogs. More importantly, he was almost totally dependent on either local natives or French-Canadian *voyageurs* to hunt fresh game for food.

The Franklin overland expedition became a perfect example of Britain's heroic failure in the Arctic during the Barrow years. It was poorly equipped, overly optimistic and soon demonstrated that when thrust into a totally unfamiliar environment, naval parties would struggle to survive. Courage alone was not enough.

While the expedition was marked by extraordinary endurance, the venture was almost consumed by terrible hardship and starvation, murder and summary execution. It is even possible that some men resorted to cannibalism to survive. Although the expedition managed to cover remarkable distances, much of the territory was already mapped and the cost in human suffering was intolerable.

Beginning on the western shore of Hudson Bay, Franklin's party travelled to the mouth of the Coppermine River and explored eastwards along the coast to the appropriately named Point Turnagain. Franklin failed to rendezvous with Parry and only emerged from the ice in 1822 after a three-year ordeal that resulted in the death of eleven of the 20-man party. Among the casualties was Robert Hood, an Irish-born naval officer who was murdered by the Iroquois Indian, Michel Terohauté who, in turn, was summarily executed by Franklin's deputy, John Richardson.

Game was scarce and starvation gripped the travellers at every stage in the horrific journey. The men were reduced to eating scraps of animal skin or repulsive lichen scraped from rocks, which they called *'tripes de roche'* (tripe of the rock). Once, they chewed the leather of their own spare shoes and Franklin earned the lasting reputation as 'the man who ate his boots'. On his return home, he was hailed as a hero and the appalling suffering and wholesale deaths were quietly forgotten.

Parry, by contrast, enjoyed the best advantage that any explorer in the field could possibly desire – a generous slice of good luck. To his credit, he exploited his good fortune and completed one of the greatest of all Arctic voyages.

He sailed from London in late spring 1819 with provisions for two years and clear orders to penetrate deep into Lancaster Sound, where John Ross had feared to go. He commanded a robust naval bomb ship, the 375-ton *Hecla*, which was supported by the 180-ton *Griper*.

Parry's good fortune was that 1819 was an exceptionally easy year for ice and he made remarkable progress, crossing the dangerous waters of Baffin Bay and entering Lancaster Sound in early August. Pushing further west than anyone before, he found considerable new land and caught sight of several inlets to the south that offered hope of a way through the ice.

Parry eventually sailed to the end of Lancaster Sound into a broad new expanse of water which he called Viscount Melville Sound. In mid-September, he reached 112° 51' west, his farthest westerly point where he faced a daunting barrier of impassable ice. He called it Cape Providence.

With the autumnal weather deteriorating fast, Parry hurried back to a bay on the newly discovered Melville Island to establish quarters at a place he named Winter Harbour.

Parry had mapped around 1,000 miles (1,600 kilometres) of new territory and was convinced that a passage to the Pacific was achievable when the ice relented the following summer. The prospects, he wrote, were 'truly exhilarating'.

Hecla and *Griper*, however, were not able to escape from the ice of Winter Harbour for ten months. When free, Parry made a fresh attempt to drive westwards and on the distant horizon he discovered Banks Land (now Banks Island). But the ice was as impenetrable as the previous year and with the short navigable season once again closing in, Parry turned for home, finally stepping ashore in October 1820.

He had penetrated about halfway through the North West Passage and had lifted the veil on more unknown Arctic terrain than anyone before. He was quickly installed as a new national hero, having demonstrated that, with good fortune, it was possible to survive unscathed through the Arctic winter and potentially complete the journey to the Pacific.

Barrow was exhilarated by Parry's outstanding voyage and did not hesitate to mount another expedition the following year to complete the task. Among those prepared to join his crusade was midshipman Francis Crozier.

CHAPTER 3

Seizing the Moment

Francis Crozier was on a downhill slope to nowhere in the early days of 1821. He was stuck in the dreary routine of Channel peacetime patrol duties and the chances of promotion in the foreseeable future were highly improbable due to the stumbling block of thousands of underemployed naval officers. When his tour of duty on *Dotterel* ended, Crozier faced the ignominy of being side-lined on half-pay, a paltry few shillings a day. Entering his mid-twenties and without an obvious alternative career in mind, Crozier had to make a choice; the choice was polar exploration.

It appears that Crozier, like so many others, was captivated by Parry's great feats in Lancaster Sound. Parry had made Arctic exploration fashionable and his men were greeted as heroes, fêted by society and rewarded with swift promotion up the navy's ranks.

Parry, the first truly heroic figure of nineteenth-century exploration, was a fine example of what polar exploration could achieve for a willing and able naval officer in the years following the Napoleonic Wars. Fresh from his Arctic triumph, Parry's near celebrity status brought an audience with King George IV, the freedom of his home city of Bath and an unexpected windfall when an eager publisher paid 1,000 guineas (over £50,000 in today's terms) for publication of his expedition journals.

Francis Crozier in his mid-twenties during the years spent exploring the Arctic with Edward Parry. The artist is unknown.

Crozier could hardly fail to notice the distinct similarities between himself and Parry. Both were born into prominent, well-to-do families and both had enlisted in the navy as boys. While the Crozier family had close ties with Ireland's landed gentry, Parry's father was an eminent doctor who practised in the upper echelons of English society. His circle of acquaintances included the great astronomer, Sir William Herschel and Edward Jenner, inventor of the smallpox inoculation.

Parry junior, dynamic and single-minded, was six years older than Crozier and ideally suited to the role of explorer as national hero. He was clean-cut, religiously sound and had learned how to network in the right places from an early age. Soon after returning to London in 1820, he was rubbing shoulders with influential men like Barrow and Sir Joseph Banks, the legendary president of the Royal Society. 'I already feel that I stand upon higher ground than before', Parry wrote, as society opened its doors to him.

In the warm afterglow of the expedition's return, Crozier took the decisive step of volunteering for Parry's next voyage to the ice. After the tedium of patrol duties and periods of half-pay, the expedition gave Crozier the opportunity he so craved – the chance to serve the navy. More than perhaps anything else, the diligent, hard-working young man was driven by a clear-cut sense of duty. In later life, the woman he loved rejected Crozier's proposal of marriage on the grounds that he was already married – to the navy.

Parry clearly liked what he saw when he first encountered Crozier. Parry was fastidious in his choice of officers and often rejected the customary naval practice of handing out postings to friends and the sons of influential men. He preferred to pick men on merit and most of the officers recruited for the 1821 voyage had already been on earlier journeys to the Arctic. While preparing for the trip, Parry explained to his parents:

> I must have the Commander of the second ship and my first Lieut. to be officers in who I place implicit confidence, without which I will not consent either to risk the loss of the little reputation I have gained, or to be cooped up for an indefinite period with people whom I do not like.[1]

The mission in 1821, Parry's second voyage in command, was to find a completely new route through the ice. Although the first venture in 1819–

20 was a great success, the passage west was blocked by solid ice in the Melville Sound area at the end of Lancaster Sound. A fresh route was required.

The likely path to the Bering Strait and the Pacific, he reasoned, lay somewhere further to the south in a parallel and as-yet-undiscovered channel closer to the Canadian mainland. He intended to approach the area from the south by exploring the upper reaches of Hudson Bay, where he confidently expected to find the elusive ice-free passage leading to the west.

At the Admiralty, Barrow listened carefully but needed little persuasion. Parry's record in Lancaster Sound made him untouchable and there was also renewed urgency as word reached London that the Russians were again active in the Bering Strait. Nothing was likely to stir Barrow's blood more than the audacity of foreign intruders stealing British glory.

Within weeks of *Hecla* and *Griper*'s return in the autumn of 1820, Barrow commissioned the new expedition and fully endorsed Parry's decision to investigate the northern passageways of Hudson Bay. *Hecla* was overhauled and made ready for the trip, but the sluggish *Griper* was discarded in favour of *Fury*, another converted bomb ship of 375 tons and *Hecla*'s sister ship. Almost all working parts of the two vessels were interchangeable – a sensible innovation allowing men and equipment to be transferred from one to the other if either *Hecla* or *Fury* became fatally ensnared in the ice.

Midshipman Crozier came under Parry's wing from the very start and was assigned as a junior officer to *Fury*, Parry's flagship. Here, Crozier discovered that, at age twenty-four, he was one of the few without experience of the ice. The most notable other figure on board *Fury* was James Clark Ross, who, at only twenty-one, was making his third trip north. *Fury*'s officers also included Lieutenants Joseph Nais and Andrew Reid from the 1819–20 expedition, while *Hecla*'s ranks featured Henry Hoppner from Parry's last voyage and George Fisher, a newly ordained vicar who had sailed with Buchan in 1818 and who was now enrolled in a dual role of chaplain/astronomer. The only newcomers among the officers were Crozier and the twenty-two-year-old midshipman, Edward Bird.

The two debutants to exploration, both quiet and conscientious officers, became firm friends.

Crozier's closest companion on the expedition was Ross. The pair quickly developed strong bonds and became close companions, a deep relationship that lasted for the rest of their lives. Ross was one of the few who called Crozier by the name of Frank.

Ross was everything that Crozier was not. Crozier was a dark-haired and solidly built man of about 5 feet 9 inches, a model of simplicity and efficiency. He was an industrious, utterly trustworthy officer who carried a little too much weight, but rarely stood out in a crowd. He was straightforward, genial and possessed a gentle sense of humour.

An unpretentious man who disliked excessive formality and pomp, he once returned to Banbridge for the opening of the town's new church opposite his family home and discovered that class-conscious parishioners were jostling to reserve the most favourable pews. Crozier walked calmly into the church and sat in a pew at the back of the building, proclaiming: 'One pew is as good as another.'

Crozier was an understated figure without a trace of vanity. His principal frailty was a low level of self-confidence that may have stemmed from insecurity about his modest formal education. The surviving correspondence of Crozier, with its occasionally erratic spelling and punctuation, reflects the limited instruction of someone who left school at thirteen.

On board ship, Crozier mixed easily with young men from similar backgrounds who had enlisted before reaching adulthood and who relied on their quick wits and sound basic intelligence to progress through the naval ranks. But it was a different matter ashore, where the untutored young officer felt a little ill at ease among the more sophisticated and scholarly types he met at receptions and dinner parties.

Crozier was nevertheless highly respected by his naval colleagues – the men who knew him best. He may have lacked flair, but his fellow officers liked his firm loyalty, unswerving dedication and ironclad integrity. John

Barrow, not a man to lavish praise, once wrote of Crozier:

A most zealous young officer who, by his talents, attention and energy, has succeeded in working himself up to the top of the service.[2]

Rock solid and reliable, Crozier was born to be a number two.

James Clark Ross, by contrast, was a striking figure with dark piercing eyes and once christened the most handsome man in the navy. He was a charismatic, popular figure with a flair that made him one of the greatest polar explorers of all time – something that more than compensated for his streak of vanity, arrogance and occasional sharp tongue. Where Crozier may have lacked confidence, Ross displayed a breezy self-assurance and a strong sense of destiny that swept all before him. Ross, a dashing figure with a strong sense of his own vocation, was a born leader.

Despite the outward differences, Crozier and Ross had much in common. They shared ancestral roots in Scottish Presbyterianism and a staunch belief in the powers of the Almighty. Ross' ancestors were soldiers and ministers on the craggy peninsula near Stranraer in west Galloway, barely 100 miles (160 kilometres) from the border homelands of the early Croziers. Both had joined the navy as boys, Ross signing up in 1812 less than a fortnight before his twelfth birthday.

Both men also overcame limited formal tuition to become leading authorities in the field of maritime science, notably on the effect of the earth's magnetic fields on navigational compasses. It was Ross – along with the acknowledged experts, Edward Sabine and Professor Humphrey Lloyd – who later made the first systematic magnetic survey of the British Isles.

Crozier also showed great aptitude for scientific observation. On successive expeditions he took responsibility for erecting observatories and the painstaking task of taking reliable readings. Years later, some of the most distinguished scholars and naval figures of the age recognised the value of Crozier's work by endorsing his election as a Fellow of the Royal Society,

The dashing and highly experienced polar explorer Sir James Clark Ross, lifelong friend of Crozier.

the country's most prestigious scientific body.[3]

Crozier's appointment to *Fury* found him suddenly catapulted into unaccustomed limelight after a decade of anonymity in the fleet. With Arctic exploration now popular among the public, crowds poured down to Deptford on the River Thames to see the two ships and the explorers before they departed.

Parry responded to the popular acclaim by throwing a grand farewell ball on the decks of *Fury*. Hundreds of guests, splashed with early summer moonlight, danced long into the night.

Below decks, the holds of *Fury* and *Hecla* were bulging with food and equipment for a journey into the unknown that might last three years.

CHAPTER 4

A Promise

*F*ury and *Hecla* sailed on 8 May 1821 with instructions to enter Hudson Bay and proceed along the western shores in search of an outlet that would take the ships towards the Bering Strait. The most likely avenue was thought to be Repulse Bay on the north-western side of the bay, or further north in the little-known waters of Foxe Basin.

In early July, the two ships – accompanied by the supply vessel, *Nautilus* – reached the mouth of Hudson Strait, the gateway to the Arctic ice that separates Canada's north-eastern coastline and Baffin Island. Tons of supplies, including twenty live bullocks, were transferred in the choppy seas and *Nautilus* turned for home, leaving *Fury* and *Hecla* alone on the edge of the frozen wilderness.

The ships sailed through the awkward currents of Hudson Strait and all on board were surprised to discover they were not quite alone. Three merchant vessels were spotted making their way into Hudson Bay, including one carrying 160 Dutch settlers seeking new lives in one of civilisation's most far-flung outposts. Parry persuaded one of the ships to carry the expedition's mail back to England and *Fury* and *Hecla* resumed their journey.

Hudson Bay is a vast inland sea some 700 miles (1,120 kilometres) wide and 850 miles (1,360 kilometres) long and the ships' progress across the icy waters in patchy fog was agonisingly slow. All hands were on constant alert to avoid collisions with loose ice floes.

The expedition faced a major decision as the ships came close to Southampton Island at the apex of the bay and headed for Repulse Bay. The only known route at the time was up the dangerous narrow channel that runs between the bleak western shore of Southampton Island and the Canadian mainland – a channel with the incongruous name of Roe's Welcome Sound. Parry gambled and decided to avoid the proven route, instead running along Frozen Strait on the north-eastern side of Southampton Island, where no ships had been before.

Visibility was poor as the vessels moved deliberately forward, taking regular depth soundings and keeping on full alert for drifting ice. 'Neck-or-nothing navigation' Parry called it. Occasionally, small boats went ashore to investigate Southampton Island and to pick up fresh water and supplies. Crozier returned from one trip with enough shellfish to feed both ships for a couple of days.

To relief all round, the fog suddenly lifted to reveal *Fury* and *Hecla* in a massive natural theatre of a bay enclosed on three sides by steep cliffs rising to 600 feet (185 metres). Without fully realising it, *Fury* and *Hecla* had passed blindfold through the unexplored Frozen Strait and into Repulse Bay. The bay, discovered by Captain Christopher Middleton in 1742, was aptly named. A quick reconnoitre showed that it was a dead end with no sign of an exit to the west.

Parry immediately withdrew and turned the ships into Foxe Basin. Progressing northwards along the largely unknown shores of Melville Peninsula, *Hecla* and *Fury* were now venturing into seas where few ships had ever gone before.

Foxe Basin, with its chunky blockade of intimidating ice floes, had rarely been visited since its discovery by Luke Foxe in 1631. Foxe, an experienced sailor, declared it a blind alley and his firm declaration brought the early search for the North West Passage to a halt for almost a hundred years.

Parry was now poised to take his ships into Foxe's cul-de-sac.

For six weeks, *Fury* and *Hecla* poked and probed along the rugged Melville Peninsula on the western shores of Foxe Basin, dodging the ice and taking frequent depths in the uncertain waters. But the elusive pathway to the west could not be found. As September gave way to October, the short season of ice-free passages in the area was coming to an end and attention turned to finding a sanctuary where the ships could spend the winter.

The refuge, found in early October, was a wide bay at the southern tip of Melville Peninsula and was given the appropriate name of Winter Island. The shelter, a few miles to the south of the Arctic Circle, was to be their home for nine months.

Over-wintering with Parry did not threaten the same terror for the combined payroll of 118 men on board *Fury* and *Hecla* as it had for men on earlier voyages to the Arctic. Most had reluctantly endured an isolated winter only after becoming trapped in the ice. Parry, by contrast, deliberately chose to pass a winter in the Arctic and had planned for the occasion.

Parry was the most accomplished of early-nineteenth-century polar explorers and his methods and routines for withstanding the long, dark months of isolation became a model for many other voyagers in both the Arctic and Antarctic. He devised a system of firm discipline and busy working schedules, combined with a comfortable living environment, a generous diet and an abundance of pastimes and amusements to keep the men occupied. It was a system that generally worked very well.

The upper masts were taken down and canvas was stretched over the decking to provide a covering against the worst of the weather. Another innovation was an early form of central heating which was rigged up below decks using a maze of insulated pipes to carry hot air from a coal-burning stove in the galley to the living quarters. The contraption – named the Sylvester stove after its inventor – was crude but highly effective. But without the benefit of thermostat control, temperatures below soared to uncomfortable levels and the men often found themselves in the bizarre position of being far too hot in one of the coldest places on earth. Anyone venturing from the sweltering heat of the lower decks to the freezing outside environment had to endure a heart-stopping change in temperature of more than 100°F (40°C) within the space of sixty seconds.

Strict discipline was observed, with regular inspections of the ship, a weekly examination of the crew by doctors and firm directives to ensure the men took frequent exercise. Classes were set up to teach the mostly illiterate crew how to read and write and Parry, a devoutly religious man, proudly announced that all hands would return home with the ability to read the Bible.

The diet, particularly the fresh food, was plentiful and explicitly arranged to avoid scurvy, the traditional curse of seamen on long voyages. Although the causes of scurvy – lack of the anti-scorbutic vitamin C typically found in fresh meat, vegetables and fruit – would not be properly identified for another century, Parry's regime was fairly successful in combating the

Hecla *and* Fury *in the ice at Winter Island during Crozier's first expedition with Parry in 1821.*

ailment. But it was not foolproof and without sufficient quantities of fresh meat or vegetables, scurvy was inevitable.

The diet was the traditional navy fare of salted beef or pork and oatmeal, along with the latest innovation of tinned soups, vegetables and fruit, which kept the men well fed but did not contain the necessary requirement of anti-scorbutic. Occasionally, the men ate fresh meat from local game, and small quantities of lemon juice, fortified with generous helpings of rum, were administered. The steaming hot pipes were dressed with trays of mustard and cress that grew rapidly in the hot-house conditions and for a time provided the men with 100 pounds (45 kilograms) of fresh greenery rich in vitamin C.

All hands were given plenty of free time to amuse themselves or participate in organised events. Regular singsongs and musical recitals – Parry was a capable violinist – could be enjoyed, while others sought a quiet corner in which to read, play chess or write up their journals.

The most popular pastimes were the magic-lantern shows and Parry's finest novelty, the Royal Arctic Theatre. The theatre was first introduced during the 1819 voyage and presented a series of popular costume dramas, with officers shaving off their whiskers and dressing up as women to thunderous applause from the captive audience. It was a stunning piece of man-management, giving the men something special to look forward to and providing sailors with the unprecedented opportunity to laugh uproariously at their officers. Such insubordination would have brought a flogging in normal circumstances, but it was positively encouraged in the Arctic outpost, thousands of miles from anywhere.

Crozier was press-ganged into participating in the first production of the 1821 Arctic theatrical season, *The Rivals*, written by the Irish playwright Richard Brinsley Sheridan. He shaved off his whiskers to play the key role of Sir Lucius O'Trigger in the classic comedy of manners set in Parry's home city of Bath.

Elsewhere, the important business of the expedition's extensive scientific

ICEBOUND IN THE ARCTIC

agenda took up much of the time for officers such as Crozier and Ross during the winter. Many astronomical readings and gravitational experiments were undertaken, officers conscientiously measured air and water temperatures every four hours, and Crozier was engaged in the painstaking mathematical task of making magnetic observations.

A curious – and hazardous – test was conducted to discover whether the spectacular aurora borealis emitted a noise. Officers soon found that their uncovered ears froze solid as they stood silently in sub-zero temperatures gazing at the heavens and listening for faint sounds from the ether. Many ears were pinched by the cold during the unusual test, but no 'sound' was ever heard.

Commander George Lyon, the colourful captain of *Hecla*, made his own oddball input by claiming he was better equipped to 'hear' than everyone else because his body retained the heat from a visit to the Sahara Desert two years earlier. By a cruel irony, Lyon would lose his sight a decade later through ophthalmia – severe inflammation of the eye – picked up in the baking heat of Africa.

Months passed slowly in the freezing darkness of Winter Island, though the monotony was relieved in February 1822 when an inquisitive band of local Inuit visited the ships. It was a friendly exchange which encouraged bouts of singing and dancing and provided a rare opportunity for both communities to examine each other's lifestyle.

The white men – known to the Inuit as *kabloonas* – were astonished at the skills of igloo-building and the comfort of the native dwellings. Some officers and seamen even followed the native example of getting garish tattoos on their bodies. Midshipman Bird made the mistake of employing an old native woman with poor sight to give him a tattoo and emerged with an ugly hotchpotch of meaningless squiggles that defied description. Lyon reported that the old woman stitched away with 'barbarous indifference as if it was an old shoe she was operating on'.

The relationship between the men of *Fury* and *Hecla* and the Inuit became increasingly close. Regular visits were made to the nearby snow houses and on occasion the Inuit slept on board the ships. It is probable that relations became intimate, although surviving records provide only scraps of evidence. But many years later, an elderly Inuit claimed to have slept with both Parry and Lyon during the months at Winter Island.[1]

More constructively, an Inuit woman named Iligliuk gave Parry useful details about the local geography, including the tantalising promise of open water to the north and an ice-free channel to the west. Iligliuk sketched a map that raised hopes that a sea passage – perhaps even the fabled 'Open Polar Sea' – was within easy reach.

Encouraged by Iligliuk's map, Parry sent small parties along the coast to scout the immediate vicinity. But while the men of *Hecla* and *Fury* were expert seafarers, they lacked any real experience or knowledge of travelling overland on the ice and quickly ran into difficulty.

A party under Lyon ventured out too early in the season when temperatures were still dangerously low and almost perished. Lyon, pulling three days' food and a single tent on a wooden sledge, ran into severe weather and a routine trip along the shoreline came close to disaster.

A howling gale and heavy snow forced the men to seek shelter in the tent after travelling barely 6 miles (10 kilometres) from the ship. Unable to steer ahead, Lyon decided to hurry back to the ship by following his outward tracks. But snow had covered the trail and the men wandered aimlessly in white-out conditions. Before long, they were hopelessly lost and one man was on the brink of collapse. Lyon was getting desperate when, by chance, someone spotted a different trail made by Inuit and within a short time the grateful men were back on board, having learned a salutary lesson about the hazards of overland travel.

By May, when the weather was thought to be more manageable, Parry began preparations to leave Winter Island. Parties of men equipped with pickaxes were dispatched to the ice to hack a channel to open water. The sailors laboured from six in the morning until eight at night, but temperatures were so low that the lanes of open water closed over as fast as the men could smash them open. It was exhausting work and two seamen died.

Fortunately, a gale in July achieved what was beyond human labour and a pathway to open water suddenly appeared. *Fury* and *Hecla* seized the moment and edged out of Winter Island, their nine-month stay at an end.

Guided by the Inuit map, the ships sailed north and reached Igloolik at the top of Melville Peninsula. To its surprise, the expedition was greeted by the friendly band of natives who had made the trek overland from Winter Island to hunt game.

Anxious to locate the strait identified by Iligliuk, Parry split his party in two, taking Crozier in one group on an overland march to find the waterway and sending Lyon inland to survey other nearby territory. Lyon found little of value, though he fully enjoyed renewing his acquaintanceship with the natives.

Parry and Crozier, by contrast, struggled northwards across broken ice to the very northern tip of Melville Peninsula, where the Inuit had promised a channel leading to the west. Climbing a high promontory, Parry and Crozier were bitterly disappointed at the view stretched out before them.

The natives were correct about the existence of a strait, but it was a narrow channel choked with ice and offering precious little possibility of a passage for the ships. In the distance, however, Parry believed he saw clear signs of open water. Gambling on the ice receding in the summer, he summoned the ships to the entrance of the channel, which he named Fury and Hecla Strait.

Initially, the gamble paid off because the ice broke away sufficiently for *Fury* and *Hecla* to sail a few miles into the channel. Parry believed that Fury and Hecla Strait held the key to the passage and all they had to do was wait for the inevitable break-up of the ice that summer before sailing triumphantly through to the Bering Strait. But the mood of optimism began to evaporate as the ice ahead became progressively thicker. Never had the frustrated Parry witnessed such a barrier.

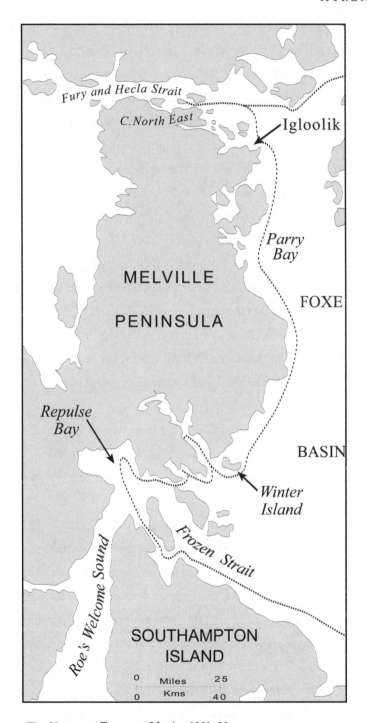

The Voyage of Fury *and* Hecla, *1821–23.*

On one occasion, Crozier and Parry left the ship with a small party to climb the high promontory named Cape North East to scan the horizon for signs of cracks in the ice. It was a treacherous march across broken, slushy sea ice, where dangerous lanes of open water threatened to cut off the retreat to the ships. As insurance, the party carried planks of wood to bridge any channels of open water it might encounter.

Crozier was the first victim of the unstable ice. While walking with Parry, Crozier found himself separated from the others by a yawning crack in the ice. The plank was far too short to bridge the gap and swimming in the freezing waters would be suicidal. But Crozier, imperturbable and resourceful, calmly dropped the gear he was carrying and moved up the open lane, finding its narrowest point and where he could see large chunks of ice floating in the flowing water. Steeling himself, Crozier began leaping from floe to floe as lumps of ice bobbed along in the current. After a few perilous leaps, he managed to find more solid ground and cheerfully returned to the ship unharmed and seemingly untroubled by his near-fatal ordeal.

The incident was typical of Crozier, a man who possessed a calm head in a crisis. Only weeks later, he was again able to demonstrate his coolness under pressure when for the second time he found himself in peril after getting cut off from the ship.

He had taken two marines ashore in a 9-foot (3-metre) boat, with four days of food supplies, to study and measure the tides at the head of Fury and Hecla Strait. It was another straightforward task, but the weather deteriorated badly soon after the men reached shore. Temperatures plunged sharply and the fast-running tidal flow was whipped up by gale-force winds.

On board *Fury*, Parry grew alarmed. He admitted to 'serious apprehension' about Crozier's safety and decided to personally lead a rescue party to fetch the young officer. Parry's searchers struggled ashore in high winds but could find no trace of Crozier and the two marines. Parties were sent in both directions along the shore and musket shots were fired to alert the missing men, but the cracks of gunfire were drowned out by the roar of the gale.

Parry suspected the worst when, to his astonishment, he found Crozier crouched beside a rock, sheltering from the winds and quietly jotting down his tidal observations. Crozier, totally absorbed in his duty, seemed oblivious to the tempest raging all around, as a mightily relieved Parry recalled:

I had the indescribable satisfaction of seeing Mr Crozier make his appearance from behind a rock, where he was engaged in watching the tide-mark.[2]

Back on board, the failure to penetrate Fury and Hecla Strait infuriated Parry, who believed he was 'stopped at the very threshold of the North West Passage'. At one point, the ships resorted to the risky tactic of charging the pack, but the pack held firm and in late September, *Fury* and *Hecla* came to a halt at 83° 29' west – not as far west as Parry managed on the great journey through Lancaster Sound in 1819–20. Parry decided to sit out a second winter in the ice and to have a further stab at Fury and Hecla Strait in 1823.

The party returned to the Inuit settlement at Igloolik to nurse its disappointment. A tough summer season had yielded little and the normally self-confident Parry admitted that 'very little had in reality been effected in the furtherance of the North West Passage'.

Igloolik – about 150 miles (240 kilometres) inside the Arctic Circle – was a colder and less hospitable haven for the crews of *Fury* and *Hecla* than that enjoyed in the more southerly latitudes of Winter Island. But the party was comforted by the close and generous presence of the friendly band of Inuit.

Crozier was popular with the Inuit community, particularly when he helped bring sick natives on board the ships for medical treatment. Having been given responsibility for the task, he personally ferried ailing Inuit back and forth over the ice, and in the process became one of the party's most accomplished ice travellers.

Crozier became a familiar sight to the natives on his hospital run and they soon devised their own name for him. The Inuit initially struggled to pronounce his Scots-French name and called him 'Croz-har', but they soon came up with their own pet name for him, which was *Aglooka*, meaning 'one who takes long strides'. More pertinently, the Inuit identified Crozier as *esh-e-mu-tar-nar* – an officer not as great as the ship's captain.[3]

During his contact with the Inuit at Igloolik, Crozier also revealed that he wanted to return to the ice in the future. According to native testimony passed down over the years, Crozier told the natives of his ambition to lead his own expedition.

An elderly Inuk from the Igloolik settlement, speaking about forty years after the visit of *Fury* and *Hecla*, told a fascinating story to Charles Francis Hall, an American who spent much time in the same region during the 1860s. She revealed that *Aglooka* (Crozier) had faithfully promised the Inuit that he would return to the Arctic regions one day as *esh-e-mu-ta* – captain of the ship.[4]

CHAPTER 5

Fatal Errors

The 1822–23 winter at Igloolik was a decisive moment in the history of British polar exploration. Never had such a large party – over 100 naval officers and crew, including the navy's finest explorers of the age – spent so much time living alongside the native Inuit population. Both communities were provided with an opportunity to observe each other's lifestyles and habits at close quarters, even though in this environment the native Inuit had far more to offer their visitors than the British could offer them. Unfortunately, the opportunity to learn was wasted.

The explorers who camped on ships alongside the Inuit community witnessed everything the natives did over a period of many months. At times there was precious little else to do but watch these aboriginal people go about their daily business and much of what the British saw was meticulously logged. Lyon, in particular, wrote detailed reports that years later encouraged professional anthropological studies of the local people.

However, the explorers wrote down much but understood little. Not once did it occur to them to ask how it was that uneducated, 'half-savage' tribes could survive and thrive in a hostile, merciless environment that defeated the educated and technically superior British.

The explorers found the Inuit interesting and entertaining and marvelled at things such as the art of building an igloo in a gale and the finely honed hunting skills that kept their communities alive. They were mildly perplexed by other traits, such as how Inuit gorged on raw meat or the casual way in which sexual favours were dispensed. But the opportunity to learn by studying the survival skills and lifestyles of the indigenous population was largely wasted.

Parry's expeditions were ground-breaking and innovative affairs. Consequently, his style and methods formed the template for decades of endeavour in the polar regions by generations of British explorers. But the opportunity to make even more progress by studying the survival abilities and adopting the lifestyles of the indigenous population was ignored, and convoys of British explorers went into the ice for another hundred years clinging to the foolish prejudices and methods which were tragically ill suited to the environment.

The critical failure of the 1822–23 party to learn from the Inuit lay in the inherent sense of superiority felt by the British towards all foreigners. When *Hecla* and *Fury* ventured into the ice in the early 1820s, Britain ruled the world, both militarily and economically. Illiterate Inuit tribes living above the Arctic Circle were dismissed as hopeless inferiors, or at best regarded as children. Lyon wrote in his journal:

> I could not look at these modest little savages, without being obliged to draw comparisons rather disadvantageous to many sweet little spoiled children in England.

British explorers, reflecting the society that sent them north, lacked a basic respect for other cultures and the humility to recognise that native tribes knew more about their own environment than refined naval officers. However, they failed to comprehend that the totally different environment of the Arctic demanded separate rules that were fundamentally alien to the British way of life.

Inuit have survived in the Arctic wilds for countless generations through a combination of sound diet, effective clothing and efficient living quarters – a simple formula that gave the native population a colossal advantage over the navy in the 1820s.

British explorers brought their own skills and technology from Europe, which they naturally considered far superior to anything the Inuit possessed. But the trappings of an advanced European culture, such as its clothing and food, had little to do with Arctic survival. Navy expedition ships of the time were little more than a small slice of Britain berthed on a foreign shore. The explorer travelled in his own cocoon, deliberately shutting out the local environment rather than embracing it.

For the explorer, the paraphernalia and comforts of home were a self-deluding reassurance that all was well. It was a system that worked well in good times, when food and shelter were in plentiful supply and especially when bands of friendly Inuit helped bolster the diet with fresh game. But explorers were horribly exposed without their ships and the comfort of naval discipline and familiar routines. Left to fend for themselves and lacking the Inuit survival skills, naval officers and seamen struggled.

The question of diet was a perfect example of the huge differences between the natives and the visitors. Inuit were meat and fish eaters, readily consuming raw flesh and blubber whenever they were successful in the hunt. Though an unedifying sight for the cultivated British officers more accustomed to dining off fine bone china and with silver cutlery, the unsightly eating habits did not alter the fact that the Inuit diet was far superior to the navy's staple of salted beef or pork as a preventative of scurvy. The enormous advantage of raw flesh over navy rations would eventually be measured in men's lives.

Navy rations on long Arctic voyages were a recipe for scurvy. Salted or tinned meat and vegetables lost virtually all value as an anti-scorbutic. Parry did make use of pemmican – a compound mixture of dried meat and fat that provided good nutrition – but it was ineffective in the battle against scurvy. The navy had administered lemon juice to seamen with some success in the eighteenth century, but the quantities were far too small for men on Arctic diets, who went without fresh meat and vegetables for twelve months or longer.

Nor were the explorers very accomplished at hunting and stocking the larder with fresh game. Inuit – using primitive bows and arrows or spears – were far more effective than British navy personnel equipped with the latest muskets or shotguns. For navy officers, hunting was a sport; for the natives, it was a matter of life and death. The British rarely managed to kill any seals or caribou and any fresh game they did catch – mostly birds – was too often boiled beyond any worth as an anti-scorbutic.

The men, weaned on salt beef and bacon, refused to eat raw meat or fish donated by kindly Inuit. Parry himself condemned the native diet as 'horrible and disgusting'. Inuit found navy rations equally objectionable.

Yet when in 1822-23 the officers and men of *Fury* and *Hecla* were displaying swollen gums and stiffness of the joints – early signs of scurvy – Parry failed to make the connection between diet and the undeniable fact that the natives were free from scurvy and healthier than his own men. It never occurred to anyone to ask how, year after year, Inuit communities across the Arctic were not laid waste by scurvy.

Parry also failed to appreciate how Inuit invariably lived in small groups because the hunting grounds could not support larger numbers. By contrast, Parry took 118 men into the Arctic with little intention or realistic prospect of ever living off the land. Officers even took manservants into the ice for the sole purpose of being waited on hand and foot. But each servant was another mouth to feed.

Parry was not alone in misreading what the local environment could support. Despite the overwhelming evidence, the navy continued to send ships into the same region for the next twenty years laden with over a hundred dependents and with scurvy in relentless pursuit. Scurvy, in fact, blighted naval expeditions for a further century and was a critical factor in the struggles and disasters which characterised the heroic age of Antarctic exploration in the early twentieth century.

The advantages of Inuit clothing in the Arctic climate were similarly overlooked. While naval seamen clung to the traditional tight-fitting wool and flannel uniforms, the natives wore loose-fitting caribou fur or sealskin parkas with hoods that allowed body heat to circulate more freely. Sailors laboured in conventional leather boots, while the natives kept their feet dry and warm with sealskin footwear. Parry did experiment with new water-proofs developed by Mackintosh of Glasgow, but these offered no real improvement on the simple Inuit garments that had evolved over centuries.

Additionally, the men from *Fury* and *Hecla* never seemed to appreciate the comfort of Inuit living quarters. Igloos can be built quickly and provide adequate and even permanent shelter. Travel is quicker too, since sledges are not burdened with the bulky tents favoured by the navy during Parry's stay in the Arctic. Yet the art of building a 'snow house' remained beyond the ken of the navy's finest.

Even more remarkable was that no one seems to have spotted the mas-terful efficiency of using dog teams to pull sledges across the ice. In the pre-mechanised age of travel, dogs were the outstanding form of transport. They move nimbly on the ice, do not consume vast quantities of food that has be carried on the sledge and they work well in teams when managed expertly. But the men of *Hecla* and *Fury* never considered it a priority to learn the essential skills of dog-driving and for many years afterwards a procession of British explorers went to the Arctic and Antarctic without ever coming to understand the importance of dog teams. In the curious logic of the time, it was considered demeaning for dogs to do the work of men. Although many later British expeditions did take dog teams, they were often more hindrance than help to men who never fully mastered the art of managing the animals.

In the absence of dogs, British parties fell back on hauling their own cumbersome sledges – an exhausting ordeal. Yet it was considered more

Lost opportunities. British explorers were fascinated by Inuit skills, such as driving dog teams, but invariably failed to adapt to native ways.

masculine and noble for navy men to drag sledges than to allow dogs to do the work – a ridiculous hypothesis that had tragic consequences during Captain Scott's ill-fated journey to the South Pole in 1912.

William Scoresby, the whaling captain, was far-sighted enough to urge the Admiralty to use dog-drawn sledges for the 1818 North Pole venture and pointed to the remarkable feat of the Cossack, Alexsey Markov, in the Arctic. In 1714, Markov used dog teams to travel an incredible 800 miles (1,280 kilometres) through the wastes of Siberia in just 24 days – an impressive average of almost 34 miles (54 kilometres) a day. Man-hauling navy sledge teams, by contrast, did well to march 8–10 miles (13–16 kilometres) during an exhausting day's work.

On most days during the winter of 1822–23, intelligent and resourceful men like Crozier, Parry and Ross witnessed the easy efficiency of Inuit dog teams scampering over the ice. On one occasion, Crozier and Parry went on a fishing expedition with a few locals. To their utter surprise, they found that a team of ten dogs travelled 40 miles (64 kilometres) in one day while pulling 1,200 pounds (550 kilograms) on a lightweight sledge across 'very indifferent' ice, a journey that would have taken man-hauling teams days of hard labour.

It is possible to understand – though not excuse – how the 'masters' failed to learn even the most glaringly obvious lessons from a race they believed to be inferior.

In the event, *Fury* and *Hecla* left Igloolik in 1823 none the wiser and unwittingly invited future generations of polar explorers to repeat the same mistakes for years to come. Had the men of *Fury* and *Hecla* possessed the humility and respect to seek answers from people they regarded as children, it is entirely possible that at least some of the subsequent disasters in the Arctic and Antarctic during the nineteenth and twentieth centuries would have been avoided. But, as Pierre Berton, the distinguished Canadian historian, concluded: 'The real children in the Arctic [were] the white explorers.'[1]

CHAPTER 6

Wreck of *Fury*

Winter passed slowly at Igloolik and illness, particularly incipient scurvy, took an increasing toll on the party. By April 1823, most Inuit had gone in search of the spring hunting grounds and the explorers were alone again.

Scurvy had first begun to take effect during the depths of winter. Surgeons noticed the revealing signs of blackened gums and aching joints. By July, almost nine months after reaching Igloolik, the general health of all hands had deteriorated badly. Fife, ice-master of the *Hecla*, was the worst case and by September he was dead.

The worsening health of the party forced Parry's hand. Prior to scurvy taking a grip, he had wanted to send *Hecla* back to Britain and continue the search for the passage with *Fury*. Despite the obvious risks of venturing further into the ice with only one ship, he began transferring extra supplies to *Fury* and volunteers were sought for a third winter above the Arctic Circle.

But Parry changed his mind as the incidence of scurvy increased and as men struggled to cope with the back-breaking work of sawing a channel through the ice to free the ships. Two men from *Fury* and another from *Hecla* died, and Lyon warned of the 'very serious consequences' of remaining another winter.

Parties were sent out to scout the local land and bring back any fresh game they could find, but the men were not natural hunters and their catches were invariably disappointing. On one trip, Crozier went ashore with Parry and the two discovered a previously unknown river running through a deep gorge more than 50-feet (15-metres) wide and flanked by magnificent mountains. It was named Crozier River.

By early August, Parry's resolve was shaken to the core. He climbed the mast to scan the horizon to the west but saw only an unbroken white sea-scape as far as the eye could see. 'One vast expanse of solid ice,' he noted.

Fury and Hecla Strait had no intention of revealing its secrets and, after thirteen frustrating months at the entrance to what Parry believed was the North West Passage, the expedition was abandoned. It was not until 1948, some 125 years after the visit by *Fury* and *Hecla*, that a modern icebreaker managed to complete the first navigation of Fury and Hecla Strait.

Fury and *Hecla* turned for home on 12 August, reaching the Shetland Islands on 10 October 1823, where the explorers were greeted by enthusiastic crowds and the pealing of church bells. Barrels of tar were set ablaze in the streets to light up their homecoming after a disappointing and frustrating journey that had lasted twenty-seven months.

Shortly before sailing, Parry had optimistically told Barrow that 'nothing short of the entire accomplishment of the North West Passage' would satisfy the expectant public. The expedition, he now conceded, was an 'extreme disappointment'.

Nevertheless, the voyage had confirmed that Hudson Bay did not hold the key to the passage although a few more blanks on the map – notably the opening of Fury and Hecla Strait – had been filled. With public opinion still highly favourable, a fresh attempt to find the passage was inevitable.

Crozier returned from the Arctic in the autumn of 1823 to find the nation abuzz over the North West Passage. The public demanded nothing less than a successful outcome, and Barrow, sensing the popular mood, decided to take the bold step of accelerating the pace of discovery.

In early 1824, only months after the return of *Fury* and *Hecla*, Barrow fired a broadside of four separate expeditions into the ice in one final push to accomplish the task. Crozier, caught up in the heady atmosphere, volunteered to sail again.

The first expedition of 1824 was handed to Lyon, fresh from *Hecla*, who was given command of the small *Griper* and ordered to undertake a highly risky venture. He was told to travel unsupported into the ice of Repulse Bay on the edge of Foxe Basin before marching 1,000 miles (1,600 kilometres) overland to Point Turnagain – the most easterly spot reached by Franklin in his search of the Canadian coastline in 1819–22.

The second expedition would take Franklin and Richardson overland and by canoe down the Mackenzie River to the western end of the continent. For the third mission, Captain Frederick Beechey was ordered to take the *Blossom* around Cape Horn and enter Arctic waters by way of the Bering Strait.

The fourth mission was given to Parry, who was asked to take *Fury* and *Hecla* back to Lancaster Sound and to explore down Prince Regent Inlet, a potentially promising channel first sighted during the 1819–20 voyage. If successful, it was assumed the strait would bring the ships to the western end of the Fury and Hecla Strait, thus eliminating the need to navigate waters that had thwarted Parry's ships a year before.

In the most co-ordinated campaign so far, Parry was asked to erect flag-staffs and place food caches along the coast to support the overland marches of Franklin, Richardson and Lyon, while Beechey was told to station *Blossom* near the western entrance of the Bering Strait for a rendez-vous with both Franklin and Parry.

Crozier, still rated a midshipman, was among a total complement of 62 assigned to Parry's ship, *Hecla*. Command of *Fury* was given to Captain Henry Hoppner. Among his crew of 60 was Ross, newly promoted to lieutenant.

Crowds flocked to the Thames to see the ships, now among the most famous in the fleet. Over 6,000 people climbed *Hecla's* gangplank to sign the visitors' book, while the officers – resplendent in crisp, blue uniforms and fine braid – were applauded at a glittering farewell ball to mark their departure. Here, Parry met his future wife Isabella Stanley for the first time.

Hecla and *Fury* sailed down the Thames on 19 May 1824, accompanied by the supply vessel, *William Harris*. But Parry's luck, which had been so crucial to his great voyage in 1819–20, had run out.

Parry began one of his missions to the Arctic by cheerfully proclaiming, 'Oh, how I long to be among the ice!' A more realistic judgement on the perils of exploring in the ice was made by Leopold McClintock, the accomplished explorer, who once wrote: 'I can understand how men's hair have [sic] turned grey in a few hours.'[1]

Parry's ships ran into severe difficulties off the west coast of Greenland soon after unloading stores from *William Harris*. The ships entered the cold waters of Davis Strait, where, to their dismay, the ice was twice as thick as when Parry last visited the area in 1819.

Hecla ran aground on a rock during one manoeuvre and the ship, battered by high seas and the grinding ice, tipped over onto its side. Just when it seemed the ship might founder, *Hecla* was righted and managed to float free.

The journey up Davis Strait and across Baffin Bay towards Lancaster Sound in unseasonably bad weather was horrendous. *Fury* and *Hecla* fought against strong winds, freezing fog and the constant threat of collision with icebergs. The decks and sails were coated with a layer of ice and the pack seemed impenetrable. It looked as though the 122 men and ships would be prevented from entering Lancaster Sound and forced to spend the winter trapped in Baffin Bay.

Fortunately, the ice eased a little and the ships were able to resume sailing. But the journey across Baffin Bay to Lancaster Sound had taken almost two months – about twice as long as expected. *Hecla* and *Fury* did not turn west into Lancaster Sound until 10 September, well behind schedule and with little time left to reach their target of Prince Regent Inlet before the autumnal ice closed in.

Hopes of making progress were further hit when heavy pack ice confronted the ships 20 miles (32 kilometres) from the entrance to the inlet. The short navigable season was now almost finished. Even the usually optimistic Parry became despondent. For a moment, he contemplated abandoning the enterprise and returning home.

Foul weather then delivered a fresh blow when very strong gales from the west drove the ships out of Lancaster Sound and back into Baffin Bay. Just when things looked at their bleakest, the winds suddenly changed direction and *Hecla* and *Fury* were thrown back into Lancaster Sound almost as quickly as they had been ejected. Propelled by powerful gales, the ships rebounded into Lancaster Sound and raced 200 miles (320 kilometres) to the mouth of Prince Regent Inlet. The inlet, a broad expanse of water running due south between the towering cliffs of Baffin Island and Somerset Island, was a daunting challenge.

In wild weather and with autumn descending, the most pressing matter was to find shelter for the winter. Clinging resolutely to the coastline, *Fury* and *Hecla* edged slowly south down Prince Regent Inlet in high winds, taking frequent depths and anxiously scanning the shoreline for a suitable harbour on the western shores of Baffin Island. After sailing about 50 miles (80 kilometres) along the coast, a small bay was spotted and the ships were quickly installed in their winter quarters.

The bay, named Port Bowen, was an austere, inhospitable spot surrounded by dark, brooding cliffs and with few diversions to help the men pass the dark winter months. There was little wildlife and no sign of kindly Inuit to provide fresh game or willing company. Parry gloomily recorded the 'motionless torpor' of the bleak setting.

It was a long, tedious winter, despite the usual sideshows and routines designed to keep the crews occupied. The traditional Arctic theatre was

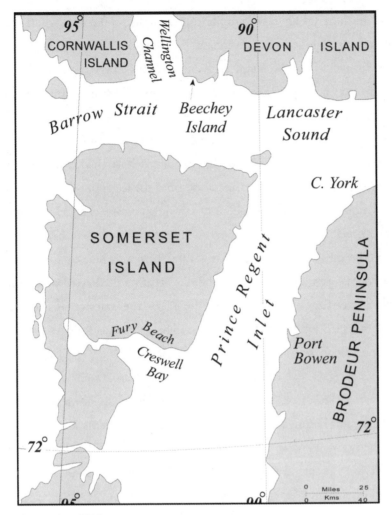

Fury Beach, 1825.

abandoned in favour of elaborate costume balls that featured officers dressed up in ever-more absurd outfits and waltzing through the night in women's clothing.

Crozier blacked himself up with boot polish as footman to a grand dame in the unlikely shape of Captain Hoppner. On one occasion – to the merriment of all – Parry disguised himself as an old tramp and shambled across the ice to *Fury* begging for a few spare coppers.

Crozier took up his now familiar role of taking copious magnetic readings, making detailed observations of the weather and acquiring regular water samples. He was happy with his scientific duties, particularly when joined by Ross and Lieutenant Henry Foster, a young officer regarded as one of the most capable scientific brains of the age.

The days passed slowly. Parry was affected by rheumatism, and a few tentative inland voyages to explore the neighbouring vicinity yielded very little new knowledge. By early July, with the release from the ice approaching, the crews were sweating from the hard labour of sawing an escape channel through the ice. One gruelling session lasted almost unbroken for twenty-six hours.

Freedom came on 20 July 1825 when the ships were able to sail unscathed from Port Bowen and resume the journey southwards down Prince Regent Inlet. Parry ordered the ships to cross the inlet – the waterway is between 40 and 60 miles (65 km to 100 km) wide – and begin looking for a passage to the west along the rocky coastline of Somerset Island.

But once again, the expedition was assailed by an atrocious combination of powerful winds, freezing temperatures and a heavy build-up of ice blocking their path. During one storm, *Fury* was driven towards the coastal cliffs where hefty chunks of ice were clinging to the rocky shoreline. Men from *Hecla* jumped over the side to help smash up the threatening ice and all hands were relieved when high tides carried *Fury* back to open water.

It was only a brief respite and the ice and winds made a fresh assault, driving the ships back towards the shore. On one occasion, the vessels came close to colliding in the high winds and again *Fury* was hurled towards the cliffs by the strong winds.

Finally, *Fury* was driven onto the shore. Beams began to buckle and crack as the ship hit the beach and a cracking sound like a gunshot announced the snapping of the ship's rudder. As water poured in, Hoppner's crew worked around the clock to stem the tide, while officers from *Fury* took the risk of venturing over the broken sea ice at the height of the storm to inspect the damage.

Fury needed urgent repairs. Men worked solidly for two weeks in hazardous conditions trying to plug the leaks and replace fractured timbers. Only when raging winds and swirling blizzards made it impossible to work did the men retreat across the sea to *Hecla* for a brief rest.

Hecla was forced to move to safer waters when violent winds threatened to drive the ship aground alongside *Fury*. In the battering which followed, *Fury* was rammed further onto the beach. From their vantage point at sea, the men on *Hecla* could only watch helplessly.

For four days, *Hecla* was forced to stand off the beach, which lies in Creswell Bay on the south-eastern side of Somerset Island. When the winds eased off slightly, men hurried back across the sea to find *Fury* beached like a dead whale. The stricken ship was lying on its side, and ice, driven by the high winds, had closed around the hulk. *Fury* was doomed.

Parry and Hoppner came ashore on 25 August for a closer inspection of the wreckage. Parry recorded the 'utter hopelessness' of the vessel. Repairing the ship would take weeks, perhaps a month, which would leave no time for exploration that season. The serious risk of *Hecla* also being driven ashore left Parry with no choice but to abandon *Fury*.

It also meant abandoning the expedition. The crew of 60 men was given an hour to remove personal belongings, while stores and equipment from *Fury* that could not be carried on *Hecla* were stockpiled on the beach as a source of life for future adventurers to the area. The bleak, windswept shore was named Fury Beach.

On 25 August 1825, *Hecla* left the mortally wounded *Fury* to the mercy of the brutal Arctic climate. John Page, one of *Fury*'s seamen, died suddenly as *Hecla* prepared to sail for home; he was the only casualty of the expedition.

Hecla, badly overcrowded with men and supplies from *Fury*, turned for home. It was a poignant moment and marked the end of Parry's long and occasionally hazardous quest to find the North West Passage. Worn out by almost eight years of endeavour, Parry effectively gave up his search at Fury Beach. But as he turned for home, he scribbled a final philosophical entry in his journal: 'The only real cause for wonder is our long exemption from such a catastrophe.'[2]

Hecla passed along Lancaster Sound and into Baffin Bay, where, to their surprise, they found little ice in the seas that had threatened so much danger only a year before. After a comfortable and uneventful trip, *Hecla* was back in British waters by October and was finally paid off on 21 November 1825. Parry's third expedition – the least successful of all his voyages – had been a dismal failure that brought the quest for the North West Passage no closer.

Barrow's three other expeditions from the salvo of 1824 produced mixed results. Lyon's venture in the *Griper* was a total failure. Faced with heavy ice and hurricane-force winds, the ship failed to reach its destination of Repulse Bay and a defeated expedition crept back into England after only five months. Lyon never went to the Arctic again.

Beechey in *Blossom* endured a mammoth 73,000-mile (117,000-kilometre) journey to the Bering Strait that lasted three and a half years and cost the lives of numerous crewmen. At one point, he was only 160 miles (256 kilometres) along Canada's northern shore from the overland expedition of Franklin and Richardson, but neither knew of the other's existence and the opportunity of an historic link-up between parties from east and west of the passage was lost.

Franklin and Richardson achieved the most, trekking thousands of miles and mapping large swathes of unknown land during their two-year journey.

Crozier emerged from Parry's expedition in a far better position than he might have envisaged given the mission's failure. Now an established Arctic hand, he had found his *métier*. Three winters in the Arctic had enabled him to make his mark and exploration, despite its rigours, was precisely the type of duty that enabled him to serve the navy. He resolved to go north again.

CHAPTER 7

North Pole

Months passed before Crozier's value to the country's programme of Arctic exploration was officially recognised. In March 1826 – six months before his thirtieth birthday – he was finally promoted to the rank of lieutenant.

Progress through the ranks had been excruciatingly slow because of the continuing surplus of idle navy officers and it had taken Crozier over fifteen years, more than half his lifetime, to become a lieutenant. But without Arctic exploration, it is likely that his progress would have been slower still. Luckily for Crozier, the ambitious Barrow was plotting to send more ships north.

By the mid-1820s, Barrow had fine-tuned his targets. After almost a decade of focus on the North West Passage, he now considered it timely to switch attention towards the North Pole. Buchan's unsuccessful expedition in 1818 was the last attempt to reach the Pole, but by 1826 Barrow had persuaded the Admiralty to fund a fresh endeavour.

Barrow's enthusiasm for the North Pole was linked to his persistent fondness for the 'Open Polar Sea' notion and he cited the reports of Lieutenant Constantine Phipps – who had made a particularly unsuccessful attempt to reach the Pole in 1774 – as justification for another expedition.

Phipps, he reminded the Admiralty, had turned back at 80° north after finding his path blocked by 'one continued plain of smooth unbroken ice'. Barrow perceived the obstacle encountered by Phipps as an opportunity, not a deterrent. Scoresby added his weight to the fanciful idea by claiming it was possible to drive a coach-and-four across the unbroken field of ice.

Barrow's theory seemed plausible. Ships would take men as far as possible into the pack, where they would unload small boats and drag them over the ice until they reached Phipps' 'plain of smooth unbroken ice'. At this point, parties could haul their small boats over the undemanding terrain until they reached the 'Open Polar Sea' where the small craft could be launched for a gentle cruise to the most northerly point on the globe.

The idea for a new North Pole expedition was first proposed by Franklin after his return from the 1818 voyage with Buchan. But Barrow sat on the scheme until 1826 when he offered the project to his personal favourite, Parry.

Barrow needed to be persuasive. Following the loss of *Fury*, Parry had returned to London convinced that his exploring days were at an end. He also had to witness Hoppner endure the statutory court martial for the loss of *Fury*, although ultimately no blame was attached.

After three Arctic expeditions, Parry was drained and within months of coming home had pursued his relationship with Isabella Stanley, the twenty-four-year-old daughter of a minor aristocrat who he had first met on the eve of *Hecla* and *Fury*'s departure. Arctic exploration had never been further from his thoughts.

But Barrow, having dusted off Franklin's plan, urged Parry to have another shot at glory. Parry dutifully abandoned his plans to retire and agreed in early 1827 to lead the North Pole expedition, driven perhaps by thoughts that he needed to repair his reputation after the embarrassment of losing *Fury*. Isabella Stanley, whom he married in 1826, faithfully gave him a silk flag to fly at the Pole.

Parry assembled his repertory company of tried-and-tested Arctic players for the North Pole expedition. There was a familiar feel about proceedings as Crozier, Ross, Foster and Bird agreed to join up. *Hecla*, too, was spruced up for one final attempt to grant Parry the triumph he so earnestly sought.

Crozier was asked to play a crucial role in the expedition, an appointment that underlined Parry's respect for the Irishman. While Parry and Ross would lead the trek to reach the Pole, Crozier was to take effective command of *Hecla*.

The plan was to take *Hecla* to Spitsbergen in the Svalbard archipelago and from there dispatch two teams of sailors north, dragging specially built boats across the ice to the edge of the 'Open Polar Sea'. The boats were equipped with wheels or steel runners and backed up by the unusual auxiliary power of eight Norwegian reindeer. The option of using dog teams to cross the ice, as advocated by Scoresby, was rejected.

Buoyed by Barrow's enthusiasm and his own in-built optimism, Parry was highly confident of making a routine hike to the Pole. 'Few enterprises are so easily practicable,' he wrote. 'I can perceive nothing whatever that should make it an enterprise of extraordinary risk.'

Hecla sailed in late March 1827 and reached the small port of Hammerfest in Norway, above the Arctic Circle, on 19 April. Here, the party expected to pick up the reindeer, but the animals were nowhere to be seen.

Crozier was then ordered to make a tricky 60-mile (100-kilometre) trip in stormy weather down the coast to Alten to acquire the animals. He returned a few days later in atrocious conditions with the mournful-looking beasts and bales of moss for fodder.

The weather was appalling during the trip to Spitsbergen – far more troublesome than anyone had expected. *Hecla* was struck by vicious storms soon after leaving Norway and it was clear from the heavily packed ice that the winter of 1826–27 had been unusually cold.

Hecla ran into further difficulties while skirting the west coast of Spitsbergen. The ship was forced to seek shelter from the high winds by pulling into the pack for protection. Entering the ice proved far easier than escaping from it, and *Hecla* was stuck in the ice for three weeks, throwing Parry's schedule into disarray. Even when a sharp easterly gale broke open the ice, *Hecla* spent a further ten days in freezing conditions hunting for a safe harbour to moor the ship.

The combination of severe gales and heavy pack ice forced Parry to consider landing supplies on shore in case *Hecla* had to be abandoned. But even the contingency plan ran into trouble.

Crozier and Foster had been ordered to ferry the emergency supplies ashore, but a fresh storm blew up immediately the operation began. After struggling for fourteen hours in treacherous seas and bitterly cold temperatures, the men were still unable to land all the stores. Crozier and Foster, weary from their exertions, returned to *Hecla* and the plan to cache emergency supplies was abandoned.

Hecla soon became trapped in the ice for a second time and a further two precious days were lost. It was not until 18 June, almost three weeks behind schedule, that *Hecla* found a suitable harbour at Sorgfjord.

Sorgfjord, a small bay at the northern end of the narrow channel that separates the islands of West Spitsbergen and North East Land, is a desolate, austere inlet whose surrounding hills are dotted by the gravestones of unfortunate whalers. Dutch sailors originally named it Treurenberg Bay from the word *treuren* – to lament.

Hecla was manoeuvred into the sheltered bay, which was renamed Hecla Cove. High above the bay, a headland offering a spectacular lookout over the planned route to the Pole, was named Point Crozier.

Three days later, on 21 June, two seven-man teams left for the Pole, about 700 miles (1,120 kilometres) away. Parry took charge of one boat, which he called *Enterprise*, and Ross took the other, which was named *Investigator*. Crozier commanded *Hecla* while the men were away.

Crozier accompanied the boat parties northwards with additional supplies for about 50 miles (80 kilometres), before bidding farewell at the small outpost of Walden Island.

Unlike the blithely optimistic Parry, Crozier had reservations about the difficult trek and knew the party faced a tougher journey than Parry was prepared to admit. Crozier's concerns were reflected in a letter to Ross that he left behind in a food depot:

> I cannot explain the mingled sensations I experienced the day I parted with you at Walden Isle. I did not think I was so soft (amiable weakness you must say). But I assure you my heart was in my mouth till I got on board. God bless you my boy and send you all back safe and sound by the appointed time is the constant prayer of your old messmate.[1]

Crozier's anxiety was well founded. The expedition was doomed to failure, partly because the boats were too heavy to drag for hundreds of miles and partly because Parry and Ross had innocently set out too late in the

North Pole. Crozier is depicted (bottom right) in the group, waving farewell as Parry and Ross embark on their failed bid to reach the Pole in 1827.

season. The hard ice that persists in the late spring months of April and May makes better travel conditions in the Arctic than the loose, slushy conditions encountered in the relative warmth of July and August. Hazardous large pools and wide lanes of open water are also created as the ice breaks up in summer.

The boats, too, proved problematic. The plan to harness the reindeer to the 20-foot-long (6 metres) craft had been abandoned even before the party set off. On a trial run, the wheels and runners attached to the heavy boats had sunk deep into the ice and they had barely moved an inch.

In their stead, the men were ordered to pull the boats, each weighing over 1,800 pounds (850 kilograms) when packed with provisions. Effectively, each man was required to pull the equivalent of about 260 pounds (almost 120 kilograms) or more than their own bodyweight. The tortuous slog meant struggling all day across the soft snow and ice. Sometimes, they crawled on all fours like the animals they had replaced.

The ever-optimistic Parry had set out with the fond hope of travelling around 15 miles (24 kilometres) a day on the 1,400-mile (2,240-kilometre) round trip to the Pole and back. But the party managed only a fraction of this.

The arduous task of hauling boats was compounded by the nature of the terrain. Instead of the promised 'plain of smooth unbroken ice', they found miles of broken, lumpy blocks of ice intersected by dangerous lanes of open water that meant frequent stoppages. Each time a lead was reached, the men had to go through the tedious process of unloading the supplies, launching the boats, carrying the supplies across the water and reloading the boats on the other side. Launching the fully laden boats into the open water was impossible since they would be too heavy to drag from the water.

Even worse, the ice was constantly on the move due to the persistent northerly wind, which drove them backwards despite hours of intensive struggle. On some days, the men made no northerly progress despite hours of intense struggle. It was like walking the wrong way up a fast-moving escalator. At the end of one particularly exhausting day, it was calculated that, though the parties had travelled northwards for 10–11 miles (16–17 kilometres), they had ended up 3 miles (5 kilometres) south of where they began that morning.

Parry never reached the 'main ice' that he believed would provide a smooth pathway to the 'Open Polar Sea'. On 26 July, it was estimated that the previous five days of back-breaking labour had taken them only 1 mile north, which left them around 500 miles (800 kilometres) from the Pole. The march was abandoned.

During the five-week slog, the party had trekked 668 miles (1,069 kilometres) but advanced only 172 miles (275 kilometres) north from *Hecla* – a heart-breaking ratio of 4 miles (6 kilometres) pulling for every single mile gained northwards. Nevertheless, the fourteen men stood at 82° 45' north, the furthest north reached by anyone – a record that stood for half a century.

The struggle back to *Hecla* brought further torture for the tired party, with the men wracked by snow-blindness, growing hunger and early signs of scurvy. Parry had badly underestimated food rations and he noted a 'wildness in their looks' as the men inched their way south towards the safety of *Hecla*.

While Parry was away, Crozier was going through some of what the polar party was experiencing. In July, he led a group of twelve from *Hecla* to lay down a line of food depots along the route of the party's return and found the going very tough. The round trip of 160 miles (256 kilometres) to the Walden, Phipps and Little Table Islands was undertaken in appalling weather and Crozier remembered, 'No small job, I assure you.'

The food depots laid by Crozier following Parry's departure proved to be vitally important for the survival of Parry and Ross. When the polar party stumbled into the depot at Little Table Island, the men had been on the march for over two days without proper food or rest. It was a grateful Ross who reported the discovery of 'various little luxuries' that

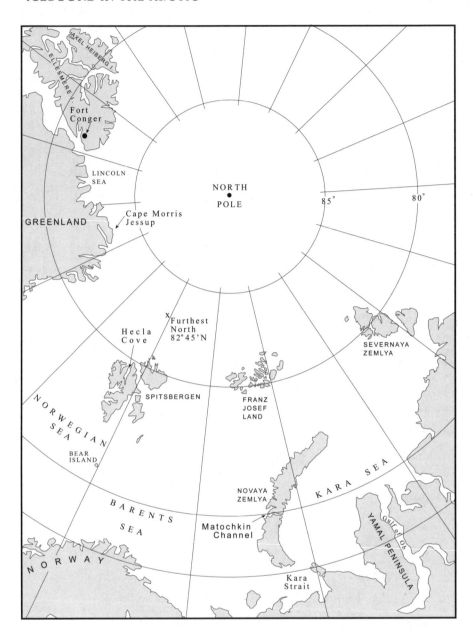

North Pole trek, 1827.

had been deposited by Crozier. Ross also found a welcoming note from Crozier, which read:

> I hope with the blessing of God you will find us right here on your arrival in due season. We think of you sometimes, always at dinner time ... how much we would give just to know whereabouts you are, whether sailing or hauling. God send the former.[2]

Crozier, too, had had a lucky escape while Parry was away. During one fearsome bout of weather, *Hecla* was driven ashore and nearly ran aground. Crozier could hear the ship's bottom scraping along the rocky beach and his thoughts may have gone back to the luckless *Fury* in Prince Regent Inlet a couple of years earlier.

Two days of intense struggle were required before he was able to take *Hecla* into safe depths. In a letter to Ross, he blamed himself for the incident: 'How short sighted is man.' It was something of an understatement when Crozier reported that he was 'quite rejoiced' to see the ship float off the shore and enter deeper water.

On 21 August, two months after setting out, the exhausted man-hauling party, suffering badly from the worsening effects of scurvy, finally reached *Hecla*. It was a close-run thing. Crozier, punctual and meticulous as ever, had the ship ready to sail for home without a moment's delay.

Unfavourable winds detained *Hecla* for a few more days at Hecla Cove and the expedition was not permitted to sail until 28 August. The Orkneys were reached on 23 September, and *Hecla* arrived in London on 17 October 1827 after a disappointing journey of nearly seven months.

By coincidence, Parry and Franklin returned from their Arctic expeditions at precisely the same time – the two men walked into the Admiralty building within fifteen minutes of each other. Both were knighted, but Parry never went to the Arctic again and Franklin headed for eighteen years of obscurity before making an unfortunate return to the ice.

Crozier, despite having completed three Arctic missions in the space of only six years, received no plaudits from above. Instead, he found himself, at age thirty-one, without a ship and resigned to living off the navy's modest half-pay which was less than £1 a day, equal to around £65 in today's terms. He also found the mood at the Admiralty changed. After a decade of chasing the North West Passage and North Pole, there had been a change of political direction in London. Barrow discovered that budgets had been trimmed and Arctic exploration, which had enjoyed unchallenged priority at the Admiralty, was put on hold.

So, too, was the career of Lieutenant Crozier.

CHAPTER 8

Arctic Rescue

Francis Crozier entered the doldrums in 1827. Despite a recognised status in Arctic circles and being at the peak of his powers, Crozier spent the next seven years in humble naval backwaters. Most of the time was spent on half-pay, interrupted by a single posting. Crozier, now into his thirties, had been promoted to the rank of first lieutenant after the North Pole expedition, but, in truth, he was a forgotten man without exploration.

Crozier's most illuminating moment on his return from the North Pole expedition was to learn that he had been elected a Fellow of the prestigious Royal Astronomical Society (RAS). The honour, which had taken effect from 11 May 1827 while Crozier was trying to reach Spitsbergen on *Hecla*, was in recognition of his valuable astronomical work conducted on Arctic expeditions with Parry.

Among his proposers to the RAS had been Lieutenant Henry Foster, the likeable scientific officer from two earlier voyages aboard *Hecla*. But some of the gloss was knocked off his accolade by news that Foster had since drowned in the swamps of Panama.

Crozier's recognition by the RAS was a rare encouragement during an otherwise melancholic period. Unable to secure a commission, he drifted aimlessly.

Surprisingly, Crozier did not join the next Arctic expedition to leave British shores. The new venture was put together by John Ross – James Clark Ross' uncle – with a view to completing what Parry had begun: to find the North West Passage. A private undertaking without official backing, it is likely that Crozier was denied permission to enlist because of Admiralty antagonism towards John Ross.

John Ross, who had been ostracised by Barrow and the polar establishment since the controversy over Lancaster Sound in 1818, emerged from semi-retirement in 1828 with his bold plan. In defiance of the official channels, he persuaded Felix Booth, the philanthropic owner of Booth's gin company, to finance the expedition.

The announcement brought a flood of volunteers, including a man who applied to be expedition cook after claiming to have dreamt about the ice. Unfortunately the man did not tell his wife about his plans for an Arctic voyage and the shocked woman – named only as Mary L – ended her husband's ambitions by informing the expedition she would not let him have his clothes for the journey. 'He must be mad ever to think of leaving a comfortable home, to be frozen in with ice, or torn to pieces with bears,' she added.

To the outrage of John Ross' critics at the Admiralty, some navy officers, most of them languishing on half-pay, promised to serve without a salary. But his much-respected nephew, James Ross, was enlisted as second-in-command.

John Ross, now aged fifty-two, had used his exile in his native Scotland to reassess Arctic exploration. Among his important conclusions was that Barrow's earlier expeditions were far too large and had used the wrong type of vessel to penetrate the ice. He proposed taking only 25 men into the ice, about one-fifth of the number taken by Parry.

The most radical part of his scheme was his choice of expedition ship – *Victory*, a steam-powered vessel. The idea of taking a motorised ship to the ice was greeted with contempt by Barrow and his reactionary cohorts at the

Admiralty who mistrusted the new-fangled steam engines almost as much as they disliked Ross.

Up to this point Britain's naval ascendancy was founded exclusively on a mastery of sail, and the Admiralty had little enthusiasm for an unproven and often unreliable emerging new technology. Lord Melville, Barrow's political master at the Admiralty, once decreed that steam engines were 'calculated to strike a fatal blow to the naval supremacy of the Empire'.

Victory proved to be an uninspiring flagship for the motorisation of sea travel which went a long way to justify the navy's scepticism. The paddle-wheel steam packet sailed north in May 1829 with its engines stuttering and boilers leaking. It suffered constant mechanical problems in the North Atlantic, yet somehow managed to cross Baffin Bay.

Victory entered Lancaster Sound and drove hard down Prince Regent Inlet, passing Fury Beach and easily surpassing the progress made by Parry under sail. Ice conditions were favourable that year and when new land south of Fury Beach was found, it was given the name of Boothia Felix (now Boothia Peninsula). The discovery was celebrated with ample measures of their benefactor's gin.

But John Ross' luck soon ran out and the expedition was forced to spend four long winters trapped in the ice. The faltering steam engine, the first experiment in motor-driven Arctic exploration, was dismantled and dumped ashore.

James Ross left the ship to survey hundreds of miles of new land, and in the spring of 1831 crowned his remarkable career by locating the North Magnetic Pole on the west coast of Boothia. On one sledging mission, he crossed the sea ice to the west and reached a desolate chunk of territory that he named King William Land.

The most-westerly headland was christened Point Victory – subsequently Victory Point – and from here Ross retreated, confident that the land was attached to the Canadian mainland. It was an unfortunate error that would later have serious implications for Crozier.

After three years in the ice, *Victory* was abandoned and the survivors marched overland up the peninsula to plunder some of the food cache which Parry had left at Fury Beach. Moving slowly northwards, the party eventually reached Lancaster Sound in small boats, from where it hoped to run into a passing whaler.

But thick ice prevented escape and the desperate men were forced to return to bleak, windswept Fury Beach, where they would spend another winter. There was no sign of *Fury* itself, which had been obliterated by the weather.

In 1833, with only 13 of the original 25 men still capable of work, John Ross took three small boats on a journey up Prince Regent Inlet. Soon after entering Lancaster Sound, the sails of a ship were spotted. To their astonishment, it was Captain Richard Humphreys in *Isabella*, the ship Ross had controversially sailed to the edge of Lancaster Sound in 1818.

John Ross lost only two men in his mammoth four-year journey. However, the lessons of the expedition were largely ignored back home.

The party survived the ordeal primarily because of its small size and was able to supplement traditional naval rations by hunting local game, which also proved helpful in preventing the deadly spread of scurvy. It is highly unlikely that a party of 120 men and two ships – typical of Parry's expeditions – would have survived four years in the wilderness on the staple navy diet of salted beef or pork.

Diet was the key and John Ross was in no doubt about the vital importance of Inuit eating habits. Unlike the men who wintered at Igloolik in 1822–23, John Ross was prepared to learn from native customs. In one prophetic statement, he declared:

> It would be very desirable indeed if the men could acquire the taste for Greenland [Inuit] food. All experience has shown that the large use of oil and fat meats is the true secret of life in these frozen countries.[1]

Yet the experience of the *Victory* expedition went unheeded in London and the Admiralty continued to send large contingents of men to the ice on a diet that invited scurvy and with no adequate means of supporting themselves in case of emergency. Among the victims of Admiralty myopia would be Crozier.

Though he was fortunate to escape the four-year ordeal of the Ross expedition, Crozier spent those years awaiting a new posting. Relief came in 1831, when he was appointed to *Stag*. However shortly after joining, his seventy-seven-year-old father, George Crozier, died in Ireland.

Stag was a newly built frigate of 46 guns, whose colourful captain, Edward Troubridge, was a wealthy peer, a Member of Parliament and aide-de-camp to the king. The ship patrolled the waters off the coast of Portugal, an awkward posting that was part guard duty and part diplomacy. Britain was Portugal's oldest ally and the navy was caught in the crossfire of the country's bitter civil war for the Portuguese throne.

When Troubridge stepped down in 1832, the captaincy was awarded to Nicholas Lockyer, a highly experienced sailor with over forty years' service in the navy. In the event, Crozier survived the difficult commission unscathed, and both he and Lockyer remained with *Stag* until the end of 1835.

These were uncomfortable times for Crozier, now in his fortieth year and still only a lowly lieutenant. Progress up the ranks was unbearably slow and his prospects more than ever rested on the Admiralty's plans for new expeditions. A man with an alternative career in mind might have resigned from the navy, but Crozier was still wedded to the sea. Nor did he know anything else.

Then, in December 1835, he received an unexpected summons from James Ross. A humanitarian crisis had arisen and Ross wanted his trusted friend to help resolve it.

A delegation from Hull whaling companies had warned the Admiralty that eleven ships were trapped above the Arctic Circle in the ice of Davis

Strait. With more than 600 sailors and millions of pounds of shipping and cargo in serious jeopardy, the whalers urged the Admiralty to dispatch a relief mission.

Initially, the Admiralty was lukewarm, insisting that the trapped ships were unlikely to be freed during the winter months and that sending relief parties north was a waste of resources. However, public pressure mounted as word filtered back to London that some of the ships had been crushed and that a number of survivors were stranded on floating bergs in Davis Strait or on an unknown headland.

One of the lost ships, it emerged, was *Isabella* – the vessel which had rescued John and James Ross in Lancaster Sound in 1833. Although *Isabella* had gone down in May 1835 off the Whalefish Islands at the northern stretch of Davis Strait, the crew had somehow managed to find its way across the ice to another ship.

Captain Humphreys – *Isabella*'s former commander – led the passionate appeals for a relief mission and he urged the Admiralty to appoint the experienced James Ross to lead it. Ross readily accepted the job, and the Admiralty agreed to commission a vessel and pay the crew on condition it was fitted out by the shipowners and manned by volunteers. Within weeks, a sum of £5,000 (around £325,000 today) was raised.

Ross was given a free hand to pick his crew and, with virtually the entire navy at his disposal, he asked for Crozier to be his second-in-command. Ross, now the most experienced active Arctic officer, selected the dependable Crozier ahead of suitably qualified men such as George Back and Dr Richard King, whose applications to join the expedition were turned down. Ross next hurried north to Hull to examine the available vessels and after scrutiny selected *Cove*, a weathered 380-ton whaling ship built at Whitby almost forty years earlier.

Cove was officially commissioned on 18 December and work began immediately to strengthen and provision the ship for the journey, a risky voyage through the stormy North Atlantic at the height of winter.

Crozier arrived in Hull on 23 December to learn that the Admiralty's instructions were to take *Cove* to the edge of the ice in Davis Strait in search of the marooned seamen and to make contact with the Danish settlements on the west coast of Greenland, where, it was hoped, shipwrecked survivors may have found their way ashore. As insurance against *Cove* itself getting trapped, the Admiralty decided to send as support vessels two navy bomb ships, *Erebus* and *Terror*.

Cove was on the brink of leaving Hull in the early days of January 1836 when good news arrived. Two of the missing ships – *Duncombe* and *Harmony* – had returned with encouraging reports that other vessels had also been released from the ice.

Cove, with 64 men on board, sailed from Hull on 6 January 1836 and immediately ran into powerful gales. One particularly violent storm to the south of Iceland lasted unbroken for five days and the ship's bowsprit was wrenched off. At the height of the storm, *Cove* toppled over and there were fears that the vessel might be lost. One officer remembered shutting his eyes, expecting to find the ship dashed to pieces when he opened them. The logbook dryly recorded: 'A tremendous heavy sea running.'[2]

Ross and Crozier inspected the damage and decided to take the battered *Cove* back to Stromness in the Orkneys for repairs. While at Stromness, news arrived that several more whalers had now been freed from the ice.

The North Atlantic winter storm had rattled even the hardened whalers and Ross and Crozier faced a minor mutiny as some crewmen refused to sail until later in the season. The mutiny was eventually extinguished and, on 24 February, *Cove* once again headed west in search of the trapped ships.

By early April, *Cove* was working along the coast of Labrador before probing northwards near the edge of the pack ice in the Davis Strait. At night, the ship fired rockets and burned distinctive blue lights in the hope of alerting castaways who may be camped on the ice.

On 15 May, *Cove* came across *Undaunted*, a Scottish whaler. Its crew reported that another of the trapped vessels – *Lady Jane* – had escaped and arrived safely in Hull. Only *William Torr*, a 286-ton whaler from Hull, was still missing.

Cove zigzagged across Davis Strait in late May before sailing towards Holsteinborg on Greenland's east coast for a planned rendezvous with the escort ships, *Erebus* and *Terror*. Seas were unaccountably calm, and Crozier was dispatched in a small boat to locate *Erebus* and *Terror* and alert them of *Cove's* imminent arrival. But Crozier found no sign of the vessels.

Cove waited for almost two weeks for the ships that never came. Assuming that *Erebus* and *Terror* had sailed up the coast to the Whalefish Islands, *Cove* followed suit and made the 200-mile (320 kilometre) journey north. While there was still no trace of *Erebus* and *Terror*, the whaler *Lord Gambier* was encountered carrying a message for the *Cove*.

The Admiralty – reassured that all but one of the whalers had returned – had abandoned plans to send *Erebus* and *Terror* to assist *Cove*. The message was reinforced a week later, in mid-June, when *Lady Jane*, one of the whalers to escape from the ice, emerged with new orders from the Admiralty that gave Ross full discretion to return home as soon he wished, the implication being that *William Torr* was lost. The navigable season was at its best, however, and Ross opted to continue the search.

Cove turned north again, entering the narrow Waygatz Strait that separates Disco Island and the coast of Greenland. Hampered by persistent fog, *Cove* edged onwards to Jacob's Bight, where a fleet of almost 50 whalers was found waiting at the edge of the ice before resuming the hunt. But there was no word of *William Torr*.

Cove retreated through Waygatz Strait to continue the search south of the Whalefish Islands, where *William Torr* had last been sighted. Venturing further south, *Cove* crossed Davis Strait again and began exploring for signs of life amid the countless rocky inlets on the northern shores of Labrador. Breaking through the dangerous offshore ice in the last days of July, the ship anchored in a small bay near the Okak Islands, where Ross discovered that a handful of hardy missionaries had established a settlement. But nothing was learnt of *William Torr*'s fate.

The search by Ross and Crozier covered an extensive area of the Davis Strait – ranging from 55°–70° north – without finding a sign of the ship or crew. Early on the morning of 4 August, it was decided that nothing more could be done and the quest was abandoned.

Three days later, *Cove* took leave of the ice and was driven home by strong westerly gales. The ship docked at Hull on 31 August and Ross and Crozier broke the news that *William Torr* had vanished.

William Torr was officially listed as lost in October 1836, but the full grisly tale of the ship's fate did not emerge until 1840 when local Inuit bands divulged a few details to a passing whaler – a ship that had coincidentally been among the vessels trapped and released in 1836. According to the natives, *William Torr* was crushed by ice off Cape Fry in December 1835, a full month before the *Cove* relief mission sailed from Hull.

Captain Smith, the *Torr*'s skipper, led a small party across the sea ice in a desperate attempt to locate *Lady Jane*, but was never seen again. The 22 seamen left behind on the shore were unable to fend for themselves and all hands perished.[3]

Failure to locate the *William Torr* did nothing to tarnish the reputation of Ross and Crozier. Ross was greeted with more public acclaim and offered a knighthood, which, surprisingly, he turned down. Amid the plaudits, Ross did not forget Crozier. To Ross, the journey had seen his friend mature into a first-class seafarer and he was determined to ensure that Crozier was promoted to a rank more reflective of his abilities.

A month after stepping ashore, Ross wrote a strong letter to the Admiralty in which he sang the praises of Crozier and urged his promotion forthwith. Employing unusually firm language, Ross warned the Admiralty that failure to promote Crozier might stain the reputation of the expedition itself. He spoke of Crozier's 'high character' and the 'high example of naval enterprise' shown during the voyage of *Cove*.

The zealous and efficient manner in which he has fulfilled his trying and difficult duties makes me anxious that an officer of such high reputation and who has given so many instances of distinguished merit should receive that promotion which it has been the invariable practice of the Admiralty to bestow . . .[4]

Ross' intervention succeeded. In January 1837, Crozier was promoted to the rank of commander.

CHAPTER 9

South

Crozier's promotion was welcome but did little to enhance his immediate prospects. He was still a junior ranking officer among a sea of unemployed officers and at the age of forty his future was almost fully dependent on exploration. Another period of half-pay and no obvious alternatives only underlined his predicament.

His uncertain career prospects echoed Crozier's equally uncertain personal life as he entered middle age. After spending his entire adult life at sea, he had not managed to lay down roots and never succeeded in developing any lasting relationships which might possibly have resulted in marriage.

Likeable and gracious, though a little shy, Crozier appears to have been unlucky in love and his affairs with women singularly failed to blossom. Years of long voyages away from home and the measly naval half-pay of an unemployed naval officer were an unattractive combination.

Typical of his relationships was a reported attraction to Jean Ingelow, then a promising young poet. It was another association which came to nothing, but it left behind an intriguing mystery.

Jean Ingelow was a petite, attractive, dark-haired woman some twenty-four years younger than Crozier. Her pious, introspective poetry probably appealed to the serious side of Crozier's character. Her biographer said, 'Her work embodied the aims and ideals of respectable Victorians.'[1]

She recovered from a difficult early life – her father was a banker who went bust in 1826 – and became popular enough to be recommended as the first female Poet Laureate. She enjoyed the friendship of literary stars such as John Ruskin and Alfred Tennyson, and it was Tennyson who once proclaimed, 'Miss Ingelow, I do declare, you do the trick better than I do.'

It is not clear how far the relationship with Crozier developed. With a suitably melodramatic flourish of the age, one contemporary observer summed up the romance by concluding:

(It was) pitched in a minor key rather than in a deep-stirring movement of two hearts beating in tune. It was a harmony of kindred minds. Beyond this Cupid never ventured.[2]

Jean Ingelow's poetry, however, included frequent references to a short and tragic romance with an unknown sailor who was later lost at sea. The doomed affair, said her biographer, lasted a year and was the 'great love affair of Jean's life'. She died in 1897, at the age of seventy-seven, having never married. In one of her poems, she wrote:

I took a year out of my life and story –
A dead year and said I will hew thee a tomb!

It is tempting to speculate that the lost love was Crozier, though there is no convincing evidence either way.

The prospect of bachelorhood for Crozier was not helped by news that James Clark Ross, his closest companion, had fallen in love with a woman named Ann Coulman and desperately wanted to marry. But the demands of exploration that had impeded Crozier's attempts at building relationships now posed similar problems for Ross. Thomas Coulman, the father of his intended bride, had severe reservations about his daughter marrying an explorer.

Coulman's concern was well founded. Ross' last major expedition to the Arctic had lasted four years and, to his dismay, Coulman now discovered that Ross was planning to take command of a new voyage. After two decades of Arctic activity, Barrow and the Admiralty had turned their attention to the Antarctic, a less-well-known and potentially more risky area. Ross, now the most experienced explorer of the age, was the obvious choice to lead the mission. Thomas Coulman was uneasy but approved the marriage on condition that it would be Ross' last expedition.

The Antarctic expedition, regardless of the dangers, was a blessing to Crozier. After more than twelve months of inactivity and, eager to serve, he wrote to Ross declaring that he was 'ready at a moment's notice' to enlist in the new venture. But Crozier's plans were interrupted towards the end of 1838 when his seventy-eight-year-old mother, Jane Crozier died and he was summoned back to Banbridge to help sort out family affairs.

The most pressing matter was to arrange for his three older and unmarried sisters to move to Dublin to be nearer their brothers, Graham, Thomas and William. The three women – Rachel, Martha and Charlotte – were soon installed in a house in Rutland Square (now Parnell Square).

The task took much longer than expected and Crozier, fearing that Ross might sail without him, became increasingly impatient. In March 1839, he remarked: 'I am almost sorry I returned here.' Concerned that he might be overlooked, he threw himself at the mercy of his friend. In a letter to Ross, Crozier said:

I have been, you may rest assured, very anxious on the subject, hoping each post to hear from you. Now, Ross, you must give me a line without delay as I conjured up in my mind a thousand things ... However I am, as you know, a volunteer for anything that I can be useful in.[3]

He need not have worried. Less than a month later, on 8 April 1839, Ross was formally appointed to lead the expedition and one of his first tasks was to send for Crozier, inviting him to become his second-in-command. Together, the men would command the nineteenth century's greatest voyage of maritime discovery in two stout ships – *Erebus* and *Terror* – that, by an ugly twist of fate, would later become synonymous with the worst disaster in the history of polar exploration.

Crozier was at the zenith of his career when appointed to the Antarctic expedition. Among those on active service, only Ross had spent more time in the ice. Crozier had been at sea for almost 30 years and was held in high regard by those who sailed alongside him. While he may not have attracted the recognition he deserved from the Admiralty, his standing among his peers was second to none.

For the second time in less than two years, Ross had the pick of the navy's most experienced seafarers at his disposal and once again he chose Crozier ahead of everyone else. Quite simply, Ross selected Crozier as his number two because he trusted him. Years of rigorous service in the Arctic had shown that Crozier was a level-headed and reliable commander who had earned great respect for his seamanship in the ice and who had developed into an authority on magnetism.

Crozier was also a stricter disciplinarian than Ross and was an unflappable officer who complemented his more flamboyant and often hot-tempered colleague. Given their considerable mutual respect, Crozier and Ross made an ideal partnership. Ross, never extravagant with his praise, summed up his warm feelings towards Crozier when he scribbled a personal postscript on an official letter to the Admiralty. Crozier, he declared, was 'a bit of trump'.

Ross immediately demonstrated his faith in Crozier by giving him full responsibility for fitting out the two expedition ships at Chatham Dockyard. He left everything to Crozier and rarely bothered to visit Chatham to inspect the work. Even the choice of crew was delegated to his willing and dependable second-in-command.

Ross was to take *Erebus* as the expedition flagship, while Crozier would command *Terror*. Although Crozier and Ross had not sailed on either before, they were familiar with this type of vessel, which belonged to the same class as *Hecla* and *Fury*.

Erebus and *Terror* were a matching pair of solid, three-masted, mortar-bomb ships, with roomy holds and shallow, flat-bottomed draughts that were considered perfect for manoeuvring through icy waters where depths might be uncertain. Designed to withstand the shuddering recoil of 3-ton mortar cannons, *Erebus* and *Terror* were ideally suited to a battering by the ice of the Southern Ocean. On the downside, the ships pitched and rolled badly in rough seas and were ponderously slow, lumbering along at little more than 4 or 5 knots.

Built in 1813, the 326-ton *Terror* had an adventurous history and played a supporting role in an important moment of American history. In 1814, at the height of the 1812 War with the US, *Terror* took part in the bombardment of Fort McHenry in Baltimore, Maryland. The battle was witnessed by poet and slave-owner, Francis Scott Key who was inspired to write a poem which was later set to music as the *Star-Spangled Banner* and became America's national anthem.

Terror also survived being run aground near Lisbon in 1828. After undergoing extensive repairs, *Terror* was pressed into Arctic service for George Back's unsuccessful attempt to reach Repulse Bay in 1836 and came perilously close to being lost in the ice. Leaking badly after severe Atlantic storms on the journey home in 1837, *Terror* was beached in Lough Swilly on the north-west coast of Ireland, not far from the spot where Wolfe Tone, the leader of the United Irishmen, was captured in 1798.

In contrast, the 372-ton *Erebus* was more modern, having been built in 1826. But the ship spent only two of the following thirteen years at sea, mostly in the gentle waters of the Mediterranean. While *Terror's* pedigree in icy seas was proven, *Erebus* was an unknown quantity.

Under Crozier's watchful eye, the two ships were strengthened to withstand the crushing pressure of the ice, with watertight bulkheads and a double lining of copper installed around the keel. Each deck was double-planked and heavy-duty oak beams were fitted to reinforce the hull. As extra insurance against disaster, each ship would take a fleet of nine small boats, including a sturdy pinnace and four cutters.

The spacious holds of *Erebus* and *Terror* were stocked with supplies and equipment for three years, including 6 tons (over 6,000 kilograms) of tinned meat and almost 7 tons (7,000 kilograms) of vegetables. Although the navy was no nearer to identifying the real cause of scurvy, the ships took the customary stocks of fresh lemon juice in the hope of combating the ailment.

As with earlier expeditions, the comfort of the officers and crew for the long journey was highly important. One feature handed down from the earlier Parry expeditions was the Sylvester heating system that had kept parties warm through many Arctic winters, though Crozier found Sylvester, the inventor, a frustrating man to handle.

Crozier, a practical and uncomplicated character, was irritated by the professorial Sylvester, who was long on philosophy and short on practice. Crozier wrote to Ross:

> Mr Sylvester seems a very strange fellow ... He talked a great deal in theory but I begged him to fit us as near as possible as he did before. He will require a great deal of stirring up.[4]

Crozier's attention to detail was mirrored in the selection of the men. He was adamant that only straightforward, proficient seamen would be suitable candidates for a long, challenging voyage where men would be expected to place their lives in the hands of their comrades and forced to endure months of close confinement with each other. 'We do not want a philosopher,' he once said.

Crozier's choice of deputy, his first lieutenant, was Archibald McMurdo, a respected, reliable and experienced officer who had been north with George Back in 1836 and who had recently won promotion for outstanding courage in saving the crew of a shipwrecked whaler from hostile natives in southern seas.

Ross turned to an experienced former shipmate, Edward Bird, as his second-in-command on *Erebus*. Bird, a friend of Crozier and Ross for almost twenty years, had ventured on three Arctic voyages with Parry and was of established quality.

Despite Crozier's best efforts, the suitability of the ordinary seamen was a concern. About two-thirds of Crozier's men on *Terror* were on their first naval posting, though some were drawn from the whaling fleets and had spent time in the ice. Joseph Hooker, the surgeon, noted that the men on *Terror* were 'much inferior' to those on *Erebus*.

Curiously, none of the 128 men bound for the Antarctic – 64 on each ship – was a qualified scientist, even though the expedition's principal aim was scientific. Ross was confident that, after years in the Arctic, he and Crozier were suitably qualified to handle tasks such as magnetic calculations, water samples and astronomical readings.

Nevertheless, as preparations neared completion, Crozier hurried to Dublin to consult the distinguished physicist, Professor Humphrey Lloyd at Trinity College. The Irish-born Lloyd, one of the world's leading authorities on magnetism, offered his much valued advice and personally assisted Crozier in choosing the instruments the expedition would take south.

Crozier bought the appliances at his own expense and arranged for the precious cargo to be shipped to London a few weeks before departure. What should have been a simple procedure, however, was soon entangled in bureaucratic red tape and it took an irritating struggle with Treasury officials to ensure he was fully reimbursed.

The frustrating diversion made Crozier even more eager to sail. In a letter to Ross, he wrote: 'I wish you were down [at Chatham] and we were off, clear of old commodores and dockyard nonsense.'[5]

Another distraction was a visit from their former commander, Sir Edward Parry, who had been knighted after retiring from active exploration and was now in charge of the Admiralty's tentative programme to develop steam-powered vessels for the navy. Parry was better placed than most to appreciate the potential of motorised vessels in navigating the ice. Equally, the Admiralty was about to send two sailing ships into unknown Antarctic waters without the back-up of auxiliary power.

All such considerations were swept aside as the ships, helped by favourable winds, sailed down the River Thames on 25 September 1839 on the first leg of the long journey to the Antarctic. But within a few hours of departure, the vulnerability of relying on sail was underlined when the two vessels were stopped in their tracks by stormy gusts of wind.

Flirting with Love

*E*rebus and *Terror* departed home shores without any of the fuss or fanfare that had surrounded Parry's earlier voyages. The mood at home was far more restrained. After two decades of effort, polar exploration was no longer so fashionable.

Yet fuss and fanfare would have been appropriate since *Erebus* and *Terror* were to enter the least-known waters on earth. People knew more about the moon from looking through telescopes than was known about Antarctica. Only a few men had seen the continent and no one had yet set foot on the mainland.

Antarctica has always occupied a curious place in the imagination. The continent appeared on maps centuries before anyone saw it. Greek philosophers as early as the sixth century BC insisted that a vast southern land existed at the bottom of the world because of the need to 'balance' the weight of the known lands in the northern hemisphere. As the discoveries in the north lay beneath the constellation of the Bear – *Arktos* – the counterbalancing lands in the south were called the opposite: *Antarktikos*.

The first modern attempt to locate the unknown lands – *Terra Australis Incognita* – was made in 1773 when the redoubtable Captain James Cook crossed the Antarctic Circle for the first time. Cook took his small sailing ships, *Resolution* and *Adventure*, to within 75 miles (120 kilometres) of the continent, but never saw land. Retreating to warmer waters, he claimed the desolate region had nothing to offer – an opinion that became the accepted wisdom at the Admiralty for more than half a century.

Others were more confident, driven by the promise of untold wealth from the southern seas teeming with seals and whales. Entrepreneurial sealers and whalers literally went to the end of the earth to make money from the Southern Ocean but were little bothered about geographical discovery and rarely spoke about their discoveries to avoid attracting rivals.

Serious exploration began again after 1820 when Edward Bransfield, the Irish-born Royal Navy Master, made the first definitive sighting of the Antarctic mainland in the small brig, *Williams*. The experienced Russian mariner, Thaddeus von Bellingshausen was in Antarctic waters at the same time but never claimed to have made the first sighting and even dismissed the idea that a continent existed.

Fresh discoveries followed, particularly as seal and whale ships penetrated further south in search of new hunting grounds. But only a small fraction of the coastline was mapped by the time *Erebus* and *Terror* sailed south in 1839, and no one, yet, had claimed to have stepped ashore on the mainland.

Britain had traditionally shown little official interest in the Antarctic, partly because of Barrow's obsession with the North West Passage and North Pole and partly because the Admiralty still clung to Cook's belief that Antarctica was a useless, frozen wasteland. But the mood changed dramatically in the mid-1830s as news reached London that American and French expeditions were heading south.

The American lieutenant Charles Wilkes came to London in 1837 to buy navigational and astronomical instruments for his proposed Antarctic voyage and the Admiralty also learned that France had approved a plan by Admiral Jules Sébastian-César Dumont D'Urville to probe the newly discovered waters of the Weddell Sea. Both expeditions were also intent on locating the South Magnetic Pole and in Britain there was mounting fear that the country, which prided itself on leading the field in scientific affairs, was falling behind in terrestrial magnetism.

Fresh impetus came when the British Association for the Advancement of Science – founded around the time Ross located the North Magnetic Pole in 1831 – set up a committee to solve the mystery of how the earth's magnetic fields affected navigation. One of the earliest conclusions was that large gaps existed in magnetic readings in southern waters. By the mid-1830s there was a growing clamour to mount an Antarctic expedition and to establish a series of observatories in the vast southerly regions of the globe between Cape Horn and Australia.

The committee, whose membership included Ross and Professor Lloyd, met in Dublin in 1835 to demand that the government launch an Antarctic expedition to find the South Magnetic Pole and to conduct a major pro-gramme of observations that would be co-ordinated with readings taken by other European countries. By 1839, with the French and American expedi-tions already underway, the government finally approved the scheme and *Erebus* and *Terror* were made ready by the eager Crozier.

The journey south began uneasily and despite an impressive Arctic track record the slower-moving *Terror* proved something of a liability. The vessel lacked speed in open seas and could not keep pace with *Erebus*, which fre-quently had to take in sails to allow *Terror* to catch up. As Crozier struggled with his ship, progress was further impeded by heavy storms and the near loss of three crewmen as the expedition passed through the Bay of Biscay.

Terror eventually anchored at Madeira, the expedition's first rendezvous point, four days later than Ross. Both Crozier and Ross cursed the slow progress made by the plodding *Terror*. 'The *Terror* has been a sad drawback to us, having every now and then to shorten sail for her,' Ross wrote.

Crozier acknowledged that the ships were moving far slower than antic-ipated. In a letter to his sister Sarah, he warned that 'our scientific friends in England' would be disappointed at the expedition's progress. 'But little do they know the heavy sailing ships we have.'[1]

Christmas was spent on the high seas and the isolated island of St Helena was reached at the end of January 1840, more than 20 years since Crozier's first visit. The island had been chosen as the location for a permanent magnetic observatory and a site was found near the former home of the exiled emperor Napoleon.

Crozier assumed much responsibility for the magnetic work and spent long periods engrossed in the painstaking mathematics of the readings. 'I think on my return I shall be fully qualified to teach accounts in a county seminary', he joked to Sarah. Unfortunately, the island's volcanic rocks interfered with the magnetic measurements and the observatory was a disappointment.

The ships ran into more thick weather rounding the Cape of Good Hope in southern Africa and all were disappointed that conditions did not improve as they entered the southern reaches of the Indian Ocean. By mid-May – following weeks of treacherous weather – the two ships stood alongside each other close to Îles Kerguelen, the archipelago of around 300 islets which lies in the Roaring Forties about halfway between Africa and Australia.

Reaching the Kerguelens in the wretched weather was perilous. Gales lashed the vessels as they approached, and *Erebus* and *Terror* struggled for days to enter the shelter of Christmas Harbour, a natural bowl-shaped haven on the main Kerguelen island. William Cunningham, a marine sergeant aboard *Terror*, described the area as the 'most dangerous place I was ever in'. He added, 'If the weather is always like this off the coast of Kerguelen's head, I don't care how soon I am clear of it.'

Gales blew for 45 of the 68 days spent at Christmas Harbour and the men from *Erebus* and *Terror* enjoyed only three days of respite from the heavy rain and driving snowstorms. Men were blown off their feet by the fury of the wind and on occasions the ships were tipped over onto their beam ends. Ross declared it a 'most dreary and disagreeable' spot, while, on shore, Crozier struggled to erect the observatory under the horrendous conditions. On 27 May, Cunningham wryly reported 'a hurricane with lulls for a few minutes'. It was, he admitted, 'very trying' for Crozier and the other officers coping with the observatory and other scientific work.

Two days later, the wind blew so fiercely that it was impossible to send boats ashore with provisions for Crozier. Cunningham reported that the officers were 'very much fatigued' when they finally managed to return to the ships and concluded that they 'seemed anxious not to go again'.

Erebus and *Terror* left the Kerguelens on 20 July with few regrets and an accompanying gale. Within hours of sailing, the ships lost sight of each other in a swirling storm and days later a fatal hurricane struck the vessels. Boatswain Roberts of *Erebus* was lost overboard at the height of the storm and four seamen were almost drowned in a desperate attempt to save him.

Crozier and Ross were separated for three weeks during the tempestuous journey through the Roaring Forties to Van Diemen's Land (renamed Tasmania in 1855). Winds surged to force ten (up to 63 mph/101 km/h), and sails were ripped in the incessant storms that left the ships rolling and pitching at gravity-defying angles. Crozier, in the logbook of *Terror*, noted 'Squalls increasing in violence'. But to the surprise of all, the slower-moving *Terror* managed to reach Hobart, the island's capital, on 15 August, some 24 hours before Ross brought *Erebus* into port.

After a brief reunion on *Erebus*, Crozier and Ross went ashore to Hobart's Government House to meet the lieutenant governor – their old friend and an Arctic veteran, Sir John Franklin.

Franklin was delighted to see his naval comrades who brought a welcome reminder of home and a rare opportunity to mix with like-minded souls. He was badly in need of the relief provided by the visit.

Van Diemen's Land was an unpleasant, half-forgotten penal colony on the fringe of the Empire. Over 17,000 of the island's population of

42,000 were convicts and many of the free citizens were former prisoners. In the words of one observer, Van Diemen's Land was 'a cage for the vultures of mankind'.

To Franklin and his feisty, strong-willed wife, Lady Jane Franklin, it was a penal sentence of its own. To round things off, many in the suffocating, reactionary frontier community disliked the Franklins, who were regarded as outsiders and dangerous liberals.

Lady Franklin, an assured, manipulative and unconventional woman in her late forties, simply grated. 'A man in petticoats', one disgruntled observer complained. They found her aggressive and disconcertingly radical, especially when she defied convention by straying into unwelcome areas, such as her attempts to improve the island's mediocre schools or to highlight the miserable living conditions of the island's unfortunate women prisoners.

John Franklin was a square peg in a round hole. He was a genial, strongly religious and inoffensive man who had little in common with the hostile colonialists or the wretched convicts. He also found himself at the mercy of wily civil servants in the Colonial Office. He was uncomfortable with the finery and pomp that went with the role of governor and had only drifted into the job because of his ambitious wife's insistence he attain a position of substance and because the Admiralty – still struggling to cope with the surplus of naval officers – could not find him a suitable commission. He was a sailor, not a diplomat nor a jailer.

Parry, normally reserved and circumspect, had tried to prevent Franklin taking up the post. Regarding it as a backward step, he warned that 'the Australian colonies are not fit for any gentleman to govern'.

The coming of Crozier and Ross brought welcome respite to the Franklin household. In Ross and Crozier, Franklin had found like-minded souls who spoke the same language. According to Lady Franklin:

> The arrival of Captains Ross and Crozier added much to Sir John's happiness ... They all feel towards one another as friends and brothers and

it is the remark of people here that Sir John appears to them quite in a new light, so bustling and frisky and merry with his new companions.[2]

Crozier and Ross spent three months at Hobart, indulging in a mixture of hard work for the expedition and frequent partying. Their primary task by day was to build an observatory and prepare the ships for the first leg of the journey into the icy waters of Antarctica. Their nights were filled with a hectic round of parties, balls, dinners and other social get-togethers orchestrated by the kindly Franklins.

Crozier also found love. He and Ross had been invited to lodge with the Franklins at Government House and it was there that Crozier met and fell deeply in love with Sophia Cracroft, Franklin's young niece.

Sophia Cracroft – known as Sophy – was the fascinating, intelligent, twenty-four-year-old daughter of a prominent Lincolnshire gentleman farmer, Thomas Cracroft and Isabella Franklin, John Franklin's younger sister. A contemporary described her as 'a young lady of beauty and fortune'.

She was one of six children who sprang from the old-established Lincolnshire family with roots dating back to the thirteenth century and who were long-time associates of the Franklins. When her father Thomas Cracroft died in 1824, the nine-year-old Sophy was immediately taken under the wing of the Franklins. John Franklin was attached to his sister Isabella and Sophy fitted easily into the family circle. While he was travelling on one expedition to the Arctic, it was Isabella who cared for Eleanor, Franklin's only daughter from his first, brief, marriage.

Equally, Sophy had become good friends with Jane, John Franklin's second wife, long before their marriage in 1828. Despite a significant age difference – Jane Franklin was twenty-four years older than Sophy Cracroft – the two became very close. Jane, who was nearly thirty-seven years old when she married John Franklin, had no children of her own and Sophy was, perhaps, the daughter she never had. In 1837, Sophy Cracroft, still only twenty years of age, had travelled with the Franklin entourage when her uncle John had taken up the post of lieutenant governor of Van Diemen's Land.

Sophy and Jane became inseparable as Sophy matured into full womanhood, and for the next four decades the lives of Sophy Cracroft and Jane Franklin became inextricably interwoven. While Jane Franklin's life was often tested by setbacks and disaster, the one constant factor was the reassuring presence and unwavering support of the resourceful, devoted and unquestioning Sophy Cracroft.

She became Jane's confidential secretary, constant companion and staunch moral support. Sophy was entrusted with the task of writing Jane's private correspondence and was even permitted to make entries in Jane's personal journals.

In later life, Sophy Cracroft carefully nurtured the public face of Jane Franklin by helping her to destroy certain letters, journals and other papers and by writing anonymous letters to newspapers – 'One of the Public' was a favourite pseudonym – to lavish praise on the 'untiring heroism of Lady Franklin'. Few photographs of Jane or Sophy have survived.

Jane Franklin marvelled at Sophy's 'acuteness and memory'. Sophy, in turn, adopted many of Jane's characteristics and once wrote of the relationship: 'We are two persons and not one.' A more recent study of Sophy's correspondence and diaries concluded that she was a '... nervous, emotional, self-centred bundle of anxiety who could be a martyr.'[3]

However, this intensely close relationship between the two women caused some friction in the Franklin household. Jane frequently quarrelled with her stepdaughter, Eleanor Franklin, and their bonds were never as strong as those between Jane and Sophy. In time, Jane and Eleanor became totally estranged.

Jane, who became Lady Franklin within months of her wedding day, was an independent and uncompromising woman who spoke her mind freely and was not afraid to challenge authority. She was also an ambitious, scheming and doggedly determined character, anxious to get her own way.

In Sir John Franklin, an avuncular and diffident man with a knighthood and a goodly place in society, Jane had found the perfect partner.

Sophy Cracroft once wrote an *aide-memoire* listing Jane's 'gifts and graces' which included, 'Clearness of perception; tenacity of purpose; delicacy of perception'. According to Sophy, Jane Franklin possessed an 'intense longing for truth' and was 'eminently critical'.[4] The observations might easily have served as descriptions of Sophy Cracroft.

The close relationship between Sophy and Jane could do nothing to help Crozier in his attempts to court Sophy. Although he did not know it, the relationship was doomed from the start. Sophy respected and liked Crozier, but she could never come to love him. She admired his professionalism and enviable reputation among naval officers but shared the same reservations about marrying into the navy as Thomas Coulman, Ross' future father-in-law.

She probably saw enough in the relationship between John and Jane Franklin to realise the pitfalls of marrying a man like Crozier, who was unreservedly committed to lengthy and hazardous voyages of exploration. On a more prosaic level, Sophy nursed a dislike of the sea as she was invariably struck down by awful seasickness.

Aside from the polite manners and quiet reserve of Hobart's Government House, there was another reason why Sophy was not attracted to Crozier. Sophy Cracroft was a snob who regarded the untutored Crozier as 'a horrid radical and an indifferent speller'.

Regardless of his steadfastness and amiable charm, Crozier was not a big enough catch for Sophy and there were plenty of other men beating a path to the doors of Government House in pursuit of her. She also enjoyed toying with the affections of men like Crozier.

Jane Franklin observed 'several minor flirtations' that came to nothing during the years at Hobart and coolly pigeonholed the fickle Sophy as a 'sad flirt'. Guests at the Franklin dinner table one night said Sophy was suitable only for two roles – 'queen or a bishop's wife.' Sophy did not challenge the judgement and wrote in her diary: 'If I were queen I should enjoy tormenting my ministers.'

Count Paul de Strzelecki, an aristocratic Polish geographer, was among those rebuffed by Sophy, despite a glittering reference from Lady Franklin, who called him the 'brightest star in your galaxy of worthies'. Captain Ainsworth, another love-struck naval officer, proposed marriage but was flatly rejected amid mutterings that he was an unread bore. 'He eats, drinks, sleeps and can do anything but read', Jane Franklin commented.

Sophy Cracroft did not always get her own way. Henry Elliot, Franklin's personal assistant at Government House and the son of the Admiralty bigwig, Lord Minto, was among the men who resisted her charms.

Sophy's most ambitious flirtation emerged when she turned her amorous attentions to Ross, who was good-looking, popular and still unmarried. She threw herself at him in a flagrant attempt to break up his engagement to Ann Coulman, an ungracious move that earned a sniffy rebuke from Jane Franklin. Here, though, there may have been an ulterior motive, as Jane Franklin had herself fallen under Ross' spell and was soon describing him as the 'most handsome man in the navy'.

Ross politely resisted Sophy's clumsy advances, which created a tangled state of affairs at Government House. Crozier was sighing for Sophy and Sophy was yearning for Ross, while in the background a strait-laced Lady Franklin kept her mild infatuation with Ross under strict control.

There was plenty of work to keep Crozier's mind on more serious matters. Building the new magnetic observatory in the grounds of Government House began within days of *Erebus* and *Terror* berthing at Hobart. John Franklin offered enthusiastic and tireless support for the project, which provided him with a welcome opportunity to escape the dreary affairs of office. He had assembled the required labour and materials many weeks before Crozier and Ross sailed into Hobart and Sophy recorded that all her uncle's spare time was spent at the site of the new observatory. She added: 'He is so much interested in terrestrial magnetism that nothing could give him greater relaxation.'

A squad of 200 convicts, press-ganged into service, worked flat out felling trees to clear the wooded area, before laying foundations for the observatory. The prisoners laboured from six in the morning until ten at night, though Ross firmly rejected all pleas to allow the men to work on the Sabbath.

Officers' quarters, a coach house and stables were also built alongside the observatory and Crozier and Ross made the site the onshore headquarters of the expedition. Their hammocks were slung alongside one another and Franklin noted the warmth and close friendship of the two men: 'It is truly interesting seeing them together,' he wrote. 'The same spirit animates each.'

The observatory was operational within nine days, with readings being taken hourly under the close supervision of Crozier. However, the solemn scientific duties were disrupted when a young woman visited the observatory wearing a steel-reinforced *bustier*. The woman's underwear, the local newspaper reported, inflicted 'so much unintentional mischief' to the sensitive apparatus.

Influence of a different sort was used by Lady Franklin to ensure that the new observatory was named after her favourite – Ross. Initially, it was planned to call the building Gauss Villa after the eminent German mathematician and authority on terrestrial magnetism, Karl Friedrich Gauss. But Jane Franklin, who freely admitted to being totally baffled by the subject of magnetism, dismissed this 'skittish title' and persuaded her husband to name it Rossbank.

To underline her authority, Lady Franklin also asked a local artist, Henry Mundy, to paint a picture of Crozier, Ross and Franklin standing alongside Rossbank. When Mundy declined the commission, Jane turned to Thomas Bock, a reformed ex-convict and artist.

Bock had to make do without the presence of Crozier and Ross for his picture, as he did not begin the task until after *Erebus* and *Terror* had sailed. But he did get some unexpected help from Crozier, who asked John Davis, second master of *Terror* and a talented artist, to sketch the scene before the ships departed for the Antarctic.

Shortly before sailing, Crozier sent the sketch to Lady Franklin, who described it as 'one of the prettiest thoughts that ever entered into Captain Crozier's head'. She passed the sketch on to Bock to assist him in his own, more famous, work. Bock's painting of the three captains was subsequently given to Edward Sabine, the leading naval authority on magnetism and a veteran of John Ross' 1818 expedition. The painting was later donated to the Scott Polar Research Institute in England and returned to Tasmania in 1948.

Crozier and Ross became local celebrities on the island and were the centre of attention as Hobart society milked their presence. Lavish dinners

(Left to right) Franklin, Crozier and Ross in 1842, standing at the Rossbank Observatory, Hobart, Van Diemen's Land (Tasmania). The artist was ex-convict Thomas Bock.

were thrown at Government House and the men were dragged to a succession of theatre parties, grand balls and the occasional inland trek for picnics. In return, Crozier and Ross hosted showy receptions on board *Erebus* and *Terror*. Before long, Hobart had adopted Crozier and Ross as the 'Two Captains'.

Thanks to Franklin, the men even found time in the busy schedule to contribute to a lasting piece of the island's heritage. On 5 November 1840, shortly before sailing to the Antarctic, Crozier and Ross attended a major public ceremony to lay the foundation stone for the new Government House, which was eventually completed in the late 1850s and stands to this day. A description of proceedings, which acknowledged the presence of Crozier and Ross, was buried under the building. In the harbour, the guns of *Erebus* and *Terror* fired a thunderous salute to mark the occasion.

An unpleasant incident occurred the following day, after Crozier and Ross had ventured north of Hobart to New Norfolk to attend a ceremony to place the foundation stone for a new college. Some coins and an inscribed account of the proceedings were buried beneath the stone, but it was lifted by thieves during the night and the articles stolen. The college subsequently failed.

The happy mood was restored when Hobart threw an extravagant party prior to the expedition's departure, with more than 300 worthies pouring into the Custom House for a grand farewell ball. The guests, said the local newspaper, were 'an ample store of beauty and chivalry' and the farewell toast to Crozier and Ross was greeted with a 'universal burst of applause and cheering'.

Crozier, though normally reserved, emerged as a highly popular figure during his time at Hobart, particularly with Lady Franklin. The two developed a lasting friendship, and Crozier responded by calling her a 'dear, good woman'. He was always comfortable in Lady Franklin's presence, despite her spirited nature and acerbic tongue. One onlooker noted that Jane Franklin's relationship with Crozier was 'less formal and more companionable' than her association with Ross.[5]

Despite his failure to win over Sophy Cracroft, Crozier had rarely been happier in his life. Jane Franklin wrote: 'Captains Ross and Crozier call [Hobart] their own home of the Southern Hemisphere.' On one occasion, Crozier and Lady Franklin pulled Ross' leg with a hint that Crozier was planning to resign from the expedition and stay behind in Van Diemen's Land when the ships sailed. Ross, however, sensed Crozier's contentment with the surroundings and took it seriously.

The episode arose after Lady Franklin had bought Betsey Island, a 400-acre island in Hobart Harbour. Crozier was attracted to the spot and Jane offered to sell it to him for the same price she had paid. Ross heard about Crozier's interest in the island and Jane Franklin said he became 'comically serious and meditative' at the possibility of his good friend deserting the expedition.

As the sojourn in Van Diemen's Land was coming to an end, Franklin's daughter Eleanor summed up the general mood. She told Ross: 'We often look back to the days you and Captain Crozier were with us, considering them the happiest we have spent here.'[6]

Understandably, there was regret all round when, on 12 November 1840, *Erebus* and *Terror* finally slipped into the Derwent River and out of Hobart for the journey to the Antarctic. The 'Two Captains' each carried a pot of jam made by Jane Franklin.

John Franklin, clearly longing to be back at sea and part of the expedition, stood alongside Ross on the deck of *Erebus* as the ships began their lengthy voyage. A little later, he transferred to *Terror* to say a personal farewell to Crozier. 'He is a nice fatherly old man,' Sergeant Cunningham reported.

Crozier had mixed emotions. He was keenly aware of his responsibilities and the enormity of the task that lay ahead. But his heart was heavy. As *Erebus* and *Terror* sailed away from Hobart, Crozier resolved to ask for Sophy Cracroft's hand in marriage.

CHAPTER 11

An Epic Voyage

Crozier and Ross sailed southwards in a mood of simmering rage. While at Hobart, they had learned that Wilkes and Dumont D'Urville had been active in deepest southern waters, which naturally upset the British sense of propriety. Crozier and Ross, in tune with the chauvinistic doctrines of Barrow, assumed that Britain possessed an inalienable right to explore without the 'interference' of foreign ships.

D'Urville, using Hobart as his base, had found miles of new Antarctic coastline between 136° and 142° east, which he named Adelie Land after his wife, Adèle. Wilkes had the courtesy to write to Ross about his sightings in the region of 100° and 160° east, but Ross, irritated by the unwelcome intrusion, did not reply.

It was decided to drive *Erebus* and *Terror* south along the meridian of 170° east, helped by encouraging recent reports from a British sealing captain, John Balleny. In 1839, only a year before *Erebus* and *Terror* first sailed, Balleny had penetrated further south than either Wilkes or D'Urville, reaching 69° south, where he discovered open sea.

Ross and Crozier had no reason to feel threatened. *Erebus* and *Terror* were far better equipped than either Wilkes or D'Urville to penetrate the Southern Ocean. Their specially strengthened vessels and their long years of service in the Arctic gave Crozier and Ross a marked advantage over the American and French commanders.

On their departure from Hobart, *Erebus* and *Terror* had initially set course for the bleak volcanic outpost of the Auckland Isles, about 250 miles (400 kilometres) off the southern coast of New Zealand and the site of the world's largest breeding grounds of wandering albatrosses. It was planned to build an observatory at Rendezvous Harbour, but a major surprise awaited the landing party as they rowed ashore. Two notice boards were discovered with hand-painted records of visits by both Wilkes and D'Urville, who had arrived at Rendezvous Harbour only twenty-four hours apart. Inside a bottle was a badly soiled note claiming that Wilkes had cruised along an 'Icy Barrier'.

High winds, much like those encountered at the Kerguelens, made the work of erecting the observatory very difficult. After three weeks of struggle, the expedition was relieved when, on 12 December, it pulled away from the island. Before departing *Erebus* and *Terror* left behind an assortment of wildlife – a ram, two ewes, a number of pigs, two goats and some poultry – to provide a source of fresh meat for future visitors to the isolated speck in the vast ocean.

The short, routine trip to nearby Campbell Island almost resulted in disaster when violent winds drove both vessels aground on unseen muddy flats. *Erebus* managed to get free, but Crozier was forced to pump out water and land stores to lighten *Terror*. The ship floated off unharmed at high tide. 'Joy and satisfaction beamed on every face,' Ross remarked as *Terror* was released.

It was an incident which further raised Crozier's stature among his crew. Crozier, though a firm disciplinarian, was always respected by fellow officers who recognised his first-rate seamanship and attention to detail. Crozier's professionalism was never in doubt.

The first iceberg was sighted two days after Christmas and even weathered Arctic hands such as Crozier and Ross were amazed at the enormity of the huge monolithic islands of ice that loomed out of the sea and dwarfed *Erebus* and *Terror*.

Icebergs in the Antarctic are often different to those that Crozier and Ross had encountered so many times in the Arctic. While Arctic bergs are more conical and resemble small floating hills, the giant Antarctic bergs are often huge, flat slabs of ice with steep perpendicular cliffs. Some Antarctic bergs have measured 100 miles (160 kilometres) in length but are more typically between 300–1,000 feet (100–300 metres).

Erebus and *Terror* pushed further south in wild weather and crossed the Antarctic Circle on New Year's Day 1841, a feat marked by the issuing to all hands of more winter clothing and extra grog. Billy, the pet goat, was given lashings of port wine and staggered around the quarterdeck to the amusement of the crews.

The mood on board was optimistic. On 6 January, Crozier transferred to *Erebus* for a light-hearted party to celebrate Twelfth Night and then invited Ross to finish off the evening with more drinks on board *Terror*. The revelry came to an abrupt halt, however, when one of *Terror*'s sailors fell overboard and had to be rescued.

The ice became more tightly packed as the ships pressed further south. Before long, the horizon to the south was filled with an unbroken field of ice, and *Erebus* and *Terror* faced the choice of seeking a way through the pack ice or retreating to warmer waters and abandoning the mission. The ships drove on southwards, looking for gaps in the ice.

The ice belt around the Antarctic continent presents a formidable barrier to ships. No vessels had entered the pack ice in this area before and sailing ships, which were at the mercy of the region's ferocious winds, were particularly vulnerable to collision.

The pack encases the Antarctic continent like a girdle, extending in width from 350–1,800 miles (560–2,880 kilometres), preventing ships from reaching the mainland for much of the year. Leads of open water, which are sprinkled with large and dangerous blocks of floating ice, open and close under the influence of currents and strong winds. Ships entering a lane of open water can find their entry and exit routes suddenly closed off by the constantly moving ice.

Crozier and Ross sailed south in strong winds, anxiously searching for inviting lanes of open water. The ships frequently sought shelter in the lee of colossal icebergs that towered over their masts. Suddenly the line of retreat was cut off when strong gales blew from behind the ships and the ice closed together.

With little option but to continue south, it was decided to ram the ice with the bows of the blunt-nosed ships. *Erebus* went first, followed by Crozier in *Terror*. Sometimes, the ships managed to break through, but often they came to a sudden halt as the ice refused to give way. On the ice, startled penguins scuttled alongside in wonderment.

For several days, the ships dodged and weaved among the leads, with visibility often obliterated by bouts of fog and white-out conditions caused by swirling snowstorms. The ships frequently lost sight of each other. On deck, the men fired muskets or rang bells to make sure they did not get too separated.

The decks and sails were covered in a ghostly shroud of ice and the sea spray froze as it fell on the ships. Steering half-blind and surrounded by heavy ice, the ships crept southwards, on constant alert for lethal icebergs. Sometimes, they brushed alongside a giant berg and the men used poles to prevent a heavy collision. On occasions, *Erebus* and *Terror* came to a standstill, waiting for the moment when a gap would appear before slipping quickly through the opening.

At midday on 9 January, the fog suddenly lifted to show the ships in open, ice-free waters. 'Not a particle of ice could be seen in any direction,' Ross gleefully reported.

Ross and Crozier, ably assisted by a skilled crew, had achieved one of the greatest feats of navigation in the history of exploration. Taking two small wooden sailing ships through the Antarctic pack ice for the first time was an achievement to rank alongside the outstanding exploits of men like Ferdinand Magellan and James Cook. It was a feat put into full context seventy years later by Roald Amundsen, the finest of all polar explorers, when he described the journey as the 'boldest voyage known in Antarctic exploration'. Writing in 1912, Amundsen applauded Ross and Crozier:

> With two ponderous craft – regular 'tubs' according to our ideas – these men sailed right into the heart of the pack, which all previous polar explorers had regarded as certain death. It is not merely difficult to grasp this; it is simply impossible – to us, who with a motion of the hand can set the screw going and wriggle out of the first difficulty we encounter. These men were heroes – heroes in the highest sense of the word.[1]

Erebus and *Terror* had breached the pack and run into open water of what is now called the Ross Sea at 69° 15' south, where the weather was mercifully clear. Optimists thought it possible that the ships could now sail freely to the South Magnetic Pole and even the South Pole itself. Barrow's popular 'Open Polar Sea', which had proved so elusive in the Arctic, seemed equally possible in southern waters.

The optimism was soon dampened. At 2 a.m. on the morning of 11 January, a yell of 'Land!' came from the crow's nest. The discovery, perversely enough, was a blow to the men of the expedition, who suddenly saw the prospect of sailing directly to the South Magnetic Pole disappear before their eyes.

Ross, aware that his ambition of being the first to stand at the earth's two magnetic poles had been dashed, recorded his 'severe disappointment' at the ominous sighting of land.

The men could pick out mountains on the far horizon, even though they were perhaps 100 miles (160 kilometres) distant. By late evening, the ships stood off the majestic Antarctic landscape of imposing white cliffs and soaring black mountains. The territory was named Victoria Land after

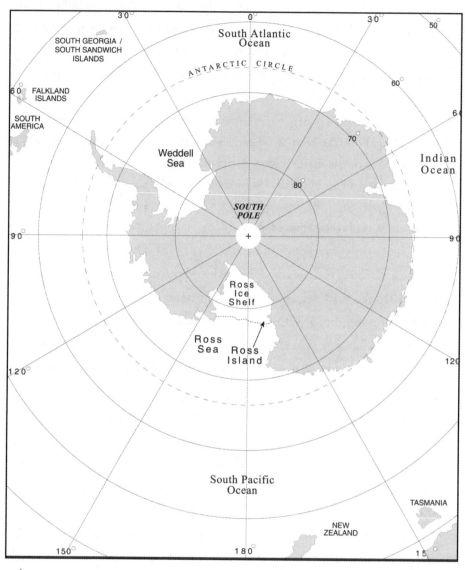

Antarctica.

the new queen and the first identifiable peak, rising to around 10,000 feet (3,048 metres), was named after the estimable naval authority on magnetism, Irish-born Edward Sabine.

When a long chain of mountains came into sight, these were immediately named the Admiralty Range, with one peak christened Barrow after the Admiralty's most potent force. Ross called Cape Ann after his fiancée and diplomatically named Coulman Island after his future father-in-law.

Crozier evoked his Irish roots by naming one headland Cape Downshire and by calling a nearby peak Mount Robinson in honour of Thomas Romney Robinson, the Astronomer of Armagh Observatory.

The next step was to claim possession of the frozen land for Britain. *Erebus* and *Terror* were brought close to the shoreline, passing Cook's 'furthest south' in the process. A boat was lowered so that Ross and Crozier could undertake the ceremony on the mainland, but a thick band of ice blocked their path and the party instead made for a small island a few miles offshore. Symbolically, it was named Possession Island.

Crozier and Ross struggled ashore in the face of foul weather and lumpy seas to perform the brief twenty-five-minute ceremony, witnessed only by a handful of freezing seamen and thousands of disinterested penguins. A flat site was found, which turned out to be a thickly impacted bed of foul-smelling penguin guano. The scent, one crewman recalled, was 'all but stifling'.

The Union flag was hurriedly planted in the most southerly outpost of the Empire, and officers, shivering in the sub-zero temperatures, toasted the day with an 'excellent sherry'.

On board *Erebus* and *Terror*, concerned colleagues hoisted signalling flags entreating the party to return to the ships because of steadily worsening weather. Crozier and Ross hurried back into the boats, arriving on board the ships just moments before a dense blanket of fog descended. Even a brief delay on Possession Island would have made their return extremely hazardous.

Erebus and *Terror* resumed their journey and on 23 January passed the record 'furthest south' of 74° 15' set by James Weddell, a Scottish sealing captain, on the other side of the continent in 1823. Extra grog was dished out to celebrate the milestone.

By 26 January, with the compass needle behaving abnormally, it was calculated that the South Magnetic Pole was barely 174 miles (278 kilometres) away.

Another small island was spotted on 27 January and again it was decided to risk a landing, despite the dangerous seas. In heavy swell, two boats were pulled towards shore and the surgeon Joseph Hooker was almost crushed when he fell between the two vessels. The landing was promptly abandoned, but the island, an undistinguished 8-mile (11-kilometre) lump of rock poking out of the water, was named Franklin Island in honour of their friend.

New land burst onto the horizon the following day and was initially named 'High Island' because of the distinctly visible mountains. As *Erebus*

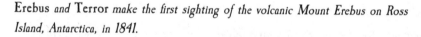

Erebus *and* **Terror** *make the first sighting of the volcanic Mount Erebus on Ross Island, Antarctica, in 1841.*

and *Terror* approached, wispy puffs of smoke laced with red flashes of spitting flames were seen drifting from the top of one large mountain whose slopes were covered in snow. It looked like flames pouring from a monstrous iceberg and Crozier and Ross realised they had discovered a volcano.

The imposing peak, which was named Mount Erebus, is the world's most southerly active volcano and rises to a height of 12,450 feet (3,795 metres). Alongside stands a smaller, extinct volcano, a 10,600-foot (3,230-metre) peak that was named Mount Terror.

It was an overwhelming spectacle that Hooker said surpassed 'anything I could imagine'. He added: 'There is a certain awe that steals over us all in considering our own total insignificance and helplessness.'

The jaw-dropping beauty of the landscape could not, however, obscure the reality that the South Magnetic Pole was slipping from their grasp. The Magnetic Pole lay inland to the west, but the ships were confronted with continuous coastline that drove them inexorably in the wrong direction towards the east. They sailed along the shore of 'High Island', which was eventually named Ross Island and seventy years later became the focal point for the heroic age of Antarctic exploration with men like Scott and Shackleton.

Ross Island was also the place where Ross decided to honour Crozier, his able deputy. A striking headland at the eastern end of the island, a little over 10 miles (16 kilometres) from the foot of Mount Terror, was named Cape Crozier. Ross dedicated the site with great affection, writing:

[It was named] after my friend and colleague, to whose zeal and cordial co-operation is mainly to be ascribed, under God's blessing, the happiness as well as success of the expedition: under the circumstances we were placed in, it is impossible for others to fully understand the value of having so tried a friend, of now more than 20 years standing, as commander of the second ship, upon whom the harmony and right feeling between the two vessels so greatly depends.[2]

The austere, windswept and rocky cliffs of Cape Crozier are home to the most southerly breeding grounds of the Emperor penguin. The site was immortalised eighty years later by Apsley Cherry-Garrard in his book, *The Worst Journey in the World*, featuring a perilous mid-winter trek to Cape Crozier during Scott's last expedition.

Cape Crozier is a fearsome place, flayed by brutal winds and unimaginable cold. Temperatures on a journey made by Cherry-Garrard in 1911, which inspired the book's title, plunged to a bone-numbing -77.5°F (-61°C). The traumatised explorer said he had never heard or felt winds like those at Cape Crozier. 'I wondered why it did not carry away the earth,' he wrote. 'No words can express its horror.'[3]

As Cape Crozier was left behind, *Erebus* and *Terror* immediately ran into another astonishing spectacle. As far as the eye could see was a colossal perpendicular wall of ice nearly 200 feet (61 metres) high. To the south, the land seemed to stretch to the horizon in one flat, featureless plain of ice.

The discovery, even more startling than the volcanic Mount Erebus, was the Ross Ice Shelf, an immense floating sheet of ice roughly the size of France and up to two-thirds of a mile (1 kilometre) thick. In a warmer climate, the area would be a huge bay. Ross called it the Barrier because it was quite literally a barrier to his ships in their bid to sail to the South Magnetic Pole or the South Pole itself. 'We might with equal chance of success try to sail through the Cliffs of Dover,' he lamented.

Ross described the Barrier as a 'mighty and wonderful object' that offered the strong prospect of 'extensive country to the southward'. He was correct in his assumption and the later expeditions of Amundsen, Scott and Shackleton duly marched crossed the Barrier's flat plain in search of the South Pole.

Ross inadvertently sparked a lengthy controversy in the scientific and geographic communities by naming the majestic feature a barrier. Deep divisions emerged in the years after the discovery as to whether the feature should be called by the more geographically correct title of ice shelf or retain the original name of Barrier given it by Ross in 1841. The bitter row lasted for over a century and it was not until the early 1950s, over a century after its discovery, that the 'Barrier' was officially named the Ross Ice Shelf.[4]

Disappointed that hopes of sailing to the South Magnetic Pole had now vanished, *Erebus* and *Terror* traced another 250 miles (400 kilometres) along the Barrier's high ice cliffs. By early February, the ships stood at a latitude just slightly over 78° south, the furthest south yet recorded by humans.

Crozier went across to *Erebus* for talks with Ross to discuss their options. The cold was intense as the short Antarctic summer season neared its end. Ice formed across the decks and in the rigging and each breaking wave brought a fresh layer of ice. From the masthead, there was no sign of an end to the Barrier and in the second week of February it was decided to halt the voyage east.

Erebus and *Terror* retraced their course along the Barrier and at Ross Island were greeted with a spectacular display of pyrotechnics from the smouldering Mount Erebus. A welcome bay running to the southwest of Ross Island was discovered and named after Lieutenant McMurdo, Crozier's first lieutenant on *Terror*.

After a further consultation, Ross and Crozier calculated that the South Magnetic Pole lay approximately 160 miles (256 kilometres) across the mountainous terrain spread out before them. But the season was closing in, with ice building up all around Ross Island and *Erebus* and *Terror* facing the unhappy prospect of getting trapped. As the expedition was not equipped for spending winter in the south, orders were given to withdraw to warmer waters.

But the return journey northwards through the pack ice was far more difficult than experienced on the inward trip. The ships ran into very heavy ice and when winds suddenly dropped, they were at the mercy of the dangerous sea swell that drove them hard into the tightly packed bergs.

Terror suffered minor damage and both crews were hugely relieved when, on 8 March, the ships emerged largely unscathed into open seas. It had been a testing voyage of high risks, bitterly cold conditions and the severe disappointment of failing to locate the South Magnetic Pole.

But morale remained remarkably high throughout the trip and not a single man from either *Erebus* or *Terror* had been lost or taken seriously ill since leaving Hobart. In a letter carried across to *Erebus*, Crozier reported, 'We are here as happy as droves.' In another memo to Ross from his cabin on *Terror*, he wrote, 'All get on famously.'[5]

Ross took a detour on the run back to Van Diemen's Land, turning westwards towards an area where Wilkes had reported seeing an impressive chain of mountains. Much to his amusement, Ross found only open sea and discovered no seabed when he dropped a line over 600 fathoms (1,100 metres) into the waters. Ross, though, was in no position to mock.

Exploration of the time was not an exact science and distant images, occasionally seen in hazy light for a few brief moments, were often distorted by refraction. Ross, too, was a victim of phantom sightings. While in the Ross Sea only weeks earlier, he had charted a range of peaks beyond the Barrier that he called the Parry Mountains. When Scott's *Discovery* expedition first travelled across the Barrier sixty years later, it was clearly established that the Parry Mountains do not exist.

A month after the encounter with Wilkes' 'mountains', *Erebus* and *Terror* returned in triumph to the familiar verdant landscape of Van Diemen's Land. The ships had been gone for five months, had spent 63 days below the Antarctic Circle and sailed further south than anyone before them. They had also managed the breath-taking feat of navigating the pack ice for the first time and had discovered vast tracts of new land, a live volcano among the new-found mountain ranges and the unforgettable Barrier. But without locating the South Magnetic Pole, the journey was incomplete.

CHAPTER 12

Dangerous Waters

Hobart was again in party mood on the return of the 'Two Captains' in April 1841. John Franklin sailed his official governor's barge down the Derwent River to greet *Erebus* and *Terror* and before long the town was in full swing.

Crozier also renewed his attempts to court Sophy Cracroft but was once again rebuffed. Sophy politely tolerated his advances but offered no encouragement. Crozier's cause was not helped by the absence of Lady Franklin, his strongest advocate and an inveterate traveller, who was touring in Australia and New Zealand.

The 'Two Captains' were again the centre of attention as they indulged in another giddy round of social events, though what they probably needed most after a long journey was rest. One glittering occasion seemed to run into another as Hobart took full advantage of the visitors, their reputations further enhanced by the brilliant results of their first foray into Antarctic waters.

The most ambitious but unhappy effort to salute the men was the staging of a specially commissioned play to commemorate the expedition. Unfortunately, the production – entitled *South Polar Expedition or the Discoveries of Captains Ross and Crozier* – was held at the Royal Victoria Theatre in the

ROYAL VICTORIA THEATRE,

CAMPBELL-STREET.

THE Public are respectfully informed, that on Wednesday next, the 14th instant, will be performed the melo-drama, entitled

MABEL'S PROPHECY.

AFTER WHICH,—

The celebrated interlude called

MY HUSBAND'S GHOST.

The evening's entertainments to conclude with the laughable farce, which was received with unbounded applause on the first night of its representation, of the

MASTER'S RIVAL,

OR A

Day at Boulogne.

In preparation, and will shortly be produced, a grand nautical drama founded on the glorious discoveries of Captains Ross and Crozier, entitled

THE SOUTH POLAR EXPEDITION,

OR THE

Discoveries of Captains Ross and Crozier.

F. B. BOOTH, Stage Manager.

April 12, 1841.   919

Poster advertising 'The South Polar Expedition or the Discoveries of Captains Ross and Crozier', a play staged in Hobart in 1841.

seedy dockside area of town and was shunned by Hobart society. Neither Crozier nor Ross, probably on the advice of Franklin, attended the play.

The local newspaper sardonically observed that the play was 'evidently much better written than it was played'. It reported that attempts to impersonate Crozier and Ross 'cast a damp upon the energies of those who represented the distinguished personages'.[1] Robert McCormick, surgeon on *Erebus*, was a little more forthright, declaring that the drama was 'rather indifferently got up and not much better acted'.

The highlight of the second season at Hobart came on 1 June when Ross and Crozier threw a gala ball on board *Erebus* and *Terror* to thank the town for its generous hospitality. The elaborate and expensively staged evening was the finest ball in the island's colonial history and was proudly remembered in Hobart for many years as simply the 'Glorious First of June'.

Erebus and *Terror* were lashed together close to Government House and Franklin built a special paddock in the grounds to accommodate the fleet of carriages bringing the 300 guests to the ball.

Visitors approached the vessels along a makeshift gangway made from a line of boats strung together and decorated with flags and wattles, the floral emblem of the island. A large canvas awning was thrown across the ships, with the upper decks of *Erebus* fitted out as the magnificent ballroom and the dazzling supper tables assembled around *Terror's* upper deck. More than 250 mirrors were arranged on the sides of the ships to reflect the flickering candlelight which threw a magical shimmering glow over proceedings.

Crozier and Ross entertained guests on *Terror* with a champagne reception and a sumptuous supper of English, French and local dishes. Later, the party transferred to *Erebus* where revellers danced until dawn to the music of the 51st Regiment orchestra and Hobart's quadrille band.

One young female guest said the ball 'far eclipsed anything else that has taken place on Van Diemen's Land'. In near breathless prose, she wrote to a friend:

> I had the honour of dancing with both Captain Ross and Captain Crozier. I told Captain Crozier that while I was dancing with him the morning of your birthday was dawning. He said he was very sorry that you were not there dancing too![2]

Crozier also provided a surprise for the evening by speaking a few words of

Grand ball. The embossed invitation to the lavish event on board Erebus *and* Terror, *hosted by Crozier and Ross at Hobart, 1841.*

Irish to the gathering. Although he is unlikely to have been a fluent Irish speaker, Crozier responded to a formal toast with the common Irish phrase, *céad míle fáilte* (a hundred thousand welcomes).[3]

Cunningham, the marine sergeant, offered a more pedestrian account of the evening. His diary of the following two days read:

> 2nd Wednesday. Clearing away the wrecks – head bad. 3rd
> Thursday, ditto.[4]

The most poignant moment, however, passed unnoticed. Crozier, as co-host, spent much of the evening on the decks of *Erebus* and *Terror* with the main guest, John Franklin. Within five years, those very decks that echoed to waltzes and quadrilles would be the setting for great personal tragedy for both men.

Erebus and *Terror* left Hobart on 7 July for a swift trip to Sydney. On the open seas somewhere between Van Diemen's Land and Sydney, Crozier sat in his cabin and drew up his last will and testament, appointing elder brother and lawyer, William, as executor and leaving the bulk of his estate to his unmarried sisters, Rachel and Charlotte. In the absence of an address while at sea, the meticulous Crozier listed his precise geographical coordinates.

Sydney saw a repeat of the hard work and ample socialising experienced in Van Diemen's Land. All hands worked flat out to erect a new observatory on Garden Island and the governor, Sir George Gipps, led the brisk round of dinners, balls and other public events for the visitors.

Magnetic observations were completed a few weeks later and in early August the expedition sailed to New Zealand, which only recently had separated from the Australian state of New South Wales to become a single British colony. The ships remained in the area for three months, building a further magnetic observatory, indulging in abundant local foodstuffs and keeping a wary eye on the restless Maori population. Maori unrest at British occupation was growing at the time and only a few years later would escalate into nearly twenty-seven years of armed conflict. Ahead of the subsequent outbreak of fighting, the expedition's officers and men carried guns whenever they ventured ashore, but the only casualty during the brief stay was a marine who drowned when his dinghy capsized.

An odd incident occurred soon after sailing when a seaman leapt overboard in high seas in the hope of avoiding a flogging for 'mutinous conduct'. He was plucked from the water and, according to the second master of *Terror*, John Davis, 'got his deserts besides his ducking'.

Dispatches were sent back to London, outlining future sailing plans and recommending promotion for several officers including McMurdo and Davis. 'The ships are now in the best possible condition, have on board about two years and a half provisions up to Febry [*sic*] 1844', a confident Ross informed the Admiralty. 'The crews are in the most perfect health,' he added.

The expedition sailed back towards Antarctic waters for a second time on 23 November 1841, with the target of reaching the edge of the pack ice along the 146th meridian by mid-December. This would bring the ships to the point on the Barrier where they had turned back the previous season.

Right on target, *Erebus* and *Terror* met the pack on 17 December. Christmas Day, the third since leaving Britain, was an occasion for a splendid dinner of roast beef and goose, accompanied by the disturbing sight of the vessels surrounded by dense ice. Picking a path through the tightly packed ice in freezing conditions was treacherous and Cunningham reported that Christmas was 'anything but a pleasant one'.

New Year's Day 1842 found the ships about 250 miles (400 kilometres) into the pack and still hopeful of emerging into open water. But when heavy ice brought the ships to a standstill, the officers and crew took the opportunity of improvising a New Year's celebration – one that lasted for two days.

A few hands climbed aboard a nearby iceberg and hollowed out a rectangular-shaped 'ballroom'. At one end of the dance floor, magnificent thrones were chiselled from the ice for Crozier and Ross. The artistic Hooker and Davis carved an 8-foot (2.4-metre) statue of a woman from the ice and named it Venus de Medici.

Drink flowed freely as the party ignored their predicament, singing and dancing into the early hours. Crozier and Ross entered the spirit of this bizarre occasion by dancing a quadrille in heavy boots and cold-weather clothing.

When the party broke up at 1 a.m., the 'Two Captains' were light-heartedly pelted with snowballs as they made their way back to their cabins. In the meantime, 'Venus de Medici' drifted slowly away towards the melting waters of the north, carrying a goodwill message signed by Crozier, Ross and the other officers.

'Venus de Medici' did not bring the expedition any luck. *Erebus* and *Terror* remained trapped in the ice for almost three weeks and on 20 January a hurricane hit the ships with astonishing ferocity. Ross reported the vessels 'rolling and groaning amidst heavy fragments of crushing bergs', and both ships lost their rudders at the height of the storm.

Terror suffered the worst. Although a spare rudder was made ready, the ice encasing the ship was too thick for the carpenters to work. Then, a potentially catastrophic fire broke out near the Sylvester stove and the quick-thinking Crozier was forced to flood the hold to a depth of 2 feet (0.6 metres) to douse the flames.

Following a consultation between Crozier and Ross, it was decided to take a huge risk by steering the ships back into the thickest area of ice, where it was expected the heavily packed ice would reduce turbulence thus making it easier to effect repairs. *Terror*'s rudder was eventually replaced, and the relieved expedition resumed the journey south, steering a fresh path through the endless miles of pack.

However, the damaging storm was a serious blow to the expedition, slowing the ships' progress and curtailing the season when the seas would be safe to navigate. It was not until 1 February, forty-seven days after entering the pack, that *Erebus* and *Terror* finally managed to locate clear water. A year earlier, the ships cleared the pack in less than five days.

Battered, broken but unbowed, *Erebus* and *Terror* had survived the Antarctic's most deadly assault and by late February the ships were running alongside the familiar sight of the Barrier. Ice conditions were tolerably good and as expected the ships steered east beyond the point where they had turned back twelve months earlier.

But it was now colder than it had been at that time the previous year. Cunningham reported layers of ice on the decks were far deeper, and the 1½ inch (4-centimetre) ropes had swollen to around 12 inches (32 centimetres) thick with ice.

A fish, dashed into *Terror*'s side by a wave, was instantly frozen against the hull of the ship, though Dr Richardson, *Terror*'s surgeon and naturalist, was thwarted in his attempts to analyse the fish when the ship's cat pounced and darted off with the prize.

The ships edged cautiously along the Barrier. On 22 February, *Erebus* and *Terror* reached 78° 10' south, about 6 miles (10 kilometres) further south than on the previous voyage and the most southerly point that any human had attained. 'No one will ever beat that in this longitude, that I may safely say,' Davis wrote.

He was correct as regards the 1842 season. Ice conditions grew rapidly worse and as February drew to a close, Crozier and Ross faced a difficult decision. As the ships came to the end of the Barrier, it was discovered that the land swerved to the north and brushed into the encircling pack. It was too late in the season to consider another encounter with the ice and on 24 February, helped by a favourable breeze from the southeast, it was decided to cut and run.

It had been a disappointing season truncated by the tortuous journey through the pack, though the expedition had reached a new 'furthest south' and, more importantly, lived to fight another day.

Erebus and *Terror* turned north, hoping for a quick voyage through the pack before exit routes were closed off by the colder autumn weather. Luck was on their side and the ships made a surprisingly easy passage, crossing the Antarctic Circle on 6 March.

Ross ordered a new course to the east to take the shortest route to Cape Horn and the Falkland Islands, where they intended to spend the winter. Most on board relaxed, assuming the worst had passed. Cunningham blithely noted: 'Have not seen any ice these two days. I think we are clear of it.' It was an unfortunate prediction.

In late-evening darkness on 12 March, the barometer plunged, heavy snow fell and hefty chunks of ice began to appear alongside. Seas became very rough and ice-blink – a reflection of ice in the distance – indicated pack ice directly ahead. Ross ordered *Erebus* to slow down by taking in his topsails, but Crozier was still running full sails on *Terror*, unaware of the imminent danger.

At 1 a.m. on 13 March, a line of massive icebergs – one standing about 200 feet (60 metres) out of the water – suddenly loomed in front of the ships. Ross turned away sharply and ran directly into the path of the faster-moving *Terror*. The two vessels collided with a sickening crunch in the pitch black. Men were knocked off their feet by the impact, wood splintered and the riggings became entangled as the ships struggled to remain upright in the heavy rolling seas. Cunningham reported a 'tremendous berg so close on our lee beam you could throw a biscuit on it'.

Erebus suffered badly, with the bowsprit, foretopmast and other smaller spars ripped away in the collision. *Terror* was carried to the top of heavy waves, almost exposing the ship's keel to the terrified men on *Erebus*. In an instant, the roles were reversed, with *Erebus* jerked out of the water on a rising wave and threatening to smash down on *Terror*.

By a miracle, the broken masts and rigging were separated as the ships rose and fell in the heaving seas. But the danger had not passed. Both ships were still perilously close to a pair of massive bergs – one at least 120 feet (35 metres) high, the other 200 feet (60 metres) out of the water. Davis

The dramatic collision of Erebus *and* Terror *while trying to avoid icebergs in the Southern Ocean, 1842.*

remembered, 'A dreadful shipwreck and death then appeared inevitable.'

Crozier reacted quickly. He spotted a dark shape between a line of six icebergs bearing down on his ship and gambled that it was an opening between the floating mountains of ice. Men, many of them still half-dressed after being summoned from their hammocks, flew to the ropes and sails as *Terror* steered for the small gap between the walls of ice.

The ship ran so close that heavy sea spray hit the bergs, splashed back over the decks and immediately froze. Officers and crew held their breath as *Terror* passed through the slender opening as though threading a needle. The gap, said Davis, was 'not twice the breadth of the ship'.

The 'horror and despair' of the incident was etched on the faces of the terrified men and Davis recalled a 'truly horrible time that will never be effaced from my memory'. One seaman reportedly went berserk with fear and three others wept uncontrollably. Cunningham said it was 'Divine providence that we were not all sent into the presence of Our

Crozier in Terror *(right) signals as Ross steers* Erebus *through the narrow gap between icebergs in 1842.*

Maker with all our sins on shoulders ...'

Crozier remained perfectly composed throughout the crisis, standing resolutely on deck, calmly issuing orders and displaying a measured authority that left his junior officers gaping in admiration. Davis observed that Crozier behaved 'as coolly as if he were steaming up the Derwent [in Tasmania]'. They were lucky to escape, as Crozier later explained to Davis:

> The Captain himself, when it was all over, said that he had not the slightest idea what he did during the time or how we got through.[5]

Crozier ordered a blue lamp to be lit as a beacon for the crippled *Erebus*, which, an hour later, managed to battle through the small gap between the icebergs thanks to the outstanding seamanship of Ross. Hooker, on board *Erebus*, concluded that 'no naval annals in the world could record such a narrow escape'. Davis admitted, 'Never till those moments did I really know what fear was.'

The first light of dawn gave both crews an opportunity to inspect the damage. Time was also taken for a brief service of thanksgiving for surviving the close brush with disaster.

Apart from the loss of masts and sails, *Erebus*' bow anchor had been driven into the hull, penetrating the extra planks and copper plating that had been used to reinforce the ship against the ice. It remained embedded in the hull for a further five days when it was released by the impact of another howling gale.

Patched up as effectively as could be managed on the high seas, *Erebus* and *Terror* resumed their journey north towards the Falkland Islands. At night, sails were brought in to avoid another unfortunate encounter with icebergs.

Days later, the expedition was hit by another blow. James Angelly, quartermaster on *Erebus*, fell overboard during a storm and was drowned. It was the ship's third loss. Crozier had not lost a man on *Terror*.

Next day, the two ships rounded Cape Horn and on 6 April 1842 *Erebus* and *Terror* ran into Berkeley Sound on East Falkland and anchored at Port Louis, the island's main settlement. The ships, which had been at sea for 135 days, entered Port Louis unnoticed under a blanket of dense fog. Thomas Hallett, *Erebus'* purser, went ashore to buy supplies of fresh beef and vegetables and to pick up the mail. To universal disappointment, the post had not arrived.

But Hallett brought back great news for Crozier. According to the Navy List in the lieutenant governor's office, Commander Francis Crozier had been promoted to the rank of captain, effective from August 1841 when the expedition was stationed in New Zealand. It had taken thirty-one years of loyal service to the navy to reach the cherished status of captain and Crozier wrote to Lord Minto at the Admiralty expressing his 'heartfelt thanks' for the promotion.

CHAPTER 13

Trembling Hands

Crozier's joy at being elevated to the rank of captain was overshadowed by growing signs of discontent aboard *Erebus* and *Terror*, where the first serious cracks had begun to appear in the expedition's façade. The ships, now at the end of their third year at sea, had been gone too long for many on board. A number of the men felt that the expedition had been forgotten back home, and Hooker complained that the English newspapers were 'more full of D'Urville's and Wilkes' expeditions than ours'.

The agitation increased further when the men discovered there was no mail from home and that Crozier was the only officer to be awarded promotion. While no one begrudged Crozier's elevation, some felt that other deserving cases had been overlooked. Both Hooker and McCormick anticipated promotion and McCormick moaned that he had been 'left in the cold'.

Morale was at its lowest ebb as the ships docked at the Falklands, particularly when the crew learned that it was intended to remain at the miserable, run-down colony for many months. Speculation was rife that a number of men had been planning to desert at the next port of call and that Ross had only decided to spend the winter in the Falklands because no sailor in his right mind would jump ship in such a dire and desolate spot 8,000 miles

(12,800 kilometres) from home. To add to the gloom, a number of crewmen became insensibly drunk on cheap rum during their first run ashore in five months and had to be carried back to the ships.

The strain had been evident even before the ships had reached the Falklands. In January, Crozier had taken the rare step of ordering John Barclay, *Terror*'s steward, to be punished with forty-eight strokes for 'drunkenness and general irregular conduct'. Discipline on board was generally very good throughout the long voyage and it was unusual for Crozier or Ross to hand out severe punishments.

Morale among the officers was also under strain. Quarrels and disagreements were regular fare and both Hooker and McCormick felt the sulphurous lash of Ross' tongue over minor issues. Davis reported the normally composed Ross looking 'anxious and careworn' in the days before the ships reached dry land.

The mood worsened when the party discovered that the Falklands were in a state of near anarchy, just nine years after Britain had annexed the islands. Organised farming had collapsed and many of the 75 inhabitants were starving.

Richard Moody, the inexperienced and newly appointed twenty-eight-year-old lieutenant governor, was struggling to maintain a semblance of law and order and to keep his community alive. The tiny population – civil servants, vagabond sailors and smallholders – was more than doubled by the arrival of the crews from *Erebus* and *Terror*, which suddenly imposed further strain on the island's flimsy resources.

Crozier and Ross paid a visit to Governor Moody, who informed them that he was unable to give the expedition even simple supplies such as fresh milk although herds of wild cattle roamed freely across the islands. To their astonishment, Crozier and Ross also learned that the island's farms could only produce enough fresh vegetables for one helping a day.

The appalling state of affairs on the Falklands left Crozier and Ross in a bizarre position. Instead of replenishing their own supplies after months below the Antarctic Circle, they were forced to dip into the expedition's provisions to provide Moody with bread and flour for his abject community.

The dismal weeks and months spent on the Falklands was the unhappiest episode of the entire voyage. Ross considered the islands a 'rather retrograding' place and Hooker said the wet and windy Kerguelen Islands were 'paradise' compared with the Falklands.

The most pressing task was to repair and refit the ships after the torrid time in the Southern Ocean and to build an observatory. Fortunately, a navy ship arrived at Port Louis and was able to carry an urgent message requesting a new bowsprit for the damaged *Erebus*.

Repair work began immediately. *Erebus* was emptied and hauled up the beach as far as possible and carpenters worked day and night mending the damaged hull. A similar task was performed on *Terror* and on 23 June the warship *Carysfort* arrived with a new bowsprit for *Erebus*. By the end of July, the two ships were ready for sea again.

In addition to overseeing work on the ships, Crozier and Ross were recruited to assist Moody in his quest to find a new capital for the Falklands. Crozier and Ross, two of the navy's most distinguished seafarers, were ideally suited to locating a new site for a community that would always be heavily dependent on shipping to sustain itself.

The choice was between two sites on East Falkland: the existing Port Louis in Berkley Sound or the more sheltered deep-water harbour of Port William in Jackson's Harbour. Although the swampy land around Port William was a tricky place to build new settlements, Crozier and Ross believed the anchorage facilities outweighed the disadvantages.

Port William was duly chosen as the new capital and renamed Port Stanley after the colonial secretary. Today, two streets running alongside Stanley Harbour bear the names Crozier Place and Ross Road. Another lasting reminder came from the methodical Crozier's wish to mark the exact high-water in Berkeley Sound by embedding a slate in a cairn on the shore-line. The marker remains in place to this day.

After five months on the islands, *Erebus* and *Terror* finally left the Falklands on 8 September 1842 for the stormy waters of Cape Horn. Few had regrets. Ross had fallen out with Moody on a grand scale and McMurdo, Crozier's deputy on *Terror*, had taken ill and was left behind to be invalided home on the next passing ship.

Many dreamed of accompanying McMurdo on his journey home. 'You can hardly conceive how earnestly we longed at the Falklands that the Admiralty would have recalled us, or ordered us on another direction,' wrote Hooker.

With Lieutenant John Sibbald of *Erebus* now installed as Crozier's first lieutenant on *Terror*, the intention was to conduct more magnetic observations around Tierra del Fuego, linked to readings taken in the Falklands. But the notoriously rough weather around the Horn hampered work. On Hermite Island, an isolated spot at the tip of South America, the observatory was erected in stormy conditions under the bemused eye of local Fuegian natives.

Erebus and *Terror* returned briefly to the Falklands in mid-November before making final preparations for their third voyage into Antarctic waters. At Port Louis, Crozier picked up his mail, which included an official notification from the Admiralty confirming his appointment to the rank of captain.

A ceremonial gun salute was fired as the ships sailed from Port Louis on 17 December 1842, though the volley could not disguise the sheer relief at leaving the depressing Falklands. Ross observed that 'not one individual in either ship [felt] the smallest regret at leaving the Falkland Islands'.

The plan was to sail as far south as possible on the meridian 55° west towards the Antarctic Peninsula in the hope of meeting Louis Philippe Land, first discovered five years earlier by D'Urville. If ice blocked their path, the alternative was to sail into the area on the other side of the peninsula which was discovered in 1823 by James Weddell.

Ross, at least, maintained an air of determination that either took no account of the simmering unrest or displayed a resolute display of authority. In a dispatch to the Admiralty from the Falklands, he boldly announced:

> I have not the smallest shadow of anxiety about our next season's operations. experience has made us so familiar with our work, now, in that quarter that we can regard it with as much tranquillity as we should approaching the English Channel.[1]

Erebus and *Terror* again headed south and the first icebergs were sighted on Christmas Eve. Christmas Day was celebrated close to Clarence Island by dining on a 'fine fat ox' which Governor Moody had generously donated to each ship.

Towards late afternoon, the main pack came into view and Joinville Island, which lies at the northern tip of the Antarctic Peninsula, was seen in the distance a few days later. To the south of Joinville, the ships found a host of unknown islands and rocky capes. The weather was blissfully fine and Crozier and Ross went ashore to a place called Cockburn Island to claim formal possession of the area for the Crown. A flurry of other naming took place in the area, including James Ross Island, Snow Hill Island and Paulet Island. An inlet was named Erebus and Terror Gulf and Governor Moody was recognised with Moody Point.

Further southerly progress, however, was blocked by an imposing line of unbroken ice. After consulting Crozier, Ross decided to head southeast, into the pack, in the hope of finding a passage towards the continent. But the ice, which had been penetrated so successfully into the Ross Sea, was crammed more tightly on this side of the continent.

Ice soon closed around the ships and by mid-January, *Erebus* and *Terror* were firmly beset in the northern reaches of King George IV Sea (later renamed the Weddell Sea).

The Weddell Sea is a potential graveyard for ships. Among the vessels subsequently lost in the same seas was Sir Ernest Shackleton's *Endurance*, which was crushed by the ice and sunk in 1915. Hooker described the sea as 'repellent'.

The Weddell Sea is a vast basin of mostly impenetrable ice surrounded on three sides by land where strong currents from the east drive the constantly mobile ice in a clockwise direction and pile it up against the 1,200-mile-long (2,000 kilometres) Antarctic Peninsula. From this area, the Antarctic pack swells to its thickest, extending at times to over 1,800 miles (2,880 kilometres) wide.

Erebus and *Terror* attempted to penetrate the waters for another two weeks, often taking a severe battering from large hunks of floating ice and frequent violent storms. By the end of January, the outline of Paulet Island could still be seen on the horizon, confirming that the ships had made barely any progress. They were not freed from the ice until 4 February, far too late in the season to contemplate seeking a new passage to the south.

Erebus and *Terror* came to a halt at around 65° south, with Crozier and Ross bemoaning the fact that, in 1823, Weddell had found open seas many degrees further south at 74° S. Even at 74°, Weddell had seen open water to the south, but he sensibly decided to turn back because of the lateness of the season.

Crozier and Ross rightly concluded that 1823 must have been a freak year. The ice in 1843, however, was unrelenting and their luck was out. In a different year, it is probable that the well-equipped and well-led *Erebus* and *Terror* might have made an historic journey, beating Weddell's 'furthest south' and may even have discovered what is today called the Caird Coast, Coats Land and the Filchner Ice Shelf on the Antarctic mainland.

Erebus and *Terror* had entered the Weddell Sea further east than Weddell, where the waters are invariably more negotiable. It was down these eastern channels that the famous twentieth-century voyages of Shackleton and Vivian Fuchs were made. It was also along this corridor that Britain established a permanent scientific Antarctic base at Halley Station on the

Brunt Ice Shelf and where 140 years after the voyage of Crozier and Ross, scientists first measured the alarming depletion of the ozone layer over the Antarctic continent.

For Crozier, Ross and the crews of *Erebus* and *Terror*, the 1843 journey was a major disappointment. Hooker described it as 'the worst season of the three, one of constant gales, fogs and snowstorms'. Calling it a 'signal failure', he added that Ross 'will not allow this'.

Strangely, there was an uncomfortable parallel with Parry's three attempts to find the North West Passage two decades earlier. Ross and Crozier's most accomplished season in the Antarctic was 1840–41, their first. But each successive year was less accomplished than its predecessor and the final season was a sorry postscript to the expedition. Parry suffered the same fate. His first expedition of 1819–20 into Lancaster Sound was a great triumph, the second a disappointment and the third a dismal failure.

Erebus and *Terror* retreated to warmer waters. Heading east, the ships ran alongside the pack and criss-crossed the Antarctic Circle. A few days later, *Erebus* and *Terror* ran into the pack again and in March a thick line of ice extended across their path from east to west with no sign of a break.

Tentative moves were made to re-enter the pack and the ships covered another 27 miles (43 kilometres) before coming to a grinding halt in front of an impenetrable wall of unbroken ice. *Erebus* and *Terror* stopped at 71° 30' south, the furthest south the ice would permit that season. A little more than 50 miles (80 kilometres) across the horizon – unknown to Crozier and Ross – was the coastline of Dronning Maud Land, an area that would remain undiscovered for another ninety years.

A weary Ross signalled to Crozier that the great endeavour was at an end. The ships withdrew from the ice, crossing the Antarctic Circle for the last time in the second week of March.

The ships turned north towards Simon's Bay at the Cape of Good Hope, hoping for better luck and easier travelling. But they immediately ran into another fierce north-easterly gale, which left them reeling from its force and in danger of being smashed into the pack ice.

The expedition was again shaken by the ferocity of the storm and the biting cold. Seas broke over the decks and froze, and the sails were soon armour plated with ice. Men stayed on deck throughout the night on constant alert for stray icebergs. A brief lull followed before the storm once again erupted with full fury as though the Antarctic was bidding a pitiless farewell.

The violence of the storm rattled even the hardened men of *Erebus* and *Terror*. Nothing experienced on the long voyage seemed to compare with those final days in the Southern Ocean, even for men who had endured three voyages through the worst seas on earth. Crozier and Ross, despite their vast experience of the southern seas, were visibly traumatised by the ordeal. Crozier's hair, once dark, was now distinctly grey.

Crozier emerged as a giant during these final demanding days in the Antarctic. His dedication, cool professionalism and outstanding seamanship were unsurpassed. Lesser men might have buckled under the strain. Danger had always been at hand, particularly as the ships battled against the treacherous waters of the Weddell Sea. Hooker reported:

> They were nights of grog and hot coffee, for the orders to splice the main brace were many and imperative, if the crew were to be kept up to the strain on their nerves and muscles.[2]

Crozier's commitment was awe inspiring. He did not sleep in his bed for weeks during the skirmish with the icy seas, remaining on deck for hours at a time and only snatching a few hours rest by dozing in a chair in his cabin. Ross had little doubt about the value of Crozier or of how much Crozier had relied on his solid Christian faith to get him through the traumatic journey. Ross noted:

> His firm and unwavering confidence in that almighty power ... when no other

power could save enabled him at all times to meet with calmness and firmness every impending danger.[3]

Ross was not a man to lavish praise too freely but his admiration for Crozier's seafaring skills and 'noble conduct' was clear. He wrote:

Too much praise cannot be bestowed upon Captain Crozier and his officers for the seamanlike manner in which the *Terror* was conducted throughout these severe gales.[4]

Crozier, too, had cemented his respect and admiration for Ross during the voyage. A contemporary observer said, 'Ross and Crozier were like brothers, so attached by their mutual tastes and dangers shared together.'[5]

Onlookers in South Africa noticed something else that was peculiar about Crozier and Ross as they were entertained at receptions soon after arriving in Simon's Bay. Mrs Bagot, the daughter of the Cape's admiral, Percy Jocelyn, spotted that Crozier's and Ross' hands trembled. She wrote:

Their hands shook so much they could hardly hold a glass or a cup ... Sir James Ross told me when he took me to dinner one day: 'You see how our hands shake? One night in the Antarctic did this for both of us.'[6]

There was another curiosity. Crozier told Mrs Bagot that doctors on *Erebus* or *Terror* had never needed to break into their medicine chests during the voyage. Only once, when a man had hurt his hand, was any surgery required. But during their stay at Simon's Bay, a few men fell ill as they adjusted to a more temperate climate. According to Mrs Bagot, 'They all felt the heat intensely, though it was the Cape winter.'[7]

Nevertheless, only three men from *Erebus* were to die during the voyage, and just two of *Terror*'s officers were invalided home, a remarkably low casualty rate for the time. A century earlier, more than a thousand men died on the four-year, round-the-world voyage of Commodore George Anson, and Cook, arguably the finest of all seafarers, lost 34 men on his first expedition of 1768–71.

Erebus and *Terror* spent almost a month in the pleasant environment of Simon's Bay, quietly refitting the ships, resting and looking forward to the return home. But there was consternation on board as a rumour spread about more instruments being shipped from London to allow the expedition to continue for another year. It proved a false alarm and the ships left the Cape on 30 April for the final leg of their mammoth journey.

The shores of England were sighted on 2 September and *Erebus* and *Terror* anchored off the Kent port of Folkestone at midnight on 4 September. The last great journey of discovery to rely solely on sail came to a formal end on 23 September 1843, almost four years to the day since the ships had sailed south. It would be another 31 years before *Challenger* in 1874 would become the first steam-powered vessel to cross the Antarctic Circle.

During the absence of *Erebus* and *Terror*, ether was used for the first time in a hospital operation, the Penny Post was introduced and Napoleon's remains were taken from the outpost of St Helena to Paris.

The voyage was the nineteenth century's most outstanding feat of navigation and paved the way for most of the great voyages of twentieth-century Antarctic exploration. Ross and Crozier, relying entirely on their exceptional seamanship, had opened the door to Antarctica and the South Pole itself for the acclaimed explorers that followed in their wake, notably Amundsen, Fuchs, Mawson, Scott and Shackleton. It was a comprehensive triumph of navigation, surveying and scientific endeavour.

Under the exceptional command of Ross and Crozier, *Erebus* and *Terror* had navigated the southern pack ice in the Ross Sea area for the first time and located thousands of miles of new Antarctic seas and coastline. The major discoveries included the Ross Sea, Victoria Land, the Ross Ice Shelf, Ross Island, McMurdo Sound and Mount Erebus. They even caught a brief sighting of a passing comet.

The location of the South Magnetic Pole, the primary objective of the expedition, was indicated, but never reached. In his kit, Ross still had the neatly folded Union flag that he had flown at the North Magnetic Pole in 1831. The South Magnetic Pole, a constantly moving location, was finally reached in 1909 by Edgeworth David, Alistair Mackay and Douglas Mawson from Shackleton's *Nimrod* expedition, though it was located some 230 miles (370 kilometres) north of where the *Erebus* and *Terror* expected to find it.

The huge amount of magnetic and astronomical data accumulated by Crozier and Ross required years of painstaking scientific exami-nation before the results were published. The expedi-tion's extensive mapping and charting of the ocean depths, the studies of marine biology, and collection of botanical specimens were all vitally important over the years as the veil was slowly lifted from earth's last undiscovered continent.

Crozier and Ross were lauded as the finest scientific navigators of the age and several of the expedition's leading officers – among them Bird, McMurdo and Sibbald – were pro-moted. Joseph Hooker, just twenty-one when he sailed, went on to become one of the great natural-ists of the Victorian age and lived long enough to advise Captain Scott before the *Discovery* expe-dition to the Antarctic in 1901.

Crozier and Ross were also among the first recipients of a curious new naval custom which applied to anyone who had sailed

Crozier's silver watch (front and back) given to Sergeant William Cunningham of Terror *in 1843 as a mark of esteem following the Antarctic expedition.*

through both the Arctic and Antarctic Circles.

By tradition, such travellers can drink with both feet on the table.

The expedition, however, never quite caught the public imagination or generated the enthusiastic acclaim at the Admiralty it so richly deserved. The suspicion that the seafarers of *Erebus* and *Terror* were forgotten men was at least partly true. Four years away from home was too long out of the public gaze and the official reports and scientific results were not released for years. To compound this situation, Ross struggled to publish his account of the voyage, and when it finally emerged four years after *Erebus* and *Terror* docked, it was a dry and pedestrian tome.

Unfortunately, no one thought to persuade Crozier to write his version of the momentous events. Writing a book would have been the perfect way to rest and recuperate from the rigours of the voyage and if successful might have provided Crozier with the recognition and public profile he lacked. It may also have stopped him going back to sea again.

Crozier was quick to salute the role played by the lower ranks. Shortly after returning home, he generously gave the silver watch he had worn for 15 years to William Cunningham, the marine sergeant who had served so well on *Terror*. The watch was engraved:

Presented by Captain F.R.M. Crozier, R.N. to Sergt W K Cunningham R.N. as mark of esteem.[8]

Less than four weeks after the Antarctic expedition was formally wound up, Ross married his twenty-six-year-old fiancée, Ann Coulman, and retired from exploration at the age of forty-three. He was knighted the following year.

Crozier was best man at the wedding. Although forty-seven years of age, Crozier did not have the luxury of opting for peaceful retirement. Nor did he seem any closer to finding a wife.

CHAPTER 14

'I Am Not Equal to the Hardship'

Crozier was drained by the four-year voyage to the Antarctic. His stamina had been sapped by the huge physical demands of the journey, and while his energy would recover given a suitable period of convalescence, the psychological wounds would take longer to heal.

In a private conversation, Crozier once admitted that he endured more danger in one day in the Antarctic than in a month in the most severe regions of the Arctic. 'He went out a young man and came home broken down and rather old-looking for his years,' a relative, John Henry Loftie, remembered.

Once more without a ship and again on half-pay, he found it difficult to adjust. As a middle-aged junior captain and with so many experienced officers to compete with, eventual promotion to the rank of admiral was unlikely, despite his fine record.

Unsure about his future in the navy and still moping over Sophy Cracroft, the normally steadfast man began to crumble and descend into depression. In his torment, Crozier may well have contemplated leaving the navy, but never followed it through.

Another arduous voyage as he approached his fifties was far from enticing, even if it remained the most realistic prospect of active service. Despite his monumental efforts in the Arctic and Antarctic, he had never won the kind of acclaim and recognition afforded Ross and Parry. He was not invited to bask in the glory of his adventures with a knighthood as Ross had done, nor settle for a comfortable desk job like Parry. Crozier, now in his late forties, knew nothing else and his only source of income was the navy's half-pay.

The disparity in fortunes between Ross and Crozier was stark. The newly married Ross picked up a knighthood and an honorary degree from Oxford University and settled contentedly into his comfortable estate in the Buckinghamshire countryside, from where he wrote a book about the voyage and dispensed wisdom on polar affairs to the grateful lords at the Admiralty.

In contrast, Crozier scratched around for a ship and a means of earning a living. He remained a peripheral figure at the Admiralty, the power base of the English military establishment, where, perhaps, his Irish pedigree was regarded as an impediment by the stuffy civil servants and admirals whose own positions owed so much to the English class system. Or that in polite society, Crozier simply lacked the refinement acquired by a classical English education.

Crozier was a reluctant public figure who, with even a modest slice of Parry's ambition and a share of Ross' magnetism, would have been recognised among the finest explorers of the age, and would have survived middle age free from niggling worries about money. In the event, it was left to Ross to do what the modest Crozier seemed unable to do for himself. He wrote of him:

> Captain Crozier was of an amiable and cheerful disposition and his unbending integrity and truthfulness won the affection and respect of those he commanded, as well as the admiration and firm friendship of all those officers under whom he served.[1]

The pity is that Ross' warm and sincere words of praise for his old friend were written after Crozier's death.

The other cause of Crozier's emotional turmoil was the unfulfilled relationship with Sophy Cracroft. Despite the earlier rejection of his marriage proposal, Crozier had not given up hope of changing her mind. Indeed, there was renewed urgency in his pursuit since marriage might be a catalyst for a new life away from the navy. In addition, Sophy, now twenty-eight years old, was reaching an age when a woman at the time considered settling down and raising a family.

Matters came to a head in June 1844 when Sophy unexpectedly returned to England with Sir John and Lady Franklin. The Franklins had been forced out of Van Diemen's Land by political manoeuvring at the Colonial Office and Franklin, by perverse fortune, found himself in much the same position as Crozier.

Crozier eagerly seized the opportunity to pursue Sophy – perhaps too eagerly. The pair met many times during the summer of 1844, with Crozier becoming increasingly insistent. But she resisted his attentions and once again turned down his proposal. Sophy was adamant, re-emphasising that she had no intention of becoming a sea captain's wife.

It is easy to understand Sophy Cracroft's reluctance. Crozier in 1844 was not an attractive proposition. His grey hair and middle-aged spread hinted at someone carrying the burdens of arduous decades at sea and looking a little more than his forty-seven years. McCormick, the surgeon on *Erebus*, described Crozier as a 'somewhat heavy man'.

Crozier had sacrificed himself to the sea and his prospects were not very promising. All he could offer was the lonely existence of a sea captain's wife or the unappealing alternative of naval half-pay – a modest 14s 9d a day (about £45 in current terms).

Crozier, without a grand estate or ample farmlands to generate a decent income, had lived most of adult life out of a trunk. He had little money and few possessions. By contrast, Sophy was more accustomed to the style and glamour of a colonial governor's household or London society, where she found no shortage of male callers. Even Crozier called himself a 'halfpay bachelor'.

The state of Crozier's mind began to alarm the two people who knew him best: Ross and Jane Franklin. Both were concerned that in pursuing Sophy his behaviour had become increasingly erratic. Lady Franklin, sensing the danger, wrote to Ross:

> There is another matter on which I wish to speak to you but I think it had better not be in writing – it relates to Captain Crozier and Sophy under present circumstances. I shall be glad of your advice ... I wish to tell you what Sophy writes to me on the subject.[2]

The precise circumstances of Lady Franklin's intervention are not clear, but a clue can be found in an apologetic letter written by Crozier to Ross a few months later, in September 1844. In his note, Crozier asked his old friend to show some understanding of his recent behaviour. Clearly chastened by events, he wrote:

> I am now quite recovered and trust with God's blessing to keep myself clear of all such scrapes in future. I ought to have had more wisdom however James dear I gave you enough bother about it.[3]

Rejected, out of work and with uncertain prospects, Crozier decided to take a long holiday. 'A few months abroad will be the best thing for me,' he told Ross. The navy, possibly aware of his depressed state, generously gave him extended leave of one year.

Yet even the prospect of a long holiday away from the emotional stress of London failed to raise his spirits. In a letter to Ross, he explained that his elderly sisters in Dublin were unhappy at the length of time he would be away. But in a melancholic footnote, he added: 'I just felt I was a bother to them and a burden to myself.'

Nevertheless, in the autumn of 1844, Crozier embarked on a 'grand tour' of Europe, the sightseeing and cultural journey around the fashionable cities of France, Spain and Italy so popular at the time. Traditionally the tour was a rite of passage taken by well-heeled young aristocrats and Romantics to mark a coming of age. After over 30 years of service to the navy and surviving five expeditions to the ice, Crozier needed no rite of passage and the 'grand tour' was pure escapism.

Yet Crozier was a troubled soul, uncertain if even the lazy trip around Europe's cultural high spots was the right choice. So uncertain was Crozier that he left England without bothering to say farewell to Ross and his heavily pregnant wife, Ann. This was uncharacteristic of Crozier and guilt caught up with him on the first leg of the excursion. While passing through France, he dropped a brief note to Ross apologising for the slight. 'It has caused me much pain,' he confessed. 'But the truth is I could not make up my mind to visit London now.'

Getting away from England was the main priority. In a letter to Ross, he explained:

I believe, after all, that a few months abroad will be the best thing for me. I have one year's leave but, I think, much less will serve me as I feel adrift wherever I am. However, a little travel will cure all, I hope.[4]

Unfortunately, the unhurried, meandering journey through Europe did little to relieve the gloom or ease the feeling of loneliness. He travelled from Paris to the south of France and made a quick detour into Spain before visiting the great Italian cities of Venice, Florence and Rome.

But loneliness was eating at Crozier. Although he promised Ross to put his 'bygones' behind him, Crozier was struggling to cope. In a poignant somewhat incoherent letter to Ross from the south of France, he confided:

I could go anywhere being so much alone as I have been, has been the best thing in the world for me, plenty of time to review times past with, I do believe, an unbiased mind. In a word I am quite happy and, under all the circumstances of age, etc, I would not if I could that it were otherwise.

Now, James dear, you know the state of the case with me, in as few words as I could put it, therefore I will pester you and dear [Ann], my kind friends, with no more bygones.[5]

A thousand miles away, in London, events were moving at a more significant pace. The North West Passage, which had been off the political agenda at the Admiralty for the best part of a decade, was suddenly the centre of attention again. The architect, once more, was the ageing but ever-ambitious figure of Sir John Barrow.

Now eighty years old, Barrow was pushing for a final triumph to cap his extraordinary forty-year reign at the seat of power in the Admiralty. The spark for Barrow's last hurrah was the return of Crozier and Ross from the Antarctic. In 1844, as Crozier was wandering through the galleries and museums of Europe, Barrow finalised a new plan to complete the discovery of the North West Passage.

In Barrow's obsessive mind, one final push could bring to a successful conclusion his personal quest to find that elusive waterway, which he had begun so optimistically in 1818. It would also allow the magnetic survey of the globe, which had taken great strides forward with the Antarctic mission, to be successfully completed. He persuaded the government that the prize was within grasp, with perhaps only a few hundred miles of the passage remaining undiscovered. 'So little now remains to be done,' he wrote.

Erebus and *Terror* were on standby after their marathon voyage and he pledged that many experienced Arctic officers were 'ready and willing to embark on an expedition'. The risks, he insisted, were small.

The public, too, was eager to support Barrow's mission in the self-assured early days of the Victorian era. Queen Victoria had ascended the throne in 1837 with Britain in the unrivalled position of being the world's most powerful nation, controlling a fifth of the earth's surface and the destinies of hundreds of millions of people. Confident, expansive and ambitious, Britain strode the world politically, economically and militarily.

From his desk at the Admiralty, Barrow was among those who encouraged Britain to use its enormous power to extend the boundaries of the Empire still further. By the early 1840s the country had embarked on a massive expansion of its domain, driving into places as far apart as Africa, Hong Kong and Afghanistan. Navigating the North West Passage, as Barrow optimistically proposed, was a natural and simple extension of this imperial endeavour.

Barrow played the patriotic card with his customary skill and issued a rallying call for the passage to be completed before any upstart foreign power stole the nation's thunder. In Barrow's words, it would be 'most mortifying' to let another naval country complete the task begun by the country's noble mariners. His message was simple and chimed perfectly with the overwhelming sense of national destiny and superiority felt by Victorian Britain:

> If left to be performed by some other power, England by her neglect of it, after having opened the East and West doors, would be laughed at by all the world for having hesitated to cross the threshold.[6]

Barrow assembled key strongholds of support for his new scheme, including the authoritative Royal Society. He approached the Prime Minister, Sir Robert Peel, with the names of seven prominent Arctic officers – including Parry, Franklin, Back and Ross – who could be relied on to support his ambitions.

The most glaring omission from the list of Arctic worthies was that of Crozier, though this may partly be explained by his absence from the country. More likely, the oversight was another indication of the Admiralty's shamefully misguided opinion of Crozier.

Barrow's carefully targeted campaign to send a new expedition worked, and Peel duly approved the plan. A few days later, Barrow retired as second secretary at the Admiralty, supremely confident that the crucial final piece of the jigsaw he had been playing with for nearly thirty years was now ready to be slotted into place.

Erebus and *Terror*, the two old warhorses, were ordered to be made ready and thoughts turned to the selection of an expedition leader. While Ross, Parry and Crozier were under consideration, Barrow, still seeking to influence events from beyond the Admiralty, had his own candidate in mind.

James Clark Ross, the most experienced and capable, was the natural choice and had served on eight expeditions to the ice. But he turned down the role. Ross, now forty-four, had faithfully promised Thomas Coulman, Ann's father, that his exploring days were over after the demanding Antarctic voyage and in the autumn of 1844, Ann Ross gave birth to their first child after a difficult pregnancy.

Not everyone was convinced of the plausibility of Ross' explanation, particularly given that leaving wives behind was a generally accepted part of being an explorer. A more likely explanation is that Ross, like Crozier, was still feeling the strain of the Antarctic voyage and there were also suspicions he was drinking heavily.

Some at the Admiralty felt that Parry, who had carried Barrow's torch in the early days, would come out of retirement for a last shot at glory. But Parry was fifty-four years old and dogged by ill health. After the early death of his first wife, Isabella, Parry had remarried, and in 1843 – three months after Crozier and Ross arrived back from the Antarctic – his new wife, Catherine delivered twin girls. In the early months of 1845, as the Admiralty plotted a new assault on the North West Passage, Catherine was again pregnant. Understandably, Parry had lost his appetite for more years of Arctic toil.

Barrow's personal choice of expedition leader was the unlikely figure of Commander James Fitzjames, an engaging and able officer in his early thirties with a good service record and friends in the right places. His best friend was Barrow's son. But Fitzjames had no Arctic experience. The Admiralty, now under new management, was wary about handing over responsibility for the expedition to a relative novice with no working knowledge of the ice.

Barrow's act of naked patronage, probably his last, was politely rejected and the Admiralty searched the ranks for a more battle-hardened commander. In the circumstances, the choice of leader came down to either Francis Crozier or Sir John Franklin. But while Crozier hesitated, Franklin leapt at the chance.

Franklin was anxious to lead the party after the unhappy events that led to his departure from Van Diemen's Land. After being so long away from sea, he was particularly eager to resurrect his reputation at the Admiralty and to resume his active naval career away from diplomatic duties.

His selection campaign was fronted by the ever-ambitious Lady Franklin, who believed that the government owed her husband a debt after the shabby treatment meted out by the Colonial Office. She worked tirelessly behind the scenes to secure the posting and was not averse to playing the emotional card in her attempts to get Franklin appointed. Seeing that Ross was advising the Admiralty on the appointment, she wrote to him with a warning of what would happen if Franklin were overlooked: 'I dread exceedingly the effect on his mind,' she told Ross.

Yet Franklin, a stout fifty-eight-year-old, was self-evidently too old and not fit enough for the job. Although he was universally liked, not everyone accepted that he should command the expedition. Sir Edward Sabine and Sir George Back, two knowledgeable Arctic hands, felt he was unsuited to the task, and Sir Francis Beaufort, the distinguished head of naval hydrography, had reservations about sending Franklin as commander. The much-respected Beaufort – creator of the internationally recognised wind-speed scale – knew Franklin's weaknesses and urged Ross to reconsider.

The man with the unenviable choice to make was Thomas Hamilton, Lord Haddington, the first secretary of the Admiralty and Barrow's former political master. Haddington was initially sceptical about appointing a man nearing sixty and preferred Crozier. With a politician's nose for trouble, Haddington – his political career stretched back for over forty years – probably sensed that the finger of blame would be pointed at him if the ageing Franklin were struck by disaster.

But Franklin was a popular character at the Admiralty and had the support and sympathy of the Arctic elite, including Parry, Richardson and Ross, who felt that he deserved a chance to become leader. Richardson, a navy surgeon, gladly offered to sign a medical certificate stating that Franklin was 'perfectly sound', and Parry took a leaf out of Jane Franklin's book by telling Haddington that 'the man will die of disappointment' if not chosen as leader.

Haddington searched for an excuse to reject Franklin and in February 1845 summoned him to a meeting where he broached the sensitive topic of Franklin's age. The apocryphal story is that Haddington insisted: 'You are sixty!' Franklin replied, 'Not quite, my lord. I am only fifty-nine'. In fact, Franklin was fifty-eight and still two months short of his fifty-ninth birthday in mid-April.

Haddington's ideal choice for leader was Crozier who, by some distance, was the most experienced of the Arctic captains still on active duty. He also possessed the most recent knowledge of the region and had intimate understanding of *Erebus* and *Terror* after spending four years in the Antarctic with the two vessels.

On the face of it, Crozier's credentials for leadership were second to none. He was widely recognised as a thoroughly reliable seafarer with an unblemished record of five polar voyages – three with Parry and two with Ross – spread over more than two decades. He had never suffered the humiliation of a court martial for the loss of a ship. At forty-eight, he appeared young and vigorous enough to lead an expedition.

Leopold McClintock, who became a notable figure in the later story, had little doubt about Crozier's abilities to command. Commenting on Crozier's standing in the navy, McClintock wrote: 'Captain Crozier had now achieved the highest professional reputation.'[7]

In contrast, Franklin had not been to the Arctic for seventeen years. His reputation as an Arctic explorer, improbably enough for a person of his generous physique, was built largely on trekking overland rather than on sea voyages. 'The man who ate his boots' had never commanded an Arctic expedition by sea. It had been twenty-seven years since Franklin had last navigated Arctic waters and he would be in his sixtieth year the next time he took a ship into the ice.

For reasons that remain unclear to this day, Haddington never spoke publicly about his preference for Crozier. According to Ross, Haddington only made the offer of leadership 'privately' to Crozier.

It is equally curious that Ross did not support Crozier's case to be leader. Although the reasons for his reluctance are blurred by time, Ross may have seen it as an act of kindness towards his closest friend, who was still suffering from depression and self-doubt. Ross knew the Irishman better than anyone and a greater act of kindness might have been to persuade Crozier to decline a role in the expedition altogether and try to build a new life away from the navy.

Letters written by Crozier at the time show his uncertain state of mind. One moment he was considering pressing for command of the expedition and in the next he suggested going north, but only as Franklin's deputy. Either way, Crozier insisted that, apart from Ross and the effectively retired Parry, Franklin was the only commander he would agree to serve under.

For two months, he fretted over his decision, desperately trying to balance his passionate sense of duty against his own fragile state of mind. He finally reached the fateful decision to stand aside from the leadership battle during a visit to Florence at the end of 1844. When informing

Ross that he did not want to be considered as commander, Crozier added the revealing explanation:

> Of course I am too late to volunteer to command but in truth I sincerely feel I am not equal to the hardship. I am, in truth, still of opinion as to my own unfitness to lead. You, on that subject as well as all others, know my whole mind.[8]

Some doubts exist about the precise wording in Crozier's important letter to Ross. Unfortunately, Crozier's handwriting is indistinct and the word 'hardship' can easily be interpreted as 'leadership', leaving the sentence to read as '... I am not equal to the leadership.'

However, Crozier had made the worst of all decisions by abandoning the leadership but volunteering to serve as Franklin's deputy. A more clear-thinking person would have retired gracefully.

Crozier's determination to sail regardless of his own frailties was a response to the call of duty. In a letter to his sisters in Dublin, which showed that his sense of obligation outweighed the psychological strain, he declared: 'It was not my place to become one of the party to be left at home.'[9]

The mystery is that, while Crozier felt positively certain he was 'not equal to the hardship' of leadership, he was prepared to push himself into travelling as Franklin's second-in-command. Physically and emotionally, there was precious little difference between being number one and number two on a challenging voyage likely to last two or more years, particularly as Franklin enjoyed delegating responsibility. Crozier's four gruelling years in the Antarctic with Ross had emphasised how responsibility was shared and each captain had full reign over his own vessel.

Traditionally, Crozier would also be expected to carry the heavy burden of responsibility for choosing officers and crew, fitting out the ships and managing the expedition's scientific programme, as well as taking full command of *Terror* for the journey. But he was not confident enough to accept the burden of total control.

Ross, having backed the claim of Franklin, now recommended that either Crozier or the experienced second-in-command from *Erebus*, Edward Bird, should travel as his deputy. 'With Franklin as its commander and Crozier or Bird as his second, I should feel no doubt of the success of the undertaking,' Ross wrote confidently to Sabine in December 1844.

Against his better instincts, Haddington accepted the recommendations of Parry, Richardson and Ross and on 7 February 1845 appointed Franklin to command the North West Passage venture. It was to be the largest, most ambitious expedition ever to leave Britain.

The appointment of Franklin was a poor one, based largely on sentiment and a faint sense of guilt within the Admiralty. As historian, Pierre Berton, later concluded, the expedition 'was to be led by a man who got the job because everybody felt sorry for him'.[10]

However, the prospect of travelling as second-in-command somehow reinvigorated Crozier. He was rejuvenated by hopes of getting back to sea and a fresh opportunity to serve the navy. 'I feel quite satisfied in my own mind,' he wrote to Ross, 'that I was right in volunteering to go second to Sir John and also in not volunteering as leader, come of it what may.'

Convinced he had made the right decision, Crozier urged Ross to use his influence at the Admiralty to ensure that he was given the position of second-in-command.

I hesitate not a moment to go second to Sir John Franklin, pray tell him so, if too late I cannot help it. I would not on any terms go second to any other, Captain Parry or yourself excepted. Act for me, my dear friend, in this as you see fit and I will carry it out in every particular.[11]

It is likely that there was another, more emotive, consideration in his mind. Despite earlier rebuffs, Crozier still clung to hopes of marrying Sophy

Cracroft and bringing back the keys to the North West Passage offered the slim and near desperate hope of impressing her. Perhaps his last.

However, Crozier's appointment as Franklin's deputy was by no means cut and dried. There were, apparently, lingering doubts within the Admiralty about his suitability, particularly if Ross had confided his knowledge of his friend's delicate state of mind. While still languishing in Florence, Crozier wrote to say he was in a 'sad state of anxiety' awaiting Haddington's decision. A week after Franklin's appointment, he wrote to Ross: 'I am all ready, should I be required.'

The Admiralty's concerns about Crozier led to the position being offered elsewhere. John Lort Stokes, an experienced naval officer who had sailed with Captain Robert FitzRoy on the epic voyage of *Beagle* in the 1830s and shared a cabin with Charles Darwin, was among those under consideration.

But Stokes turned down the post and went on to become an Admiral in the navy. There was also speculation about appointing Edward Charlwood, a close friend of Fitzjames, who later wrote: 'I received private intimation from the Admiralty that I was to be appointed.' However, the Admiralty was uneasy about Charlwood's past record and eventually looked elsewhere.

Haddington turned to Ross, who once again urged the Admiralty to appoint Crozier. It was a critical intervention and on 3 March 1845 Crozier was officially appointed captain of *Terror* and the expedition's second-in-command.

A bust of Crozier. The alabaster likeness was sculpted in Florence in early 1845 while Crozier was considering the planned North West Passage expedition. The self-effacing Crozier said the bust made him 'much too young looking'.

He hurried back to London, seemingly eager to get back to work on the familiar decks of *Terror*. On the way, he wrote to the family in Dublin – the 'old sisters' he called them – to break the news of his new expedition. He said:

> Of course, you are aware that this is a service more congenial to my feelings than any other and we all know that the same God rules in all places. Whether on sea or shore, He is ever with us.[12]

CHAPTER 15

A Sense of Tragedy

Francis Crozier was in the wrong frame of mind to make another long, punishing and hazardous voyage into the icy reaches of the North West Passage. A different man, one with a different focus in life or not needing to impress Sophy Cracroft, would never have gone north in 1845.

Crozier soon found another reason to be concerned. Not long after his appointment, he began to develop serious reservations about the expedition itself. He was right to be worried.

After arriving in London, Crozier discovered that the Admiralty had delivered an amazing snub to its most experienced serving Arctic officer. The Admiralty had given James Fitzjames, a newcomer to the ice, responsibility for handling many of the expedition's most crucial affairs in the run-up to departure.

Crozier, in effect, had been stripped of his responsibilities as the expedition's second-in-command in favour of a younger man who, in all probability, had never seen an iceberg. To his chagrin, Crozier also discovered that the likeable Fitzjames had become a personal favourite of Franklin.

Fitzjames, he learned, had been placed in charge of the vital issue of appointing the expedition's 21 other officers and the rest of the crew. Traditionally this was the role of the second-in-command. It was an extraordinary decision since no one still active in the navy knew as much as Crozier about seamanship in the ice – this was his sixth polar voyage – and the behaviour of *Erebus* and *Terror* in Arctic seas.

Crozier was a hard taskmaster, but his judgement in picking officers and crew, as he demonstrated in the Antarctic, was often right. Ross, the most experienced of all, had left the selection of officers and crew entirely in the hands of Crozier and trusted him implicitly. Moreover, the low casualty rate on the four-year Antarctic expedition showed the wisdom of his selections. Death was commonplace on long sea voyages, but only three men died on *Erebus* during the voyage and there were no fatalities on *Terror* under Crozier's command.

Even more extraordinary was the Admiralty's decision to hand over responsibility for the expedition's magnetic studies to Fitzjames. The only concession was that Crozier was permitted to buy the magnetic instruments for the voyage, which implied that the Admiralty had not entirely lost trust in him.

Nonetheless, it was an astonishing rebuke to Crozier, who at the time was the navy's most experienced magnetic authority still on active service. He had been involved in magnetic work for close to thirty years, often in very trying conditions, and his expertise was recognised at the highest level.

In December 1843, three months after returning from Antarctica, Crozier was invited to become a Fellow of the Royal Society, the distinguished scientific body. Only 22 men were elected to the exclusive Royal Society that year and it was a measure of his standing in the scientific community that some of the most prominent men of the day lined up to support his election. His sponsors included the world-famous astronomer, Sir John Herschel, and from navy circles he was backed by Barrow, Beaufort, Sabine and Sir George Cockburn, the Navy's First Sea Lord. In accepting him into the select fold, the Royal Society saluted Crozier's 'untiring assiduity' in the field of magnetism.

With his distinguished record, it is not known why the Admiralty relieved

Crozier of his natural responsibilities. Or was it just one more example of the lack of respect for Crozier among the hierarchy of the Admiralty?

There is little doubt that Crozier was wounded by the slight. But, as ever, he kept his feelings to himself. His only recorded comment on the rebuke was a typically dry and whimsical observation:

> I find by the [Admiralty] instructions that Fitzjames is appointed to superintend the magnetic observations. I will therefore take just so much bother there as may amuse, without considering myself as one of the staff.[1]

However, despite having undermined Crozier's authority in the scientific field, the Admiralty had no doubts about the line of succession. Clause 21 of the Admiralty's formal instructions to Franklin declared: 'Should Sir John Franklin suffer a fatal accident Captain Crozier may take command of the *Erebus*.'[2]

The decision to give Fitzjames control over the selection of officers and crew was altogether more serious. Though a popular, well-meaning and affable character with a distinguished service record in the Middle East and China, his choice of men for the expedition was poor and reflected his inexperience in the ice.

The men appeared to be picked at random or were carried to the commission with a nauseous whiff of patronage. Many of the expedition's officers came to the expedition on the personal recommendation of Fitzjames and most, like him, were new to the ice. While some had distinguished service records, the obvious weakness among the ranks of officers was limited experience of the conditions which the expedition faced.

Only seven of the 24 officers chosen for *Erebus* and *Terror* had been to the ice before. But only four – Crozier, Franklin and two ice-masters recruited from the whaling fleet – had any recognisable polar background. Barrow's proud claim that many old Arctic hands were clamouring to serve was quietly forgotten as Fitzjames lined up a collection of Arctic beginners.

The two ice-masters, Thomas Blanky and James Reid, stood out. Both were hugely experienced men with impressive records in the Greenland whaling industry. Blanky, who was assigned to Crozier on *Terror*, had served on three Arctic expeditions and had stood alongside Crozier on the decks of *Hecla* during Parry's unsuccessful attempt to reach the North Pole in 1827.

But the records of the three other officers were far less convincing. Lieutenant Graham Gore, a busy and energetic officer on *Erebus*, had spent only one season in the ice, during Back's failed bid to reach Repulse Bay in 1836. Charles Osmer, the forty-six-year-old ship's purser, travelled to the Bering Strait as a clerk with Beechey and had some knowledge of the region. The experience of Dr Alexander Macdonald, the assistant-surgeon on *Terror*, was limited to a single season on a whaling ship.

The lopsided selections of Fitzjames were quite extraordinary considering the large pool of seasoned officers available after more than twenty-five years of relentless naval endeavours in the polar regions. The inexperience of the party was particularly severe on Crozier. Only Macdonald among *Terror*'s naval officers had seen the ice before. In the event, Crozier's first lieutenant on *Terror* was Edward Little, who came from the Mediterranean fleet and had been on half-pay for eighteen months, while the second lieutenant, George Hodgson, was last engaged repelling pirates off the coast of Sumatra.

The crew of just over 100, according to Fitzjames, were all 'fine hearty fellows' and a small number had served in the Antarctic with Crozier and Ross. Over a quarter had never served in the Royal Navy. Even the Admiralty was worried at some of the selections and three young officers selected by Fitzjames were removed even before *Erebus* and *Terror* sailed. Among the replacements was Frederick Hornby, an unemployed junior officer with no Arctic record, who probably owed his appointment to having spent time with Franklin in Van Diemen's Land.

Crozier also found it necessary to jettison a further two of the men selected by Fitzjames for *Terror*. The men – an armourer and a sail maker – were branded 'perfectly useless either at their trade or anything else' in Crozier's damning appraisal.

Crozier was obliged to participate in a public display of unity when the Admiralty threw a reception to honour the departing expedition in May 1845. The guests of honour were Crozier and Franklin, but also there was Fitzjames, ostensibly third in the expedition's pecking order, but by now a more influential figure than Crozier. Three weeks earlier, Crozier was absent when Franklin and Fitzjames met a deputation from the Admiralty to inspect the ships.

The larger reception, held at London's Somerset House on 8 May, was a notable event – the last rollcall of the ageing generation of polar explorers cobbled together by Sir John Barrow in the years following the end of the Napoleonic Wars. Or 'Barrow's Boys', as one writer called them. Among the Arctic dignitaries in full dress uniform sipping drinks and making polite conversation were Sir George Back, Sir Edward Parry, Sir James Clark Ross and Edward Sabine, while the eighty-one-year-old Barrow presided over his champions like a proud Roman emperor.

The grand occasion reflected the general mood of supreme optimism that swept the country in the weeks before the ships sailed. Completing the last few miles of the North West Passage was regarded as inevitable. Only a few irritating troublemakers even considered the possibility of failure.

Confidence was so high within the expedition that officers urged their wives and girlfriends to write to them via Russia. The effusive Fitzjames summed up the buoyant mood when he announced: 'You have no idea how happy we all feel – how determined we all are to be frozen and how anxious to be among the ice.'[3]

Such blind optimism permeated from the top down. The complacent chiefs at the Admiralty were so convinced of success that it was not considered necessary to prepare the contingency of a relief expedition in the event of *Erebus* and *Terror* becoming trapped in the ice.

Sir John Franklin, the ageing leader of the 1845 North West Passage expedition, pictured shortly before departure.

Neither did the Admiralty think it prudent to name a predetermined spot in the Arctic where relief ships could be sent if, at worst, *Erebus* and *Terror* failed to emerge from the ice on schedule. The chilling reality that Parry's *Fury* and John Ross' *Victory* had been lost in the same area was barely discussed.

The only acknowledgment of possible misfortune came in the form of a polite request to the Hudson's Bay Company, which exercised enormous authority over large swathes of the Canadian Arctic, for its wandering emissaries to render assistance if required. How a handful of Hudson Bay trekkers in hundreds of thousands of square miles of barren territory could possibly feed or assist well over a hundred seamen trapped in the ice was never fully explained. Beyond the tenuous involvement of a few Hudson's Bay travellers, the men from *Erebus* and *Terror* were on their own.

Some, such as Barrow, sincerely believed there would be no need for outside assistance. Barrow's clique thought the ships would complete the journey in one season and emerge through the Bering Strait into the Pacific Ocean to spend the winter of 1845–46 basking in the inviting waters of the Hawaiian islands. It was much the same rhetoric used prior to John Ross' voyage in 1818, the first of the Barrow-inspired attempts to find the passage.

The official mood of optimism was fuelled by the certain knowledge that the expedition would be the largest, best-equipped undertaking ever to leave British shores. It was a symbol of national virility and power. Defeat was unthinkable.

Erebus and *Terror* were to carry a huge complement of 134 officers and men and enough supplies to last for three years. The ships were refurbished at Woolwich Dockyard and fitted with an extra layer of sheet iron around their bows as protection against the ice.

Both vessels were also equipped with the newest technology of the industrial age. The Admiralty, under the direction of Parry, had decided that the time had come to use steam engines in the ice and the ships were fitted with innovative screw propellers that could be lifted out of the water if the ships were beset. It was arranged to purchase two reliable steam locomotives from local railway companies. *Terror*'s 20-horse-power vehicle came from the London and Birmingham Railway, while *Erebus*' loco of the same capacity came from the nearby Greenwich Railway Company.

The front wheels were removed and a team of ten horses dragged the cumbersome locomotives – each weighing 15 tons (15,241 kilograms) – to the quayside, where they were lowered sideways into the holds of *Erebus* and *Terror*. The propeller shaft, measuring 32 feet (9.8 metres), ran a third of the length of the ship before being attached to a 7-foot (2.1-metre) propeller.

Crozier, using a steam-powered engine for the first time, took *Terror* on trials up and down the Thames and found that the old bomb ship, now thirty-two years old, could generate a top speed of 4 knots in the tranquil inland waters. Lieutenant John Irving of *Terror* reported that the ship made 'dreadful puffings and screamings and will astonish the Esquimaux not a little'.

Not everyone was convinced that the newly invented steam engines were necessary. James Ross, whose twenty-four years of service had been entirely under sail, told the Admiralty in 1844 that he was not prepared to use steam power. '[Engines] alone would be a sufficient reason for not wishing to undertake the service,' he had written to Beaufort when rejecting the chance to lead the expedition.

The inventory of supplies was daunting, even with precious space in the holds taken up by the bulky steam locomotives. The holds were stuffed full of provisions and equipment, including over 43 tons (43,700 kilograms) of preserved meat, 61 tons (62,000 kilograms) of flour and more than 16 tons (16,500 kilograms) of biscuits. As an antiscorbutic against scurvy, the ships took more than 4 tons (4,200 kilograms) of lemons, which were to be administered at the rate of 1 ounce (28 grams) per person per day.

It was intended that officers and crew would exist for up to three years on the staple navy diet of salted beef or pork and tinned vegetables. It was later discovered that much of the tinned food was probably tainted and unfit for human consumption even before the ships left London. Modern research suggests the canned meats were riddled with botulism. The cost-conscious Admiralty accepted the lowest bid to provide the expedition's foodstuffs without adequate checks on the unscrupulous supplier and unwittingly shortened the odds of survival for the men of *Erebus* and *Terror*.

The antiscorbutic value of the diet was largely worthless and the prescription of a few spoonfuls of lemon juice a day, though helpful, would not be enough to combat the effects of scurvy.

Officers were to dine off the finest china and use their own neatly engraved silver cutlery, but there was no contingency for living off the land if the ships ran into trouble or the food ran out. Few on board, if any, were skilled hunters.

The ships were also stocked with goods to help the men survive the winters in comfort. Over 3 tons (3,100 kilograms) of tobacco and 1.5 tons (1,524 kilograms) of soap were loaded and each vessel was provided with a library of 1,200 books together with slates, pencils and arithmetic tables that would provide the sailors with a modicum of learning during the long, dark nights. Both ships were given a hand-organ that could turn out a repertoire of fifty different tunes, and a daguerreotype apparatus that would take the first-ever photographs of an Arctic expedition was also loaded.

The idea of photographing the expedition aroused some excitement. Crozier, Franklin, Fitzjames and a few other officers sat for photographer, William Beard, a few days before the ships sailed and some were impressed by the new-fangled device. But Crozier, looking slightly anxious under his peaked cap, was the only man from *Terror* whose image was captured for posterity.

The aura of invincibility was all-pervading, and a stream of distinguished visitors and friends in a mood of growing expectation – among them Ross, Parry and Haddington – poured down the Thames to catch a final glimpse of the men and ships.

Barrow heightened expectations with the audacious claim that there could be 'no objection with regard to any apprehension of loss of ships or men'. Sir Roderick Murchison, president of the Royal Geographical Society, put it more simply: 'The name of Franklin alone is, indeed, a national guarantee.'

But the cocksure atmosphere surrounding the official preparations masked serious concerns felt elsewhere. Men with personal experience of the polar regions were able to pick holes in the plans and urged the Admiralty, even at this late stage, to rethink. Commander McMurdo, a veteran of the Antarctic enterprise with Crozier and Ross, bluntly warned that Franklin would never return from the ice.[4]

The shrillest notes of alarm were sounded by Ross' uncle, Sir John Ross, and Dr Richard King, who had accompanied Back down the Great Fish River in the mid-1830s. A prickly outsider with few friends in the right quarters, King predicted unmitigated disaster. He passionately believed that the North West Passage could only be accomplished by deploying a smaller, lightweight party travelling overland along the Canadian coastline in the region of the Great Fish River.

King solemnly warned the Admiralty that the vessels were doomed to entrapment in the ice and insisted the expedition would be 'a lasting blot in the annals of our voyages of discovery'. The Admiralty, he concluded, was sending Franklin to the Arctic 'to form the nucleus of an iceberg'.

King was not a navy man, and his opinions, like those of Scoresby decades earlier, were imperiously swept aside by the naval establishment. But Franklin did pack a copy of King's book about his 1833–35 journey with Back.

The claims of Sir John Ross were not so easily swept aside. Although frozen out of the Admiralty inner circle, John Ross spoke as a man with two Arctic expeditions to his name and his well-founded claims could hardly be ignored. Specifically, he was the first to argue that the expedition – two ships and 134 men – was too large and too cumbersome to manage. Smaller expeditions were easier to handle in an emergency, as he had found when *Victory* was trapped a decade earlier. He also argued that the ships' 19-foot (5.8-metre) draughts were too big for the shallow Arctic waterways. *Victory*, which was lost in Prince Regent Inlet, had a draught of only 9 feet (2.7 metres). He further feared that the officers and men selected by Fitzjames did not possess enough experience of the ice.

Ross also urged Franklin to erect a chain of easy-to-spot cairns along the proposed route, each containing notes of the expedition's positions if anything went wrong. Franklin politely ignored his advice, but dutifully placed a copy of John Ross' book on the *Victory* expedition in the library of *Erebus*.

John Ross grew more insistent as departure date neared and he was horrified to learn that the Admiralty had no plans to send a relief mission if *Erebus* and *Terror* did not emerge from the ice as expected. In desperation, he offered to mount his own relief expedition if the ships did not reappear by February 1847, two seasons after entering Lancaster Sound. It was a measure of his anxiety given that, by 1847, John Ross would be a few months short of seventy years of age. But Franklin, irrepressibly confident and reluctant to even consider failure, once again dismissed his concerns. John Ross' proposals, he rashly concluded, were 'absurd'.

Lady Jane Franklin had different concerns about her husband. Franklin was tired and struck down by flu in the days before *Erebus* and *Terror* sailed. One afternoon, he fell asleep while she was putting the finishing touches to a silk Union Jack for the voyage. He looked cold and Jane threw the flag over his feet. Franklin felt the touch and leapt up exclaiming: 'Why there's a flag thrown over me. Don't you know that they lay the Union Jack over a corpse!'[5]

The deathly allusion summed up Crozier's dark mood. The hustle and bustle of preparation and the heady all-round expectation made little difference to his demeanour and even the warm support of Ross did nothing to ease the depression.

In the three months before *Erebus* and *Terror* departed, he lodged with James and Ann Ross at their splendid house in Eliot Place, Blackheath,

London. It was a convivial setting with fine views over Blackheath, where he enjoyed the warm embrace of friendship and the type of comfortable family surroundings he had not known since his childhood in Banbridge. It was to be Crozier's last home.

The weeks before departure brought little relief to Crozier. The Admiralty's insensitive treatment still rankled, while the *affaire du cœur* with Sophy Cracroft continued to gnaw at him. Sophy was now the permanent companion of Lady Franklin at the Franklin residence in London's Mayfair

Last home. The Georgian home of Sir James Clark Ross in London's Blackheath, where Crozier stayed before sailing to the Arctic in 1845.

and she and Crozier met frequently on the Thames dockside or at one of the formal receptions thrown for the expedition. Only twenty-four hours before the ships departed, Crozier stood beside Sophy Cracroft and Lady Franklin on the decks of *Erebus* as the deeply religious John Franklin read Divine Service.

It is thought that Crozier made one final attempt to persuade Sophy to change her mind and become his wife. In the warm glow of anticipation enveloping the expedition, she might have been tempted. But if she was, she resisted. Sophy Cracroft had not changed her mind about marrying a naval captain. Each day, she witnessed at close quarters the torment and worry of Jane Franklin as her elderly husband prepared to sail away for up to three years. Crozier himself noted that Lady Franklin was in a 'sad state' in the days before departure.

Sophy Cracroft was not prepared to endure the same burden. Instead, she coolly observed that Ross, now retired from the sea, had been 'improved' by marriage to Ann Coulman.

Nor had Crozier's prospects improved very much since his first attempts to marry Sophy. He had few possessions and his savings amounted to little more than £100 (about £6,000 today). Crozier, the itinerant sailor, had no permanent home, having spent the best part of thirty-five years as a wandering servant of the Royal Navy.

It was left to Lady Franklin, who understood Crozier and Sophy Cracroft better than anyone, to sum up the fractured relationship. Many years later, McClintock asked Jane Franklin to reveal Sophy's true feelings for the lovesick Crozier. Lady Franklin paused for a moment and replied: 'The pity is, Sir Leopold, Sophy liked the man, but not the sailor.'[6]

North West Passage

A dove flew onto one of the masts as *Erebus* and *Terror* were towed out of their berths at Greenhithe and into the Thames shortly after ten-thirty on the morning of 19 May 1845. Some hailed it as a good omen. On the quayside, crowds cheered and waved in a final outpouring of national optimism. The roar of approval from the shore was 'deafening' according to one of *Erebus'* officers.

Crozier, from the decks of *Terror*, could pick out the presence of Sophy Cracroft standing on the quay alongside Lady Franklin and Franklin's daughter, Eleanor. Franklin energetically waved his handkerchief. Crozier kept his emotions in check.

Crozier was subdued and seemed almost detached from the boisterous occasion. In contrast to everyone else on the Thames that day, he was a forlorn, disconsolate figure. Though surrounded by more than 60 men on the cramped decks of *Terror*, he was overcome by a feeling of being alone.

The men on board *Terror* were all strangers and he soon discovered he had no natural friends or soulmates such as Ross or Bird. While he professed to liking his junior officers, Crozier wrote home to his sisters: 'We shall never be the same intimate friends as I was with Robertson.' (John Robertson, a ship's surgeon, had been his closest confidante during *Terror's*

Captain Francis Rawdon Moira Crozier. This is the only known photograph of Crozier. The image was taken with the newly developed daguerreotype process in May 1845 on the eve of launching the North West Passage expedition.

Antarctic voyage.) More pointedly, Crozier confessed to Ross: 'In truth I am sadly lonely.'[1]

The canny Jane Franklin had also observed Crozier's despondency on the eve of departure. Crozier, she remembered afterwards, was 'so ill and dispirited when he left'.[2] In one of the last letters he ever wrote, Crozier explained to a friend, John Henderson: 'Living alone is the great drawback to me but I know well it cannot be otherwise.'[3]

Crozier's depression may also account for an altogether different sensation as the ships prepared to sail. Shortly before leaving London, he had an eerie premonition of disaster. Crozier, usually reserved and cautious about revealing his emotions, let his guard slip in a private conversation with the wife of the Arctic officer, Captain Edward Belcher. According to her recollection, Crozier told Diana Belcher that he did not expect to return from the Arctic.[4]

The ships, freshly painted and polished, headed down the Thames Estuary and turned into the North Sea for the short trip to the Orkneys, pulled by

Erebus and *Terror* on London's River Thames in May 1845, preparing to sail on the ill-fated North West Passage expedition.

tugs and accompanied by the transporter, *Barretto Junior* under Lieutenant Edward Griffiths. Prophetically, a sudden storm hit the flotilla off the East Anglian coast and they were forced to seek shelter near the port of Aldeburgh.

Days later, the expedition suffered its first casualties. *Erebus* and *Terror* carried ten live bullocks on deck, all destined to be slaughtered for fresh meat as soon as the expedition encountered the ice. But four animals perished on the stormy leg up the east coast of England and were replaced when the ships pulled into Stromness in the Orkneys. At a nearby island, one of Crozier's seamen on *Terror* was taken ill and invalided home.

During the brief stay in the Orkneys, the officers dined with local islanders, including the family of John Rae, the explorer who was making a name for himself with his prodigious feats of overland travel in the Arctic. The mood was overwhelmingly optimistic and one visitor to *Terror* reported that 'A general feeling of sure success pervaded them all.'

Far less sure footed was Fitzjames on *Erebus*, who made the mistake of allowing four of his sailors to venture ashore prior to departure. Inevitably, the seamen got drunk and managed to smuggle more liquor on board. Fitzjames had to interrupt his sailing preparations to make a thorough search of the ship, wasting over two hours in the process. On board *Terror*, the more worldly-wise Crozier had refused to allow his men to go ashore in the hours prior to sailing.

Crozier's mood again turned sour when he learned that the London shopkeepers, Fortnum and Mason's, had mistakenly shipped his personal stock of tea and sugar to Fitzjames on *Erebus*, and he complained:

> But by some strange accident they discovered my name sufficiently accurate to send me the bill and I was fool enough to pay it from their declaring that the things were absolutely delivered on board.

The ships, weighed down with food and supplies, crossed the North

Atlantic in very rough seas and the first ice was seen off the coast of Greenland on 25 June. Crozier, writing to a friend, reported a 'very boisterous'
crossing. On the last day of June, the ships crossed the Arctic Circle for the
first time.

The general mood on board remained cheerfully optimistic. Franklin,
dispensing easy charm and goodwill, was like a kindly uncle in charge of
a family outing. Fitzjames reported 'an incessant laugh from morning to
night' and Lieutenant James Fairholme, a junior officer on *Erebus*, said
Franklin 'looked ten years younger'. A jolly Franklin wrote to Parry:

> It would do your heart good to see how zealously the officers and men, in
> both ships, are working and how amicably we all pull together.[5]

The jaunty self-confident mood even encouraged Franklin to claim that he
was a better leader than Ross, a veteran of polar expeditions. In a letter to
his wife, Franklin said:

> I think perhaps that I have the tact of keeping officers and men happily
> together in a greater degree than Ross ... who is evidently ambitious and wishes
> to do everything himself.[6]

Crozier, however, was not convinced. He ran a tight ship and was a more
business-like captain than Franklin. Irving, *Terror*'s third lieutenant,
reported that 'nothing seems to be left undone' with Crozier in command.
'Our Captain reads prayers on Sundays,' Irving wrote; 'I like my skipper
very well.' Although the tightly packed decks and holds of *Terror* made life
uncomfortable, Crozier told Irving brusquely: 'We have not shipped for
comfort.'

Crozier took a thoroughly practical view of proceedings and began to see
Franklin in a different light. Although the two men had developed a good
friendship during their spells in Van Diemen's Land, this was the first time

they had been on the high seas together. Watching Franklin close at hand, Crozier's opinion of the man began to change.

Hardened by two decades of exploration, Crozier realised that Franklin's genial, easy-going style was more suited to an ambassadorial life in a governor's mansion than in charge of a demanding expedition into treacherous Arctic seas. Franklin was everyone's friend, whereas experience had shown Crozier that calm leadership and firm discipline were vital and that commanders needed to keep a respectful distance from those under their command.

Shortly before sailing, Crozier had described Franklin as 'my old and kind friend', but he took a different view once the expedition was underway. On observing Franklin's casual approach, Crozier commented:

> Look at the state our commander's ship is in, everything in confusion. He is very decided in his own views but has not good judgement.[7]

To make matters worse, Franklin insisted on frequently inviting Crozier to dine on board *Erebus* as the ships headed westwards across the Atlantic, a practice Crozier found tiresome and which he kept to a minimum. The rowing back and forth to *Erebus* in the rough seas prompted Crozier to tell Ross:

> I cannot bear going on board *Erebus*. Sir John is very kind and would have me there dining every day if I would go.[8]

At the same time, Franklin started to become slightly uneasy about Crozier. In a letter to Jane Franklin in early July, he noted that '... *entre nous* – I do not think he [Crozier] has had the former flow of spirits since we sailed.'

Opposite: Arctic bound: portraits of Francis Crozier, Sir John Franklin and other members of the North West Passage expedition as depicted by the Illustrated London News *six years after the men were last seen.*

Lieut. Couch

Lieut. Fairholme

C.H. Osmer

Lieut. Des Vœux

Captain Crozier, *Terror*

Captain Sir John Franklin

Commander Fitzjames, *Erebus*

Lieut. Graham Gore (Commander)

Stanley (surgeon)

Lieut. H.T.D. Le Vesconte

Lieut. R.O. Sargent

James Read

J.H. Goodsir (asst. surgeon)

H.F. Collins

Crozier, he reported, 'has never mentioned Sophy – nor made the slightest allusion to her.' He wondered whether it would be 'agreeable or proper' to speak of her, but we will never know if he did.

Yet a few days later, Franklin pronounced Crozier 'cheerful and happy' and was content that the ships were making good progress. Noting that Crozier had not made many trips to come aboard *Erebus*, he explained that this was 'on account of the weather'.

Crozier had other concerns apart from Franklin. One of his last letters was written to a nephew as *Terror* travelled up the west coast of Greenland towards the Whalefish Islands and shortly before crossing Baffin Bay. The letter reveals a mixture of emotions, ranging from a lingering sense of pride in doing his duty to a clear anxiety about the dangers ahead. He wrote:

> All is getting on as well as I could wish. Officers full of youth and zeal, and indeed, everything is going on most smoothly. The Admiralty were exceedingly kind to us, all our demands were readily granted; if we can only do something worthy of this country which has so munificently fitted us out, I will be only too happy; it will be an ample reward for all my anxieties, and believe me Henry, there will be no lack of them.[9]

Crozier's greatest anxiety, based on years of experience, was that *Erebus* and *Terror* had sailed too late in the season to make real progress towards the North West Passage in 1845. Crozier clearly regarded the first season as crucial to the success of the mission. To John Henderson, he wrote:

> This season [1845] will have a good deal to do with our future operations, if we can only make a good hit at the first it will be most glorious.[10]

His fear was a grim repetition of the journey with Parry in 1824 when *Hecla* and *Fury* arrived late in the season and were forced to endure a long, dismal winter at Port Bowen in Prince Regent Inlet. A year later, *Fury* was wrecked and abandoned. Crozier expressed his concerns in a letter to Ross, who, more than anyone, fully understood the significance of the warning:

> All things are going on well but I fear we are ... sadly late. From what we learn the weather has been very severe, with much easterly wind. What I fear from our being so late is that we shall have no time to look around and judge for ourselves but blunder into the ice and make a second 1824 of it.[11]

The ice was stubbornly thick in the summer of 1845, a sign that the previous winter had been severe. 'Bergs are numerous this year,' Crozier wrote home.[12]

On 4 July, *Erebus*, *Terror* and the support vessel, *Barretto Junior*, assembled at the Danish settlement on Disco Island to begin transferring the extra supplies from the transporter. 'How full we shall be,' Crozier wrote to Henderson. 'But I am still in hopes that we shall be able to stuff into her three years provisions.'[13]

Even with the benefit of exceptionally fine weather, it took six days to shift the boxes of supplies and equipment from *Barretto Junior* to the holds of *Erebus* and *Terror*. The men worked fourteen hours a day in dazzling sunlight and Franklin wrote a last optimistic note to Parry, expressing his hope of making Barrow Strait at the western end of Lancaster Sound in the first season:

> I think it must be favourable for the opening of the ice and we all feel happy in the idea that we shall be quite in time to avail ourselves of any openings westward of Barrow Strait.

The men wrote their final letters and handed the correspondence to Lieutenant Griffiths on *Barretto Junior*. Confidence in successfully navigating the passage was so high that families and friends were advised to send their next letters to the port of Petropavlovsk on Russia's Kamchatka Peninsula.

Griffiths also took with him three petty officers and a marine, who were invalided home, leaving 129 men on *Erebus* and *Terror* to begin the journey proper.

Griffiths sailed on 12 July, cheerily claiming that 'better fellows never breathed'. In his official communiqué to the Admiralty in London, he reported that the men of both ships were in excellent health and full of confidence.

In the mail bag carried by Griffiths, Franklin's official correspondence to the Admiralty formally reported knowledge that the previous winter in the Arctic had been severe. But, said Franklin, spring was not later than usual and 'our prospect is favourable of reaching Lancaster Sound without much obstruction'.

Franklin also paid full tribute to Crozier and the expedition's other officers, writing:

> It is unnecessary for me to assure their lordships of the energy and zeal of Captain Crozier, Commander Fitzjames and of the officers and men with whom I have the happiness of being employed on this service.

Crozier, he declared, was an 'excellent instructor and fellow worker'.

Among the correspondence carried in Griffiths' mail bag was the last known letter written by Francis Crozier. Addressed to James and Ann Ross, it was the dark, brooding missive of a troubled man harbouring major doubts about the undertaking which lay ahead. He wrote:

> James, I wish you were here. I would then have no doubt as to our pursuing the proper course. I must have done with this croaking. I am not growling, mind. Indeed, I never was less disposed to do so. I am, I assure you, beginning to be a bit of a philosopher and hope that before the season is over to have so tutored myself that I will fret for nothing.
>
> All goes smoothly but, James dear, I am sadly alone, not a soul have I in either ship than I can go and talk to. No congenial spirit as it were. I am

generally busy but it is after all a very hermit-like life. Except to kick up a row with the helmsman or abuse Jopson [the captain's steward] at times I would scarcely ever hear the sound of my voice .... Well my dear friends I know not what else I can say to you – I feel that I am not in the spirits of writing but in truth I am sadly lonely and when I look to the last voyage I can see the cause and therefore no prospect of having a more joyous feeling.[14]

Erebus and *Terror*, sitting low in the water under the weight of the extra provisions, sailed on 12 July, soon after the departure of the *Barretto Junior*. The vessels headed north up Davis Strait into Baffin Bay towards the Greenland port of Upernavik, before turning west across the bay towards the entrance to Lancaster Sound. On 19 July, Captain Straiton of the whaler *Eagle* sighted a pair of three-masted vessels in the distance off Upernavik. The ships, almost certainly *Erebus* and *Terror*, were sailing west in latitude 72° 45' north, close to the same latitude as the entrance to Lancaster Sound.

Erebus and *Terror*, as Crozier suggested, may well have sailed late in the season, but the ice of Baffin Bay was still too thick to penetrate in late July 1845. The ships were forced to hang around on the edge of the pack waiting for a break-up. While they waited, *Erebus* and *Terror* were joined by *Prince of Wales* and *Enterprise*, two whalers working the area. Captain Robert Martin of *Enterprise* reported that on 25 July 1845, *Erebus* and *Terror* were both made fast to an iceberg in the eastern reaches of Baffin Bay at 75° 12' north, 61° 6' west.

Martin, an experienced sailor in his mid-forties, was the most successful whaling master from the Scottish port of Peterhead. He almost certainly knew the expedition's two ice-masters, Reid of *Erebus* and Blanky of *Terror*, both of whom came from the same whaling fleets.

The vessels drew alongside and Martin spoke to both Reid and Franklin, an exchange that has baffled historians ever since. According to Martin, Franklin boasted that the expedition was provisioned for five years and might be able to stretch supplies out for seven years, particularly if they could kill extra game during their voyage. A day or two later, several of Franklin's officers from *Erebus* dined on board the 350-ton *Enterprise* and Martin recalled that the expedition expected to be away for four to six years.

Officially, *Erebus* and *Terror* were provisioned for only three years – a fact confirmed by Crozier's letter to Henderson. In addition, the ships had sailed with the expectation of making the journey in one season or two at most. The third year's supplies were an insurance against unforeseen events.

Either Martin was wrong or Franklin's officers were carried away with the air of optimism on board. *Erebus* and *Terror* could never have sustained a journey of five, six or seven years without restocking or by an unprecedented and sustained feat of game-hunting spread over several years.

Franklin invited Martin to dinner on board *Erebus*, but the whaler, anxious not to lose time in the hunting season, politely declined. The chance to clarify the expedition's intentions was lost.

Captain Dannet on *Prince of Wales* also had a brief meeting with officers from *Erebus* and recorded its position at 74° 48' north, 66° 13' west. He too turned down the chance to have dinner with Franklin because he was anxious not to lose the favourable winds.

Martin later told the Admiralty that the crews of both vessels were in 'excellent health and spirits' and calculated that in the prevailing ice conditions, the ships would cross Davis Strait and reach the entrance to Lancaster Sound by the middle of August.

Martin sailed to the hunting grounds sometime between 29 and 31 July 1845 and for the next two days could see the masts of *Erebus* and *Terror* on the distant horizon.

The vessels remained moored to an iceberg while waiting for the ice to break up and to resume the journey across Baffin Bay. All was normal.

Erebus, *Terror* and all 129 souls on board then vanished into the silence.

CHAPTER 17

Ice

*E*rebus and *Terror* crossed Baffin Bay and went into Lancaster Sound sometime in early-to-mid-August. What happened next is a tantalising mixture of fact and fiction, with assorted fragments of hard evidence blended with almost 170 years of rumour, conjecture and pure fantasy. While it is possible to piece together a reasonable account of some important developments, the simple truth is that the fate of the 1845 expedition to find the North West Passage remains an enduring mystery.

The expedition's first step, in line with Admiralty instructions, was to retrace Parry's route west to the end of Lancaster Sound to Barrow Strait, avoiding the temptation to venture into Prince Regent Inlet, which had already claimed *Fury* and *Victory*. At Cape Walker, on the brink of Melville Sound, the ships were to steer southwest into unexplored seas in the direction of the Bering Strait and the Pacific.

If the pathway ahead was blocked by ice, the expedition was urged to turn on its heels and steer northwards out of Lancaster Sound through Wellington Channel, the uncharted stretch of water that runs between Cornwallis Island and Devon Island. By penetrating far enough up Wellington Channel, it was assumed the party would run into the 'Open Polar Sea' championed by Barrow and his supporters.

The ice around Cape Walker, which lies in Barrow Strait at the western end of Lancaster Sound, was evidently impenetrable in 1845 and the proposed course to the southwest was abandoned for that season. Reverting to the alternative plan, *Erebus* and *Terror* turned north towards Wellington Channel.

The change of plan suited Crozier and Franklin, both of whom felt more optimistic probing the Wellington Channel than they did about pressing along the unexplored south-westerly route from Cape Walker. Both Crozier and Franklin subscribed to 'Open Polar Sea' theory and were confident that one of the northern passageways out of Lancaster Sound or Barrow Strait – such as Wellington Channel – offered the best prospects for emerging into temperate seas for a smooth run to the North Pole. From there, it was regarded as a relatively short journey to the Bering Strait and the completion of the mission.

Franklin had confided as much to his family shortly before the expedition left London. The Wellington Channel, Lady Franklin later explained, was 'not only the uppermost object in my husband's mind when he left England, but it was also in Captain Crozier's'.

Emily Tennyson, the wife of Franklin's nephew, Alfred Tennyson, recalled her final conversation with John Franklin in the days before the expedition sailed. He told her: 'If I am lost, remember Emily, my firm belief that there is open sea at the North Pole.'[1]

In the event, *Erebus* and *Terror* made a remarkable journey into Wellington Channel during the final sailing days of the 1845 navigation season. The ships sailed about 150 miles (240 kilometres) up the unexplored strait between Devon Island and Cornwallis Island, but ran into heavy ice and were stopped at 77° north, one of the most northerly points ever reached by a vessel.

The area lies at the very edge of the permanent sea ice. Beyond lay assorted islands and the vast, unoccupied Arctic Ocean. In other circumstances, this feat alone would have been recognised as a major triumph

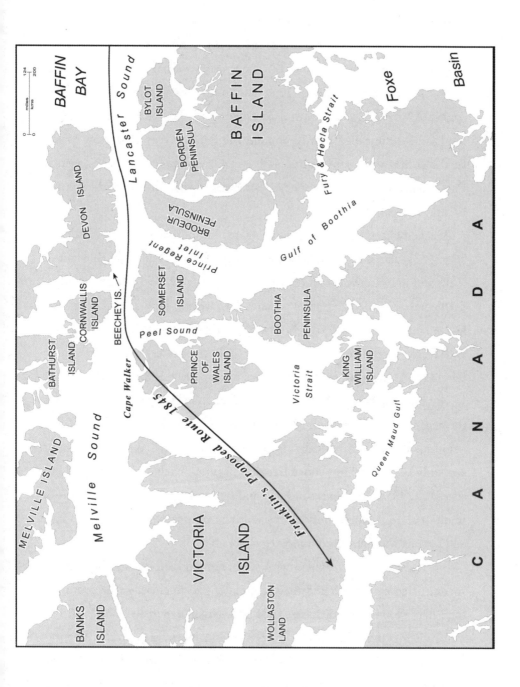

The proposed route of 1845 North West Passage expedition.

of navigation and perhaps help lay to rest the belief that moderate open waters are to be found at the top of the world.

With autumn closing in and the short season of navigable seas coming to an end, *Erebus* and *Terror* retreated south. Travelling down the west coast of Cornwallis Island – thus completing the first circumnavigation of the island – the expedition re-entered the familiar seas of Barrow Strait. In the search for a safe winter harbour, the vessels turned back towards Lancaster Sound and at Beechey Island, at the western end of the Sound, found the ideal spot.

Beechey Island is a barren, wind-blasted lump of land, barely 3 miles (5 kilometres) across and linked to the far larger Devon Island by a thin spit of rocks and gravel. It was first discovered by Parry in 1819 but considered so desolate that he did not bother to land. An excellent natural anchorage was located on the island's north-eastern coast and subsequently named Erebus and Terror Bay. Lying over 500 miles (800 kilometres) inside the Arctic Circle, it was the most northerly place a naval party had ever spent a winter.

The bleak winter of 1845–46 was colder than many of the men, with the exception of Crozier and Franklin, had ever before experienced. Temperatures in the area typically drop below -30° F (-35° C) in mid-winter and only begin to climb above freezing in June. A few trips were made to survey the bleak local surroundings and before long the party settled into traditional over-winter routines of scientific readings, school lessons, recitals and passing the time as contentedly as possible.

But it was to be a troubled winter. Three men died during the months spent at Beechey Island and their shipmates had to chisel graves from the rock-hard ground with pickaxes. The first two men to perish – John Hartnell, a twenty-five-year-old seaman on *Erebus* and John Torrington, a twenty-year-old stoker from *Terror* – died within days of each other during the first week of January 1846. William Braine, a thirty-two-year-old marine private from *Erebus*, was dead by early April.

Based on the experience of earlier Arctic expeditions, it seems likely that

First casualties. The graves of three men on Beechey Island who died in 1846 during the expedition's first Arctic winter. The bodies were exhumed for examination over 140 years later.

Erebus and *Terror* spent at least ten months at Beechey Island, not being released until July or August 1846. Countless relics of the party's winter quarters were later found on the small island, including three outhouses, piles of empty food tins and a pair of cashmere gloves apparently left out to dry and never retrieved by the owner.

A cairn was built at the southern end of the island overlooking Barrow Strait, but, surprisingly, no written records of the expedition's stay or future intentions were found inside. The cairn may have been raided by passing Inuit, or it is possible that no record was ever left because the expedition, seeing a favourable change in the weather, left in a hurry. It was the first of many mysteries.

After the unsuccessful examination of Wellington Channel, the expedition next turned to the Admiralty's first choice of route and headed for the southwest. Prince Regent Inlet, which lies almost opposite Beechey Island, was ignored and the vessels ventured further west to the next passage trending to the south between Somerset Island and Prince of Wales Island.

Erebus and *Terror* turned south into the strait, which is today known as Peel Sound. The ships made decent progress in the first few days of September and successfully navigated the channel separating the two large islands. At the end of Peel Sound, the ships reached Franklin Strait and *Erebus* and *Terror* continued south, entering a broader expanse of water where Franklin Strait meets the wider McClintock Channel. Directly ahead lay Victoria Strait and the imposing sight of King William Island. Beyond the horizon was the Canadian coastline.

The expedition now faced a critical choice. It could either take the south-westerly track around the conically-shaped King William Island in line with Admiralty orders or steer around the landmass to the southeast. As the expedition's orders were to head west towards the Bering Strait, Franklin made the logical decision to take the south-westerly route. It was a fatal mistake.

In 1846, King William Island was known as King William Land because most believed it was attached to the Boothia Peninsula and therefore the Canadian mainland. But King William Land (Island) is cut off from the mainland to the east by two channels: the James Ross Strait and Rae Strait. From the south, the island is separated from the Canadian mainland by the narrow Simpson Strait.

For a brief period in the late summer, the James Ross Strait and Rae Strait are navigable and Simpson Strait is open water, leading eventually to the Bering Strait some 2,000 miles (3,000 kilometres) to the west. It was the final section of the North West Passage which had eluded generations of ships for centuries. (At least six other navigable channels have since been discovered.)

The logical route to the southwest of King William Island, the seas of Victoria Strait, are a jumble of heavily packed and impenetrable ice. The area is a repository for huge floes of ice that originate far to the west in the Beaufort Sea before being driven down the waterways of McClure Strait,

Melville Sound and McClintock Channel. Once in Victoria Strait, the ice stockpiles against the landmasses of the Boothia Peninsula and King William Island.

James Ross, the first European to encounter the scene, reported ice driven half a mile inland by the force of the pressure build-up. Awestruck by the immensity of ice piled up before his eyes, he wrote a graphic description of the area:

> The pack of ice which had, in the autumn of that year, been pressed against that shore, consisted of the heaviest masses that I have ever seen in such a situation. With this, the lighter floes had been thrown up, on some parts of the coast, in a most extraordinary and incredible manner; turning up large quantities of the shingle before them, and, in some places, having travelled as much as half a mile beyond the limits of the highest tide-mark.[2]

It must be assumed that Crozier discussed conditions in the Victoria Strait area with Ross while staying at Blackheath in the weeks before the expedition sailed and therefore knew what to expect. But Franklin pressed on, apparently convinced that the passage was within easy sailing. Entrapment was inevitable and the grim warnings of Dr King – that the expedition would be forced to abandon its ships – were about to become a chilling reality.

It is unfair to blame Crozier or Franklin for making the wrong choice of route. Since Admiralty charts showed King William Land as part of the Canadian landmass, Franklin understandably believed that, by taking a more easterly route, he would be steering his ships into a cul-de-sac.

Even if the expedition *had* chosen the correct route to the southeast, it is not certain that *Erebus* and *Terror* were capable of navigating the dangerous reefs and shallows in the 100-mile (160 kilometre) stretch of water which separates King William Island from the Boothia Peninsula, today known as James Ross Strait which in turn leads to Rae Strait.

An even bigger hurdle awaits ships at the end of Rae Strait, the 40-mile (60 kilometre) Simpson Strait. That channel, running along King William Island's southern coast, is shallow, filled with irregular ice formations and studded with more dangerous reefs. At its narrowest, the Strait is less than 2 miles (3 kilometres) wide and little more than 18 ft (6 metres) deep. The heavily laden vessels, with a draft of at least 19 feet (6 metres), may have found it impossible to plot a course through the waterway.

In August 1846, *Erebus* and *Terror* pressed on southwards directly into the region where Ross had witnessed the 'heaviest masses' of ice he had ever observed. On 12 September, only a few weeks after entering the Victoria Strait, the ships came to a halt, surrounded by a mass of solid ice. They were never to be released.

The expedition was also desperately unlucky. Peel Sound at the time would normally be open for about eight years out of every ten and solidly blocked by ice for only two years in ten. *Erebus* and *Terror* entered the seaway in an open year but were trapped when trying to sail further south in what was one of the bad years.

Erebus and *Terror* were beset at 70° 5' N, a few miles to the north west of King William Island. Trapped in the ice, the ships were carried very slowly southwards by the currents and for the coming months ran alongside the north-western shores of King William Island. On board, the 126 men sat through the second long, bleak Arctic winter.

By May 1847, the ships were still firmly locked in the ice. Experience would have encouraged the party to predict release sometime in July or August 1847 when temperatures edge above freezing and the ice begins to break apart. Franklin was evidently so confident of being released that he sent an eight-man party ashore to inspect the immediate King William Island area and to scout the ice conditions in the general direction of Simpson Strait. The expedition probably felt their ordeal was coming to an end when, in reality, it was just beginning.

The shore party was led by Lieutenant Graham Gore, a capable and intelligent officer who had sailed on Back's misadventure in the Arctic a decade earlier. Taking six crewmen and Charles Des Voeux, the mate from *Erebus*, he travelled along the barren western shores of the island and made some progress to the south, probably by tracing the coastline. It is not known if Gore's group was able to reach Simpson Strait in the south and therefore establish the existence of the North West Passage. What is known is that Gore deposited several records of the expedition in copper cylinders along the shoreline.

The notes, written by Fitzjames, were signed by Gore and Des Voeux and placed in cairns a few days after the shore party left the ships on 24 May 1847. The brief message reported the short journey up Wellington Channel in 1845, the winter spent at Beechey Island in 1845–46 and Gore's exploratory trip to King William Island in the spring of 1847. It read:

28 May 1847
HM ships '*Erebus*' and '*Terror*' wintered in the ice in
Lat 70° 5'N Long 98° 23'W
Having wintered in 1846–47 at Beechey Island in Lat 74°
43' 28" N Long 91° 39' 15"W after having ascended
Wellington Channel to Lat 77° and returned to the West
side of Cornwallis Island
Sir John Franklin commanding the expedition.
All well.
Party consisting of 2 officers and 6 men left the ships
on Monday 24th May 1847.
Gm Gore, Lieut.
Chas. F. Des Voeux, Mate.[3]

The document contained an obvious error: the expedition had wintered at Beechey Island in 1845–46, not 1846–47, as the marked graves on the island could solemnly testify.

Any finder of the document would also have been encouraged to see that the words 'All Well' were underlined. Less than three weeks after Gore left the cheery message, Sir John Franklin was dead.

Crozier, the reluctant venturer, formally assumed full command of the North West Passage expedition on 11 June 1847, the day of Franklin's death. After five expeditions spread over twenty-six years of dedicated service, the fifty-year-old Crozier was finally in command.

He had promised the Inuit bands at Igloolik two decades earlier that he would return to the Arctic as *esh-e-mu-ta* – the captain of a ship. But while Crozier now held office, he was not in power. Control of events rested with the merciless Arctic environment.

CHAPTER 18

'No Cause for Alarm'

The death rattle of the expedition was already sounding as Captain Crozier took command in June 1847. *Erebus* and *Terror* were irretrievably trapped in the ice, scurvy was probably taking its deadly grip on the men and the inexorable countdown to disaster was gathering speed.

Matters had taken a severe turn for the worse in mid-1847 and all of Crozier's long experience in the ice must have alerted him to the severity of the crisis ahead. On the face of it, there was only enough food for another twelve months, yet with the relentless build-up of ice in Victoria Strait, he could not be certain *Erebus* and *Terror* would be released in the following summer.

The most pressing problem was feeding over 100 men. The holds of *Erebus* and *Terror* were once filled with enough food to feed the party for at least three years, but it was now necessary to dispense supplies more carefully, while making sure not to damage morale by cutting back too hard. Well-fed men were less likely to complain – or worse – than the starving and desperate.

Crozier, a practical and unruffled man, doubtless tried to augment supplies by sending hunting parties across the sea ice to King William Island in search of fresh meat. However, British naval expeditions sent to the

Arctic in the nineteenth century were invariably ill-prepared and lacked the know-how to live off the land. There was little thought of practising marksmanship or developing hunting skills when navy ships – a 'home from home' – were stocked with ample quantities of salt beef and bacon.

While officers sat down to dinner in dress uniforms and stewards served their meals on fine bone china and with engraved cutlery, the urgency to hunt fresh game and live off the land was missing. As a result, successive expeditions to the Arctic never bothered to learn the Inuit skills of stalking caribou or bear, trapping foxes or patiently waiting hours over a hole in the ice for a seal to stick its head out. Most of the weapons from the expedition later found scattered on the Arctic tundra were shotguns, the type of weapon more suited to popping pheasants on a country estate than felling a caribou or a 9-foot (3-metre) bear.

Hunting in the Arctic was often considered a spot of fun for British naval officers and it was probably already too late when it became apparent that killing wildlife was a matter of life and death. As food supplies began to dwindle, the men were cruelly vulnerable.

Crozier was also highly unfortunate that the ships had come to grief on the western shore of King William Island. The area is a barren wildlife desert, incapable of supporting a handful of people, let alone over 100. Even the native Inuit, who invariably moved around in small parties, largely avoided the western flank of King William Island because it offered little chance of sustaining life. Large animals such as bears or muskoxen were rare and Crozier's men, at best, might have shot the odd hare or bird.

This lack of fresh game raised the most serious concern for Crozier's leadership. Although he did not fully appreciate it, fresh meat offered the party's only hope of escaping the fatal grasp of scurvy.

Parties leaving the ship for the short trip to King William Island also discovered there were few helpful Inuit on the west of the island. In fact, Inuit were mostly found at the south eastern side of the island where precious wildlife was more abundant. Crozier's party was effectively alone in

1847 – alone to contemplate their fate.

The Inuit have a word for the depression that often afflicts humans during the perpetually dark months of winter in the polar regions: *per-lerorneq*. It means to feel 'the weight of life' – a sentiment with a special resonance for Crozier and his beleaguered men.

Although the expedition had been gone for two years, few in the country felt any cause for concern and the majority felt it was simply a matter of time before word of a triumphant mission reached London. Even James Ross was sanguine.

'I do not think there is the smallest reason of apprehension or anxiety for the safety and success of the expedition', Ross wrote from the comfort of his study in March 1847. Ross' upbeat tone typified the general feeling about the expedition.

The main voices of concern were those of James Ross' uncle Sir John Ross and Dr King, both of whom had expressed serious reservations about the whole enterprise from the beginning. But neither man had the ear of the establishment.

John Ross did not share the optimism of his nephew James. He had pledged to send rescue ships to the Arctic if *Erebus* and *Terror* had not reappeared by February 1847 and by March, with still no word of Franklin and his men, he was demanding that the Admiralty send a relief expedition without delay to reach the Arctic before the 1847 navigable season came to an end. The men, he warned, were facing the dire prospect of a third winter in the ice unless they were rescued in the summer of 1847.

John Ross, now seventy years old, was so concerned that he volunteered to come out of retirement and personally lead the rescue. However, the pleas fell on deaf ears. The Admiralty took little notice, preferring the more politically acceptable advice of men like Barrow, Parry and James Ross.

Even further removed from the seat of power was Dr King, a man the polar establishment regarded as an irritant. But King would not be silenced and his prescience, with hindsight, was remarkable.

In 1847, two years after the expedition was last seen, he insisted that the expedition had come to grief on the western shores of Somerset Island – close to the waters of Peel Sound where *Erebus* and *Terror* now lay trapped. King's solution was to send a rapid relief force along Great Fish River (now called Back River) from the mainland, which would bring the rescuers to an area around the southern expanses of King William Island or the west coast of Boothia Peninsula. King warned that, without relief, the expedition faced a potentially serious outbreak of scurvy.

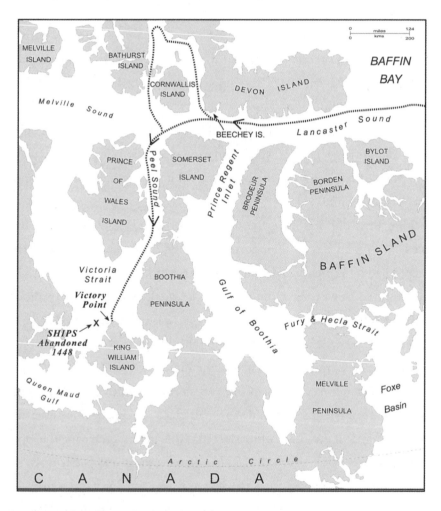

The path of Erebus *and* Terror, *1845–48.*

The Admiralty consulted its Arctic experts over King's bold asser-
tion. Parry dismissed King as a self-publicist and warned that 'it would
be scarcely safe to follow his views' on where to send relief. The official
view on the expedition within government was reflected in a civil-service
memo sent from the Colonial Office in June 1847, the month Crozier
took command:

> The Admiralty and those persons who are qualified to form an opinion on the
> matter, do not entertain at present ... any apprehension concerning the fate of
> Franklin and his party.[1]

James Ross was undoubtedly best placed to judge the expedition's situation.
He knew the region better than anyone else alive and was familiar with the
mindset of Crozier and Franklin. But his judgement on this occasion was
sadly mistaken. He stuck with his bold assumption that there was no need
to worry, despite the absence of any word from the Arctic. He rejected the
concerns of people like King and his uncle John, explaining:

> Captain Crozier was staying with me at Blackheath nearly all the time the
> expedition was fitting out, and with Sir John Franklin I was in almost daily
> and unreserved communication respecting the details of the expedition,
> and neither of them made the least allusion to any such arrangements or
> expectations beyond mentioning it as an absurdity what Sir John Ross
> proposed to Sir John Franklin.[2]

Ross' blasé attitude echoed the general sentiments of the Admiralty as well
as those of the Arctic Council, an informal group of the navy's most senior
Arctic hands who were called in to advise on the situation. The Council,
which included Back, Parry, Richardson and Ross, was the best informed
and most experienced centre of excellence the country could muster and
was unanimous in advising against mounting a relief expedition in 1847.

The Arctic Council also rejected a rescue plan from within the naval

The Arctic Council advising the Admiralty on the search included Back, Beaufort, Bird, Richardson, Ross, and the paintings on the wall behind show Barrow, Franklin and Fitzjames watching proceedings. Crozier, who was then in command, was not included.

establishment. Captain Frederick Beechey, an Arctic veteran, urged a two-pronged relief expedition. One party, he suggested, should follow *Erebus'* and *Terror's* proposed route through Lancaster Sound to Barrow Strait, and another would approach from the south by way of the Great Fish River towards the King William Island area. His plan, which bore a strik-ing resemblance to King's proposal, was never implemented.

Unknown to all concerned, some measure of relief was tantalisingly close at hand in the spring of 1847. John Rae, the Scot who worked for the Hudson's Bay Company, made a remarkable overland journey in 1846–47 that brought him within striking distance of the doomed *Erebus* and *Terror*. But at no time did he realise their peril.

Rae was the most accomplished overland traveller of the age, mapping hundreds of miles of new territory and establishing that Boothia was a peninsula attached to the mainland and not an island. It was said that Rae could travel 100 miles (160 kilometres) in two days.

Rae's great skill was that he absorbed the Inuit ways, mastered the art of driving dogs and building igloos, wore furs and snowshoes and lived off the land by hunting game and fishing. In defiance of conditions, Rae celebrated Christmas Day in the wilderness in 1846 with a feast of fresh venison, plum pudding and brandy punch.

In mid-April 1847, Rae stood at Lord Mayor's Bay on the east coast of Boothia. Less than 200 miles (320 kilometres) to the west, *Erebus* and *Terror* were stuck in the ice, Franklin would be dead in less than ten weeks and the expedition was on the brink of disintegration.

Rae would never have been able to supply provisions for over 100 men, particularly around King William Island. But he could have directed Crozier to areas where game was more plentiful and have returned to London with the expedition's precise location for his rescuers.

On board *Terror*, Crozier must have watched in silent horror as the summer of 1847 came and went without the two ships being released. A third winter above the Arctic Circle was inevitable. Little of substance had occurred to alter the outlook. The only minor change was that the vessels, wedged firmly in the ice, had drifted a few miles to the south with the slow-moving current. As the autumn hours of daylight grew shorter, *Erebus* and *Terror* stood imprisoned about 15 miles (24 kilometres) off the north-west coast of King William Island.

Crozier prepared his men for the ordeal. Although the food position was not yet critical, it was finely balanced. Supplies were scheduled to run out in the summer of 1848, precisely the moment when the men from *Erebus* and *Terror* were hoping for release from the ice.

The winter of 1847–48 was the critical time for the expedition. It was an appalling nightmare of bitterly cold isolation, growing illness and a mounting casualty rate. The silence was broken only by the battering winds and grinding noises made by the build-up of ice pressure. It was an eerie cacophony that McClintock once described as like 'trains of heavy wagons with ungreased axles slowly labouring along'. Jammed in the ice and with little to do but contemplate their fate, the expedition suffered a long drawn-out execution.

The weather was especially severe, with very low temperatures and ferocious winds. For about three months during the depths of winter the sun never rises above the horizon. Rae reported temperatures down to a paralysing -47° F (-44°C) in January 1847 while over-wintering to the east. Local Inuit gave a vivid account of their conditions which Crozier probably experienced when they told the American explorer Hall years later that 'there was no summer between two winters' in this period.

The biting cold provided the backdrop to growing sickness and death on board *Erebus* and *Terror*. Although no medical records were ever found, it is reasonable to assume that, by this stage, the party was struck down by rampant scurvy.

The condition usually develops in humans after three months or so without an adequate intake of Vitamin C, found in fresh vegetables or fruit and, to a lesser extent, in fresh meat. Vitamin C cannot be stored by humans for long periods and the small amount of lemon juice taken by the party was not sufficient, particularly as the Vitamin C in lemons loses potency in very cold temperatures.

Although the onset of scurvy varies from person to person, the condition is usually fatal after a period of six months or more. Early symptoms are lethargy, sore joints, blackened gums and loose teeth, followed by fever and convulsions.

Scurvy had cursed sailors for centuries and was called the 'plague of the sea' during the Age of Exploration from the late fifteenth century onwards as ships ventured further and further from land. It was probably the largest occupational disease in history.

Some modern-day analysts have claimed that the party was also weakened by lead poisoning caused by the crude lead soldering on the tins of meat and vegetables, which is thought to have leaked into the contents. Any exposure to high levels of lead would have accelerated the decline in health, with symptoms ranging from fatigue to irrational behaviour. A post-mortem on the three men buried on Beechey Island in 1846 – carried out in the 1980s some 140 years after their deaths – showed abnormally high levels of lead in their systems but stopped short of being fatal.

It seems more likely that scurvy was the probable cause of the rapid decline in the party's condition during the awful winter of 1847–48. Towards the end of winter, the decline was being measured in the growing numbers of dead and seriously ill. By April 1848, only eleven months after Lieutenant Gore had left his reassuring 'All well' note on King William Island, one in five of the expedition was dead.

The expedition, which sailed into the ice with 129 souls, was now reduced to 105 unfit and increasingly desperate men. Without Vitamin C, the expedition was devouring itself from the inside.

The mounting toll presented Crozier with a grave test of his leadership. As winter slowly passed, he had ample time to consider the two realistic options for survival: remain on *Erebus* and *Terror* and hope the ice relented in the following summer, or take the desperate step of abandoning the ships for a perilous overland march across the ice in search of supplies or rescue ships.

Neither choice offered much hope, but with food stocks declining and summer escape by no means certain, a decision simply had to be made. It is likely that the ice forced Crozier's hand.

By early 1848 it was probably apparent to Crozier that *Erebus* and *Terror* would never be freed. The greatest fear was that if they remained on board, the vessels would eventually be crushed against the shores of King William Island.

Hoping that the summer thaw of July or August would free the ships was dangerous if, by then, the men were too ill or too hungry to march. Where once it was possible to measure provisions in terms of years, the party could now calculate their rations in terms of months and weeks. By the spring of 1848, scurvy had probably reached epidemic proportions and another winter in the ice was unthinkable.

On 22 April 1848, Crozier took the momentous decision to abandon *Erebus* and *Terror* and set out to walk to freedom with all 105 survivors under his command. The expedition, conceived and equipped as a sea-going enterprise, was now dependent for survival on overland travel – an expertise which the party did not possess.

Leaving the ships in late April, though a desperate gamble, showed that Crozier was thinking rationally. From experience, he understood that the best times for travel in the Arctic are the weeks of late spring, when the ice is still firm underfoot. Travelling during the slightly warmer mid-summer months runs the risk of the ice floes breaking up to leave lanes of open water in testing slushy conditions.

It was these treacherous conditions that Crozier had witnessed first-hand in 1827 as Parry and Ross made their exhausting attempt to reach the North Pole. They marched in July and August and found the going tortuously difficult. Crozier evidently did not want to make the same mistake.

Anxiety about the missing men had crept up very slowly on the naval establishment in London. In November 1847, as Crozier faced the twenty-four-hour-a-day darkness of another Arctic winter and a rising tide of death, the penny dropped. Finally shaken from complacency, the Admiralty and the Arctic Council suddenly burst into action. Plans were finally made to send three separate expeditions in the spring of 1848 to begin the search. The ships would be despatched at much the same time as Crozier was abandoning *Erebus* and *Terror*.

The sheer scale of the massive area of sparsely populated land and waterways which had to be searched is daunting. In broad terms, the area where *Erebus* and *Terror* disappeared equates to the modern Canadian territory of Nunavut, which covers nearly 800,000 square miles (over 2,000,000 square kilometres) of Canadian land and seaways. The combined territories of Germany, France, Spain and the British Isles would fit inside Nunavut. Large chunks of the search area are easily accessible for only a few weeks of the year.

Ross volunteered to come out of retirement and take two ships – *Enterprise* and *Investigator* – into the principal thoroughfare of Lancaster Sound. Two others would go to the Bering Strait and an overland party under Richardson and Rae was ordered to probe the vast wilderness around the Mackenzie River area.

At the same time, huge rewards were offered to anyone finding the lost men and ships. An incentive of £10,000 was offered to whoever could locate *Erebus* and *Terror* in the Arctic labyrinth and the princely sum of £20,000 would be awarded to the man who rescued the party. In today's terms, £20,000 is worth close to £1,500,000.

Plover, the first ship sent in search of *Erebus* and *Terror*, left England in early January 1848 on a mammoth journey around Cape Horn to approach the Arctic from the Bering Strait. Some hoped they would discover that the missing ships had completed the passage and were already celebrating in the Pacific.

Captain Thomas Moore, *Plover*'s captain, carried personal letters to Crozier from members of his family and a slightly apologetic note from Ross, who evidently felt pangs of guilt about not embarking on a search earlier. Writing to 'My Dear Frank', he told Crozier: 'The Admiralty have behaved throughout with admirable liberality and I am sure will leave nothing undone that ought to be done.'[3]

The sentiment was echoed by Ann Ross, who also wrote to Crozier, saying: 'It will be a satisfaction to think that the government has not been dilatory on this occasion in arranging a very complete system of communication with you.'[4]

The Admiralty initiative sparked another furious row with the increasingly

£20,000
Sterling
REWARD.

TO BE GIVEN BY HER
MAJESTY'S GOVERNMENT

to such private Ship, or distributed among such private Ships, or to any exploring party or parties, of any Country, as may, in the judgment of the BOARD of ADMIRALTY, have rendered efficient assistance to

SIR JOHN
FRANKLIN,
HIS SHIPS, or their Crews,

and may have contributed directly to extricate them from the Ice.

H. G. WARD,
SECRETARY TO THE ADMIRALTY.
LONDON, MARCH 23, 1849.

The attention of WHALERS, or of any other Ships or parties disposed to aid in this service, is particularly directed to SMITH'S SOUND and JONES'S SOUND, in BAFFIN'S BAY, to REGENT's INLET and the GULF of BOOTHIA, as well as to any of the Inlets or Channels leading out of BARROW's STRAIT, particularly WELLINGTON STRAIT, or the Sea beyond, either Northward or Southward.

VESSELS Entering through BEHRING'S STRAITS would necessarily direct their search North and South of MELVILLE ISLAND.

An advertisement for the government's offer of £20,000 reward to whoever found the missing expedition. In today's money, this is worth around £1,600,000.

strident Dr King. He dismissed the seaborne searches and re-emphasised his belief the search should be conducted around King William Island and Boothia. He argued that Richardson and Rae's search around the vast and thinly populated Mackenzie – the area is over 1,000 miles (1,600 kilometres) from King William Island – was being conducted too far to the west to find any traces of the men.

He also dismissed Ross' mission into Lancaster Sound, which he called 'a single throw in the face of almost certain failure'. In an impassioned plea to the Colonial Office at the end of 1847, King wrote: 'It is a hard thing that 126 men should perish when the means to save them are in your Lordship's power.'[5]

The Admiralty, acting on the advice of Ross and others, ignored King's assertions and continued preparations with its own plans for a three-pronged attempt to find the men.

By any standards, the Admiralty was cutting things fine. The expedition's provisions were scheduled to run out at precisely the moment Ross was expected to arrive in the Lancaster Sound area, while the overland trek of Richardson and Rae and the approach from the Bering Strait were unlikely to reach their goals in the summer of 1848. Dr King's warning of 'a single throw' at relief was chillingly accurate.

But while King agitated, the general public seemed blissfully unconcerned. At around the time that Ross, Rae and Richardson were preparing to leave Britain, *The Times* was proclaiming: 'We do not ourselves feel any unnecessary anxiety as to the fate of the ships.'

CHAPTER 19

Breakout

The long, slow death march of the 105 survivors from *Erebus* and *Terror* began on 22 April 1848 – Easter Saturday. Some may have linked Christ's resurrection with their own ambitions.

The party took to the sea ice and travelled about 15 miles (24 kilometres) to the shores of King William Island, the nearest land. At its head, Crozier must have realised that the chances of all 105 surviving were already very slim.

The north-west coast of King William Island was a desperately bleak and austere starting point for a mission of survival. The men came ashore near Victory Point, the spot first reached by Ross in 1830. Leopold McClintock, who visited the site a decade after Crozier, wrote of it:

> Nothing can exceed the gloom and desolation of the western coast of King William Island. [It] is for the most part extremely barren and its surface dotted over with innumerable ponds and lakes.[1]

Thousands of miles away in England, the main relief expeditions were finally underway. Rae and the sixty-year-old Richardson left Liverpool on 25 March. Rae carried a pocket sewing kit for Franklin from his daughter,

Eleanor. Ross sailed on 12 May, less than three weeks after Crozier abandoned *Erebus* and *Terror*.

James Ross, in command of the 450-ton *Enterprise*, was accompanied by Captain Edward Bird, Crozier's old shipmate, in the 400-ton *Investigator*. The voyage was a complete failure.

Enterprise and *Investigator* arrived in Arctic waters too late in the season and by September 1848 were halted by the ice on the edge of Barrow Strait. The party was frozen in for eleven months at Port Leopold on the northern coast of Somerset Island, hundreds of miles to the north of where Crozier's party was fighting for its life.

In November, John Barrow, architect and agent of Britain's ambitious but unsuccessful endeavours, died in the comfortable surroundings of his home. He was eighty-four and his thirty years of promoting exploration was book-ended by devastating failure. Barrow's first expedition, before turning to the Arctic, was the ill-prepared attempt in 1816 to explore Africa's Congo River which left 38 of the 56-man party dead and Barrow none the wiser. When he died in 1848, Barrow's most ambitious attempt to find the North West Passage was concluding with the biggest single disaster in the history of polar exploration and the deaths of all 129 men.

During the winter of 1848, Arctic foxes were trapped alive and fitted with copper collars carrying details of the relief expedition before being released into the immense wilderness in the faint hope that they might be discovered by the missing men. The noble but futile gesture summed up the hopelessness of the situation.

At one point in the summer of 1849, Ross stood on the west coast of Somerset Island, peering into the ice-choked waters of Peel Sound. *Erebus* and *Terror* had somehow navigated the same seas three years earlier. But Ross saw nothing to the south except an unbroken panorama of tightly packed ice stretching as far as the eye could see. He was convinced no ships could possibly have penetrated those waters.

Having decided to leave the ships, the biggest gamble facing Crozier was determining the direction of his party. The crucial factor was food. He had left England with the knowledge that no plans had been laid down for relief and, as far as he knew, Crozier had to find his own way out of the Arctic.

The nearest outposts of civilisation – the Hudson's Bay Company settlements at Fort Resolution or Fort Providence on Great Slave Lake – were 1,000 miles (1,600 kilometres) to the southwest along the Great Fish River. Fortunately, the Great Fish River would provide an abundant source of fish and a wide range of game, including bears, foxes, caribou and hares, if he could keep the men alive long enough.

On the other hand, Crozier also knew that a large stock of supplies was stashed to the north in the more remote region of Fury Beach. He chose the Great Fish River. As events unfolded, it was the wrong choice.

The most obvious direction was north to Fury Beach, some 250 miles (400 kilometres) away in Prince Regent Inlet, where twenty years earlier he and Parry had stockpiled tons of provisions from the wreckage of *Fury*. Blanky, the ice-master of *Terror* had also been a member of the same expedition.

The cache of supplies would sustain his men for a while and, once revived, Crozier could follow the example of John Ross who in 1833 camped at Fury Beach before leading his men northwards over the relatively short distance of around 100 miles (160 kilometres) to Lancaster Sound, where they were picked up by a passing ship. Whalers were active in Lancaster Sound and the chances of rescue were fairly high.

But there was a good reason for not going to Fury Beach. Shortly before leaving London, Franklin and Crozier heard rumours that rogue whalers planned to salvage *Fury*'s hoard of provisions and sell them for a quick profit. The risk of trekking hundreds of miles overland to find the food depot empty was too great for Crozier to contemplate.

The tragedy is that the cache was never plundered. In the event, Ross and Bird did head for Prince Regent Inlet and Fury Beach. But after over-wintering, sledging parties did not reach the area until the summer of 1849 – a year after Crozier abandoned his ships – where they found the cache of supplies largely intact.

Crozier's chosen route was to strike south and then east along the shores of King William Island to the mouth of the Great Fish River, at least 200 miles (300 kilometres) away. From the estuary, the party could hope to reach one of the settlements on Great Slave Lake – a daunting trip of many hundreds of miles along a treacherous stretch of river.

Back, who explored the region a decade earlier, reported a large amount of wildlife in the area and it was also known as one of the most popular hunting grounds for the Inuit. The libraries of *Erebus* and *Terror* each carried a copy of the book about Back's voyage in the mid-1830s and Crozier almost certainly knew the territory was teeming with wolves, caribou, muskoxen, bears and fish.

The challenge of navigating the river, and the portage of his boats across perilous countryside, even for an experienced mariner like Crozier, was immense. The journey was widely regarded in Arctic circles as the most difficult territory to traverse and was long written off in London as unmanageable. Ross considered navigation of the river as 'impossible', and Back saw no hope for the men from *Erebus* and *Terror* if they struck out for the river. He declared: 'I can say from experience that no toil worn and exhausted party could have the least chance of existence by going there.'

According to Back, the river was punctuated with a succession of eighty-three dangerous rapids and waterfalls on its long, winding route. He called it a 'violent and tortuous course' and warned that in one area the river ran through a particularly desolate stretch of country – the Barren Lands – where animal life was notably scarce. Travelling with a small group, Back took six weeks to descend the river whereas Crozier would be leading over 100 exhausted men with heavy boats and provisions. Franklin, the only man in the party who knew the area from earlier journeys, would probably not have taken his men to the Great Fish River.

However, Crozier was alone and would have to make the journey without help. None of the Admiralty's three-pronged search – around Bering Strait, along the Mackenzie River and through Lancaster Sound – would take his rescuers anywhere near the Great Fish River.

It seems evident that, after making up his mind, Crozier sent advance parties ashore to King William Island to lay down depots of provisions and equipment. The boats, though still enormously heavy, were modified slightly to reduce their weight but were nevertheless a cumbersome burden.

At Victory Point, a short note was left that provided history with its only written account of the loss of the ships, the death toll and the expedition's attempt to reach the Great Fish River. The note was written around the margin of the original message left by Gore on King William Island a year earlier. Like the earlier communiqué, it was mostly written by Fitzjames.

The message, the last official word from the expedition, contained news of Franklin's death and the date of the ships' abandonment. A postscript, which appears to have been written almost as an afterthought, was added by Crozier and gave notice of the planned march to the Great Fish River. Eleven years would pass before it was found.

CHAPTER 20

A Slow Execution

Crozier's escape plan was hugely ambitious. David Woodman, a modern-day authority on the expedition, once suggested that if a jet aircraft with 129 passengers crashed landed on the west coast of King William Island today and was unable to receive the necessary support, everyone would die.

Crozier was further hampered by the unexplained high mortality rate among the officers of *Erebus* and *Terror*, which left the chain of command, a mainstay of naval discipline and routine, severely stretched. By April 1848, nine of the expedition's 24 officers were dead.

From the scraps of information and theories pieced together over the years, it appears that Crozier intended to reach the trading outposts some 1,000 miles (1,600 kilometres) away on the Great Slave Lake in a single season. Another winter in the ice was unthinkable.

Leaving the ships in April implies he intended to reach the estuary of the Great Fish River by early June – the time when the first migratory flocks of birds and herds of animals would arrive from the south. After the party had fed on freshly killed game, it was hoped the waters of the Great Fish River would have thawed sufficiently to enable the men to launch the boats for a dash to one of the settlements before the autumn freeze descended.

Crozier's plan to reach Great Fish River – a distance of at least 200 miles (320 kilometres) – depended on weeks of heavy labour dragging the bulky ships' boats across the ice on specially adapted sledges. Even a wildly optimistic target of advancing five miles (8 kilometres) a day would require almost two months of back-breaking work, even without hold-ups from bad weather. For men struggling to cope with scurvy, fatigue and restricted rations, the party would be fortunate to make two miles (3 kilometres) a day, which suggests a more realistic four months of unimaginable toil – even before tackling the rapids of the Great Fish River.

For historians, the well-documented ordeal of Sir Ernest Shackleton, trapped in the Antarctic over sixty-five years later, provides a chilling insight into the scale of the task facing Crozier in 1848. In 1915, Shackleton attempted to drag his one-ton lifeboats across the ice to open water after the loss of his ship, *Endurance*. Teams of fairly well-fed and generally fit men laboured for hours in vain. On some days they managed only one mile (1.6 kilometres) and after a week of colossal effort, the boat-haulers had advanced less than 10 miles (16 kilometres). The march was abandoned.

Crozier's unwieldy sledges were made from planks of oak fitted with steel runners, each weighing about one-third of a ton (300 kilograms). The boats, which measured almost 28 feet (8 metres), weighed up to 800 pounds (350 kilograms) unladen. When loaded with supplies and equipment, the huge physical effort was almost certainly beyond the capacity of Crozier's flagging men. McClintock later estimated that the retreating party could not have carried more than forty days' supplies to feed over 100 men.

Crozier initially retreated in orderly fashion along the west coast of King William Island towards Simpson Strait, a longer route than travelling due south, but preferable because the smoother sea ice made trek a little easier than traversing broken land. However, the weakened men soon began to fall by the wayside.

Crozier was now presented with a terrible dilemma: should he leave the weak and dying to save the strong? His priority, undoubtedly, would have been to get as many men as possible to fresh food, even if this meant abandoning the weakest members of the party, who were already doomed.

The party was reduced to a pathetic procession of weak and dying men, still dressed in wholly unsuitable woollen uniforms and navy boots and clinging resolutely to the useless paraphernalia of life at home. Despite the enormity of the life-and-death crisis, the men still carried their 'home from home' on the sledges. At a time when the situation cried out for carrying only food and essential gear, the sledges were crammed with a desiderata of Bibles and other books, engraved cutlery and china dinner plates, changes of clothing and an assortment of footwear, soap and toothbrushes, cigar cases and sealing wax. And silk handkerchiefs.

McClintock, who found the trail of discarded objects a decade later, concluded that the already exhausted and sick men were hauling 'a mere accumulation of dead weight'. The unnecessary baggage, he said with classic understatement, was 'very likely to break down the strength of the sledge-crews'.[1]

The retreating party was struck by a major emergency soon after beginning the march south. About one-third of the party, probably those suffering from acute scurvy, was too ill to march. A field hospital for the sick was erected at Terror Bay, on the south-west corner of King William Island. It was here that, for the first time on the expedition, the party became divided.

The sick were left behind, with some finding their way back to the ships and some, according to later Inuit accounts, breaking off in search of their own independent sources of game. They were never seen again.

Under the leadership of Crozier, the main body of men continued the march towards the Great Fish River, and it is likely that Crozier would have sent the most able hunters ahead to forage for game. He almost certainly intended to return to Terror Bay with fresh meat for the ailing men once the bulk of his party had reached the hunting grounds. But rescue never came and Inuit later found the remains of about 30 men in the area

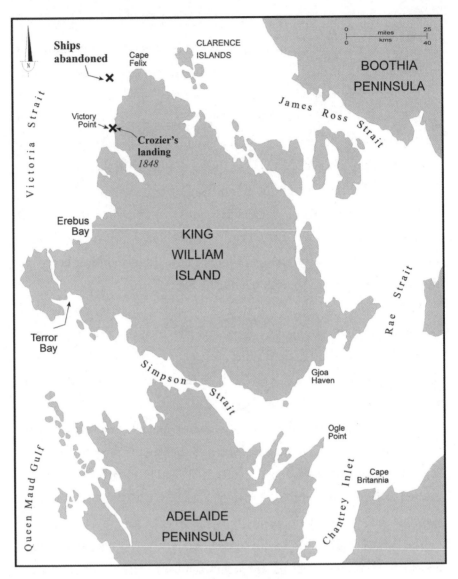

King William Island area, where Crozier abandoned the ships.

around Terror Bay, where the retreating party had first been split.

Crozier's plight was little better than the condemned men at Terror Bay. It was a predicament brought into sharp focus when Crozier's party met a group of Inuit families a short distance away. The retreating men ran into the small band near Cape Herschel in Washington Bay on the southern shores of King William Island, a headland that overlooks the western entrance to Simpson Strait.

What followed was among the most painful and illuminating episodes in the history of Arctic exploration. Inuit accounts of the meeting indicated that the men under Crozier now numbered around 40. Charles Francis Hall, the American explorer, came to the area some years later and met some of the locals who remembered the encounter. Hall was convinced from their oral descriptions that the party's leader was Crozier. Some Inuit knew of Crozier and one told Hall that he was '… so poor and nearly starved'.[2]

Crozier explained to the natives that his ships were trapped in the ice and persuaded them to give the men some fresh seal meat, which they devoured. The men, according to the Inuit, were all thin and ravenously hungry.

The explorers and the natives, in a scene faintly reminiscent of Crozier's winter at Igloolik in 1822–23, camped together for the night. In the morning, Crozier pleaded with the Inuit to stay with his men and help them find fresh game. He rubbed his hand over his stomach, repeatedly saying *netchuk* (seal) as he beseeched the natives to stay.

Inuit knew from bitter experience that the hunting grounds around Cape Herschel were incapable of supporting their own families and dozens of starving men. It was an uncompromising reminder of the most basic of all survival necessities. There was no room for sentiment and the seamen could only watch in dismay as the natives ambled away to fend for themselves.[3]

The heart-breaking exchange between the hungry seamen and the brutally pragmatic Inuit was the most striking illustration of how little naval explorers had learned about the Arctic in thirty years of endeavour. The bitter irony was seeing Crozier's decimated party reduced to begging for scraps of food from people that polite British society regarded as inferiors and savages.

The main body of survivors struggled on throughout the summer of

1848, hugging the southern coast of King William Island as they made their way very slowly towards the Great Fish River. In their wake, they left a trail of dead. In the words of the Inuit, men fell dying as they walked.

One skeleton, believed to be that of Lieutenant Henry Le Vesconte from *Erebus*, was discovered by Hall in the 1860s and subsequently returned to England for burial at Greenwich Hospital, London. However more recent examination suggests the remains are not Le Vesconte's and we may never know for sure who lies buried in the chapel at the Old Royal Navy College, Greenwich. The remains of another body, later identified as Lieutenant Irving of *Terror*, were found years after at Victory Point and interred with full military honours at Dean Cemetery, Edinburgh.

The bones of two more victims were found in 1905 by members of Roald Amundsen's *Gjøa* party when he completed the first-ever navigation of the North West Passage. In a ceremony heavy with symbolism, Amundsen's men buried the skeletal remains of the vanquished and sailed into the history books as the victors.

It was a bitter-sweet occasion for Amundsen, who ventured into polar exploration as a young man after being inspired by tales of the Franklin expedition. But despite his admiration for the sheer guts of those who ventured into the ice, he could never fully understand how the expedition had descended into such a catastrophic debacle.

Amundsen's expedition spent two winters at Gjoa Haven on the southeast coast of King William Island, about 100 miles (160 kilometres) from where almost sixty years earlier Crozier struggled ashore after abandoning *Erebus* and *Terror*. In contrast to the armada of British naval expeditions to the region, Amundsen took a small boat with a shallow draught. He and his crew lived like the Inuit, wearing furs, stalking game and even learning the language.

Gjoa Haven lies on the caribou migration routes and is an infinitely more fertile hunting ground than the west coast where Crozier landed. The Inuit name is *Uqsuqtuuq* which, loosely translated, means a 'place of plenty blubber'.

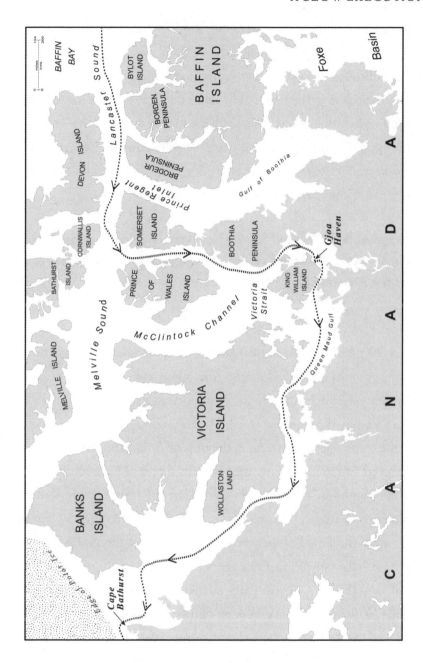

Route taken in 1903–06 by Roald Amundsen in Gjoa, *during the first-ever navigation of the North West Passage.*

Amundsen's party fished and shot copious amounts of wildlife and threw away the surplus remains. Amundsen never underestimated the severe difficulties of survival in the Arctic and respected the efforts of the early adventurers to the region. He once said: 'It is difficult for men living in comfort in civilised countries to realise the harshness of the Arctic.'[4]

But he was astonished that so many British seamen starved to death in the same region where his men, only 50 years later, lived in comparative luxury and dumped surplus stocks of food. He wrote:

> [Franklin] and his men had perished from starvation – oddly enough, at a spot where, when we reached it, we happened to find an abundance of game on land and fish in the water.[5]

At one stage during the 1848 retreat, Crozier's men stood only approximately 20 miles (32 kilometres) from the Gjoa Haven area and the rich hunting grounds that would sustain Amundsen half a century later. As *Gjøa* sailed along Simpson Strait in the short open water season to complete the maiden voyage through the North West Passage, Amundsen respectfully flew the ship's colours in salute to the men of *Erebus* and *Terror*.

Crozier's last journey along the southern shores of King William Island and into Simpson Strait in 1848 bristles with historic significance. In reaching the channel, Crozier had confirmed that the waters of Simpson Strait were the final link between east and west of the North American continent – the North West Passage.

The stragglers of Crozier's party reached Point Hall on the southern tip of King William Island overlooking Simpson Strait during the middle of 1848. On the Todd Islands, a cluster of tiny islets, more of the party fell dead. It is impossible to know how many had survived at this stage. Recent research suggests that only a handful of men were still standing. The small group of survivors dragged themselves a further 10 miles (16 kilometres) across the strait to the mainland of Canada.

Moving slowly over the sea ice, the exhausted men passed Point Rich-ardson and entered a narrow inlet on Adelaide Peninsula. The site, less than 200 miles (320 kilometres) from where *Erebus* and *Terror* were abandoned, was among the last camps for survivors. The inlet was later given the maca-bre name of Starvation Cove.

Modern research by Woodman argues that a few men clung to life around Starvation Cove until 1851, some three years after the ships were abandoned, though it is impossible to say for certain. The bones and relics scattered around King William Island and the sometimes conflicting and confusing Inuit stories which emerged over the years about what happened to the *kabloonas* (white men), have left a bewildering trail of unknowns. All that can be said with certainty is that no one truly knows.

It appears that a small number of the 105 men who set out in April 1848 survived to fight another winter. In the desperate struggle, Crozier lost the battle to keep the expedition together, and there are indications that perhaps naval discipline broke down and the men fractured into smaller, independent groups.

A handful, it seems, managed to return to the ships, while others struck out in different directions, in the hope of reaching either Fury Beach or Inuit settlements along Prince Regent Inlet. Lancaster Sound, the most likely place to find a passing ship, lies to the north.

At home, the mystery remained a closed book. Any prospects of search-ing in the right area had disappeared by the time Ross and Bird returned empty-handed in late 1849.

The search expedition was a shattering experience for Ross, a man more accustomed to triumphs and accolades. Six men died and he never went back to the Arctic. His view of Peel Sound's thick ice reaffirmed his con-viction that the Admiralty should search northwards around the region of Wellington Channel, well over 500 miles (800 kilometres) from where Crozier was to be found.

Ross was supported by McClintock who wrote that any attempt to force a ship down Peel Sound would lead to 'almost inevitable destruction in consequence of it being choked up with heavy ice'. Significantly, McClintock would later change his mind about the chances of navigating Peel Sound.

It was a conviction that ignited ten years of frantic searches for the lost expedition, a massive effort involving over forty ships and hundreds of men. Search parties combed thousands of miles of territory and, in the process, helped to map much of the uncharted region. Sometimes, rescue ships had to be sent in search of rescuers who had themselves become trapped in the ice.

Heavily influenced by Ross' view of the inaccessible waters in Peel Sound, they searched everywhere but the right place.

CHAPTER 21

Unsolved Mystery

What think you of the whaler now?
What of the Esquimaux?
A sled were better than a ship,
To cruise through ice and snow
Popular ballad, c.1850

The hunt to locate the lost souls from *Erebus* and *Terror* accelerated after the return of James Ross in 1849. In 1850 alone, no fewer than twelve ships were dispatched to the ice, including a private yacht and a schooner commanded by the redoubtable Sir John Ross, then approaching seventy-three. Others followed in the ensuing years.

Initially, the search was conducted by the Admiralty, but before long, Jane Franklin became the driving force in the frantic hunt to find the lost party. She embarked on a feverish ten-year personal quest to find traces of the expedition and refused to give up the search for information even when the fate of the men was finally established. It became an obsessive crusade that captured the public imagination and created a perfect Victorian melodrama. Jane Franklin was invariably centre stage of the drama.

Lady Franklin generated huge public sympathy as she lobbied ministers, the Admiralty, influential men on the Arctic Council such as Ross and just about anyone who would listen. She took her pleas to Zachary Taylor, the new US president, and appealed to the Tsar of Russia to send search parties to the Siberian coast in case the ships had been wrecked in the Bering Strait.

She skilfully cultivated influential people and moulded public opinion for her cause. Her biographer, Alison Alexander, said Jane Franklin developed an 'almost saintly public image' as she campaigned. She reacted badly to criticism and tried to micromanage anything written about the search, almost as though it was a private quest. At her side, always, was the faithful and unquestioning Sophy Cracroft and among those offering sympathy and support was the emerging young poet, Jean Ingelow.

Jane Franklin and Sophy took premises in Pall Mall, near to the Admiralty offices, to be close to the epicentre of events and to ensure that the issue remained in the public eye. Friends called it 'The Battery' because of the bombardment of letters that were fired at the authorities from Jane's study.

Lady Franklin raised thousands of pounds from private sources and helped persuade Henry Grinnell, the wealthy American philanthropist, to finance two expeditions. The family of Frederick Hornby, the mate and late recruitment to *Terror*, donated £130 (approximately £10,000 in today's terms) to the campaign.

She also poured some of her modest wealth into the venture, helping to outfit four different vessels from her own pocket. In the process, she further alienated her stepdaughter, Eleanor Franklin.

In between showering the press with emotional letters about the fate of the lost explorers, she made long trips to ports as far apart as Hull and the Shetland Islands to urge departing whaling captains to keep a sharp lookout for the missing ships. At Stromness in the Orkneys, Jane and Sophy sipped cherry brandy with Margaret, the elderly mother of John Rae.

Her influence even extended into the upper reaches of the Admiralty, where at one stage she encouraged them to stray from tradition by appointing a commander from the whaling fleet to lead one of her privately financed expeditions. The captain, an experienced whaler called William Penny, named his ships *Lady Franklin* and *Sophia*, but they, too, came back without finding a trace.

Jane Franklin asked all the search expedition commanders to carry a personal letter to her husband and one note provided an indication of her regard for Crozier: 'Next to you I think of dear Captain Crozier,' she wrote. 'I trust you have never been forced to separate and that you have been a mutual comfort to each other.'

One notable diversion came in 1851 with reports that two abandoned ships had been seen alongside an iceberg off the coast of Newfoundland. It was claimed the vessels were *Erebus* and *Terror*, even though Newfoundland lies an improbable 2,000 miles (3,200 kilometres) from King William Island. Under orders from parliament in 1852, the Admiralty launched a full inquiry but failed to reach a conclusion. No other ships were reported missing in the area at the time and the episode of the 'ships in the ice' remains a mystery to this day.

In 1850, Jane Franklin and Sophy Cracroft turned to the unorthodox world of spiritualism in the faint hope of uncovering clues to the lost expedition. Dabbling in the occult had become increasingly fashionable during the Victorian era and Jane and Sophy, despite firm religious beliefs, were ready to clutch at any straw.

The women were approached by numerous mystics claiming to have knowledge of the expedition, including one who solemnly declared that Franklin was still definitely alive. At that point, Franklin had been dead for three years.

The pair attended séances around the crystal ball of Lieutenant Morrison and others, including several sessions with Ellen Dawson, another popular clairvoyant. She reported seeing an old gentleman 'looking well and happy'. Franklin had been dead for two years.

Ellen Dawson, described as a diminutive woman, preferred Jane Franklin sit outside the room during the sessions to avoid any upsetting revelations and confided her visions through the soft focus of Sophy. In one sitting Dawson reported seeing the captain of the other ship, presumably Crozier's *Terror*. According to Dawson, he was thinking of the lady he loved who would not marry him. The lady, said Dawson, would be sorry and would never marry. Sophy Cracroft never married.

But the most bizarre incident involved the dubious case of Louisa 'Little Weesy' Coppin, a dead Irish child. The daughter of Captain William Coppin, a prominent shipbuilder from Derry, 'Weesy' Coppin died in 1849 at the age of four. Soon after her death, the little girl reportedly 'appeared' to her family.

In answer to questions she allegedly pointed to the precise location of *Erebus* and *Terror* in the Arctic. Ann Coppin, the seven-year-old sister of 'Weesy', was the intermediary for the messages and drew a picture of the scene. In the picture, she added key words such as 'Erebus' and 'Terror', 'Sir John Franklin', 'Victory Point on King William Island' and 'Victoria Channel'.[1]

Captain Coppin visited Jane and Sophy and gave them little Ann's drawing of his deceased-daughter's vision. In their desperation for news, Jane and Sophy apparently took the eerie claims seriously.

The oddity is that the area indicated by 'Weesy' Coppin was precisely where the ships were initially held in the ice, and Victoria Channel, now called Victoria Strait, had not been named at this stage. It was also many miles from the principal thrust of the navy's search around Wellington Channel.

However, Captain Coppin had his own agenda. He was a dedicated disciple of the supernatural and had become captivated by the disappearance of the expedition. He wanted to get involved in the search in some way or other and at one point offered to finance a further relief expedition. He secured the backing of Liverpool's mayor, Sir John Bent, to petition the

Admiralty to send ships in the direction identified by the ghostly visions of his dead child. The pleas were politely ignored at the Admiralty, where Jane Franklin's flirtation with the supernatural went down badly.

But the mystery of 'Little Weesy's' revelations did not disappear altogether. Sophy Cracroft promised to return the child's sketch to Coppin after Jane Franklin's death, but for some reason never did. While accounts of frequent visits of Jane and Sophy to various other clairvoyants in the 1850s have survived in the archives, virtually all traces of the 'Little Weesy' Coppin affair have been lost.

The episode only came to light in 1889, many years after Jane Franklin's death. J. Henry Skewes, an eccentric vicar from Liverpool, published the strange tale in an obscure book that claimed to reveal the true secret of how Franklin's fate was uncovered. The assumption is that Sophy Cracroft – loyal to the end – deliberately censored the Franklin family papers to remove records of the brush with the supernatural in an attempt to preserve Jane's credibility.

John Franklin, an evangelical man, would certainly not have approved of his wife's dalliance with the spiritual world, and Sophy Cracroft, with her finely tuned sense of public opinion, clearly felt that Lady Franklin's perfect image would have been tarnished by the affair. In the event, Jane Franklin's fling with spiritualism did nothing to enhance the search.

The confusion over the expedition's whereabouts deepened after the first traces of the lost party, including a heap of meat tins and the three gravestones, were found on Beechey Island in 1850. The discoveries gave no hint of the true scale of the disaster and no written records were found. Crucially, there was no real indication of the direction the ships had taken after leaving Beechey.

Beechey Island lies at a crossroads in the vast Arctic archipelago of seaways and landmasses. From the intersection of Beechey, it is possible to sail north into Wellington Channel, south into Peel Sound or Prince Regent Inlet, east into Lancaster Sound or west into Barrow Strait.

Even the discovery of one small clue on Beechey Island only served to deepen the mystery. A white board was found with a hand painted on it. The index finger of the hand pointed outwards. But the board had been knocked over by strong Arctic winds and it was impossible to know which way the enigmatic finger was directing the searchers.

In 1850, the Irish-born Robert McClure in *Investigator* and Richard Collinson in *Enterprise* led their ships into the Bering Strait to approach the area from the west. In 1852, the cantankerous and unpopular veteran, Sir Edward Belcher, took five ships into Lancaster Sound with orders to search Wellington Channel north of Beechey Island. He returned two years later with only one vessel. The resultant and inevitable court martial exonerated him of blame, but Belcher never received another naval command.

One of Belcher's ships, *Resolute*, was abandoned in 1854 and improbably found its way to the heart of the American political system. After being abandoned near the western end of Lancaster Sound, the ship drifted over 1,000 miles (1,600 kilometres) into Baffin Bay, where it was picked up by an American whaler and returned to Queen Victoria as a gesture of friendship between the two nations. Victoria subsequently commissioned a high-quality writing desk be made from *Resolute*'s oak timbers and in 1880 presented the desk to US President Rutherford Hayes. Since then many US Presidents, including Kennedy, Reagan and Obama, have conducted the nation's affairs from behind the ornate *Resolute* desk in the Oval Office at the White House.

In contrast to Belcher's misadventure, McClure's voyage in *Investigator* was memorable. At one point, he sailed to within 60 miles (96 kilometres) of Melville Island, first reached from the east by Parry thirty years earlier. From the crow's-nest, open sea could be seen 20 miles (32 kilometres) away and for the first time a passage across the roof of the Canadian mainland seemed possible. But the ice in the region was relentless and *Investigator* was seized and later abandoned.

After an appalling three-year ordeal of starvation and scurvy, McClure's party trudged the last miles by foot to reach *North Star* from Belcher's ravaged fleet off Beechey Island and thus became the first men to traverse the North West Passage on foot. Leaving many of his crew dead in the Arctic, McClure finally returned to Britain in 1854 and was knighted for his achievement.

However, 1854 was a bad year for Lady Franklin. On 12 January, the Admiralty formally announced that the 129 men from *Erebus* and *Terror* were to be removed from the navy's books unless news of their survival arrived before the end of March. It was the first official acknowledgement that the men, now gone for almost nine years, were dead.

A devastated Jane Franklin refused to accept the inevitable. She declined a naval-widow's pension and refused to wear the traditional black of a mourning widow. She called the Admiralty notice a 'knell of departed hopes' and lamented the 'abandonment of those unhappy men to their fate'.

At the same time, the long naval career of Francis Crozier, which began in the summer of 1810, officially ended on April 1, 1854 after almost forty-four years of service when his name was formally struck off the Navy List.

The Admiralty's decision to remove the men from the navy payroll, Jane Franklin cried, was 'presumptuous in the sight of God, as it will be felt to be indecorous, not to say indecent ... in the eyes of man.'[2]

But she had misread the mood both at the Admiralty and in the country. After weary years of fruitless search, the Admiralty's patience had run out, and the public, too, was tired of the North West Passage saga. One newspaper proclaimed in 1854 that the 'mania of Arctic exploration has lasted long enough'.

Besides, there were more pressing matters. On 28 March 1854, just three days before the Admiralty's deadline for locating the lost expedition, the Crimean War between Britain and Russia broke out. The navy fleet, which had spent almost forty years largely idle or deployed in sideshows like Arctic exploration, was quickly reassembled for its primary purpose of war.

The Admiralty never sent another ship to the Arctic in search of the

Franklin expedition. At the same time, the national focus of expanding the Empire quietly switched from the Arctic to Africa and to the exploits of men such as David Livingstone, Richard Burton and Henry Morton Stanley.

Thousands of miles away in the Canadian Arctic, the nine-year-old mystery of the missing expedition was beginning to unravel thanks to the diligence of John Rae. It was typical of the perplexing affair, however, that Rae was not actually looking for the ships or the men when he stumbled across the clearest evidence yet of the expedition's fate.

Rae had ventured north in 1853 to complete the mapping of the Canadian coastline on behalf of his employer, the Hudson's Bay Company. During his travels he discovered the Rae Strait on the east side of King William Land and established that it was, in fact, King William Island.

The most significant moment of his journey came in 1854, when Rae and four other men headed towards Pelly Bay on the east coast of Boothia Peninsula. It was relatively close to where Ross had stood five years earlier.

Rae ran into a group of wandering Inuit and noticed something strange: one man was wearing a gold cap band. The man, called In-nook-poo-zhee-jook, told him a shocking story of 35 or 40 white men seen heading south towards a large river four years earlier. The group was led by a stout, middle-aged officer with a telescope strapped over his shoulder, who may have been Crozier.

Sometime later, the natives found the bodies of many white men scattered over an area near the big river, which was identified as Ogle Point and Montreal Island in the mouth of the Great Fish River. Rae bought the gold band from In-nook-poo-zhee-jook and headed back to Repulse Bay, where he promised to pay for any other relics or information about the dead men.

Rae's reward was a rich cache of objects. The hoard included a gold watch, a fork and a plate inscribed 'Sir John Franklin'. He also collected a silver tablespoon which bore Crozier's initials, FRMC.

Over the following weeks, Rae, through an interpreter, interrogated the

John Rae, the outstanding Arctic explorer from Scotland, who discovered the first evidence of the expedition's fate in 1854.

natives about the dead men. What he learned was explosive. According to the Inuit, the starving *kabloonas* (white men) had eaten the flesh of their dead comrades. In a written report summarising the oral testimonies, Rae concluded:

> From the mutilated state of many of the corpses, and the contents of the kettles, it is evident that our wretched countrymen had been driven to the last resource – cannibalism – as a means of prolonging existence.[3]

Rae now faced the dilemma of whether to trek miles to the Great Fish River to examine the evidence for himself or to return to London with the disturbing news. As it was too late in the season for a long overland journey, he chose to speed back to London.

Rae's revelations unleashed a storm of controversy, despite providing the most telling evidence yet of what happened to the expedition. Victorian London was repulsed and outraged by the claim that the navy's finest had been driven to the most heinous crime known to humans. To add insult to injury, the only evidence came from Inuit.

Rae's gruesome story was a dagger to the heart of Victorian sensibilities. If true, the account reduced the nation to barbarians and undermined the whole concept of British superiority in the world. The reaction grew even more hostile when Rae insisted he believed the Inuit accounts.

Charles Dickens, probably the most influential writer of the age, attacked the innocent Inuit as 'covetous, treacherous and cruel' and claimed it was impossible that the 'flower of the trained adventurous spirit of the English navy, raised by Parry, Franklin, Richardson and Back' could have descended to such depths. In *Household Words*, the magazine he edited, Dickens said it was 'in the highest degree improbable' that navy officers and crew would 'alleviate the pains of starvation by this horrible means'. *The Times* simply concluded: 'Like all savages, they are liars.'

Research in the 1990s showed that Rae and the 'savages' were perfectly correct in their diagnosis. An investigation around Erebus Bay on the west coast of King William Island in 1993 found nearly 400 human bones or fragments of bone, with 92 of them showing distinct cut marks, which, it appeared, could not have been made by animal teeth.

What was not generally known to disbelieving Victorians was that Sir John Richardson, a former companion of Franklin and a highly respected member of the Arctic Council, had also once descended, perhaps inadvertently, to the 'last resource' on an earlier expedition to the Arctic.

The incident occurred in 1821 during the terrible overland expedition undertaken by Richardson and Franklin, during which Franklin earned the reputation as 'the man who ate his boots'. Richardson, travelling near the Coppermine River with seaman John Hepburn and the Irish midshipman, Robert Hood, was starving and exhausted.

The three men met Michel Terohauté, an Iroquois Indian who had recently killed two French-Canadian *voyageurs* and who would later murder Hood. In a ruthless example of frontier justice, Richardson subsequently executed Michel. Before he was shot, Michel had given the hungry men strips of meat that he claimed had been taken from a slain wolf. But, Richardson wrote, the men became 'convinced from circumstances ... that [the meat] must have been a portion of the body of [the voyageurs].'[4]

Richardson's journal of the 1820–22 expedition was not written for publication and remained unpublished in his family's hands for over 150 years. When it was eventually published, in 1984, the journal's editor, a Canadian academic, declared:

We shall never know whether Richardson ate the flesh of one of the *voyageurs* knowingly or unknowingly. But eat it he did.[5]

There was another odd twist to Rae's uncomfortable revelations. He arrived in London with his sorry tale on 22 October 1854, just three days before the infamous Charge of the Light Brigade at Balaklava in the Crimea, another of the Victorian era's great blunders.

An irresistible parallel exists between ordering the reckless cavalry charge into the teeth of Russian gun batteries at Balaklava and the disastrous charge into the ice by the expedition to find the North West Passage. Both were calamitous imperial adventures that ended in needless deaths and yet, over the years, have become acclaimed as symbols of gallant national heroism.

A link to the two events was provided by Alfred Tennyson, the Poet Laureate, whose *The Charge of the Light Brigade* was significant in glorifying the misadventure in the Crimea. Tennyson was a nephew of John Franklin. With hindsight, two lines from his famous verse have a ghastly significance for Crozier, Franklin and the unfortunate men of *Erebus* and *Terror*, dutifully following orders as they ventured into the Arctic wilderness:

> *Theirs not to reason why,*
> *Theirs but to do and die.*

All such considerations were swept aside in the clamour to condemn Rae. His many critics were astonished that he chose to return home instead of visiting the Great Fish River to corroborate the lurid Inuit stories. Nor could he provide any substantial proof that the natives were telling the truth. None of the men he cross-examined at Repulse Bay in 1854 had seen the bodies of the dead men for themselves. The stories, it emerged, were second-hand accounts and Rae's belief in the honesty of the Inuit testimony carried no weight against the tide of popular opinion.

The controversy over Rae's news added to Jane Franklin's torment. In a matter of months, the explorers had been declared dead and now her husband's reputation was sullied by allegations of cannibalism. Additionally, McClure's historic journey had robbed Franklin of the honour – posthumously – of being the first to traverse the North West Passage, albeit partly overland.

Lady Franklin refused to accept that Rae's relics proved beyond doubt that Franklin was dead, even after nine years of silence. Instead, she lobbied against Rae receiving the £10,000 (about £750,000 today) reward for discovering the expedition's fate and renewed her campaign for the Admiralty to despatch another search party to the ice. Under increasing pressure from Lady Franklin, the Admiralty paid for the Hudson's Bay Company to send a small party to the Great Fish River area to verify the Inuit accounts.

James Anderson and James Stewart, two of the Hudson's Bay Company's most experienced fur traders, made an impressively rapid journey north in the summer of 1855 and found a few more useful remnants of the expedition, including some fragments of a boat from *Terror*. But, inexplicably, Anderson and Stewart did not take an Inuit interpreter on the trip and they were therefore unable to 'cross examine' the natives. Nor did they find any bodies or documents that might have answered so many unanswered questions.

Soon after, John Rae was given the £10,000 reward but was denied any official recognition. Unlike most other Arctic explorers of the era – Parry, Richardson, Franklin and John and James Ross – Rae did not receive a knighthood for his prodigious efforts. In that sense, his experience matched Crozier's.

Anderson's and Stewart's journey in 1855, which had failed to substantiate Rae's story, instilled new energy into Jane Franklin's crusade. She maintained her hostility to Rae – 'hairy and disagreeable' – and argued that public money should be spent on the search rather than on rewarding him.

At the age of sixty-six, she launched another vigorous campaign to unearth the truth. From 'The Battery', the iron-willed Lady Franklin once more turned her guns on the Admiralty. She deployed her full armoury, including her own 'last resource' of pleading that finding traces of the expedition should not be left to a 'weak and helpless woman'.

Her PR campaign worked in some quarters. In June 1856, a few months after the end of the Crimean War, a group of eminent men of the day presented a petition to the Prime Minister, Lord Palmerston, urging the

Admiralty to approve a further search.

But the Admiralty had lost its appetite for the Arctic regions and privately many were tired of Jane Franklin's relentless campaign. Too many men, too many ships, and too much money had already been ploughed into the search, even if as late as February 1857 – nearly twelve years after *Erebus* and *Terror* sailed – odd newspapers continued to carry reports that some of the men were still alive in the Arctic wilderness.

It is estimated that the Admiralty alone ploughed close to £700,000 into its search efforts. Today, this would be the equivalent of around £50,000,000. American investors, too, had spent heavily on private expeditions and Jane Franklin had invested around £35,000 (over £2,500,000) of her own and her supporters' money in the quest to find her husband. It was little comfort that years of probing every seaway and inlet of the Canadian Arctic had resulted in the most comprehensive mapping of the area ever undertaken.

In a spirit of compromise, the Admiralty agreed to help fit out an expedition if Lady Franklin could find a ship and crew. She mustered £7,000 from her own funds and raised £3,000 from sympathisers, including a donation from Count Strzelecki, the generous Polish aristocrat who had vainly courted Sophy Cracroft on Van Diemen's Land.

In 1857, Lady Franklin purchased *Fox*, a small, screw-propeller yacht of only 177 tons. She arranged for Captain Leopold McClintock, by now one of the navy's most experienced Arctic commanders, to lead the expedition. The little ship, reinforced against the polar ice, sailed from Aberdeen on 1 July 1857, with Jane and Sophy standing expectantly on the quayside.

For once, an expedition left British waters suitably equipped for the rigours of the Arctic. The shallow draught of *Fox* was a blessing in the variable depths of the icy waterways and seventeen of the hand-picked crew of 25 had Arctic experience. As further insurance, McClintock took teams of dogs and an Inuit interpreter, perhaps taking a leaf out of Rae's book.

McClintock, a thirty-eight-year-old career naval officer, hailed from Dundalk which lies 30 miles (48 kilometres) from Crozier's home turf

Leopold McClintock, the Irish-born explorer, whose Fox *expedition found Crozier's final message in 1859.*

of Banbridge. He was a sensible choice as commander of the party and a practical, level-headed character with an unflappable temperament and an impressive track record of overland sledging in the Arctic. He sailed with Ross in the fruitless first search of 1848, captained *Intrepid* on Belcher's unfortunate expedition in 1852 and – unusually among naval officers – had partly adopted native Inuit methods to improve the efficiency of sledge travel and survival. During the Belcher debacle, McClintock once trekked over 450 miles (720 kilometres) in just fifteen days, a feat beyond most naval sledging parties.

His mission was to explore the general area around Peel Sound down to King William Island, and the coastline between the mouths of the Great Fish River and Coppermine River, the very area Dr King had for ten years urged the Admiralty to search.

Fox ran into trouble immediately after leaving. The ship was trapped in the ice of Baffin Bay in August 1857 and forced to spend a perilous winter in the pack, drifting aimlessly for over 1,000 miles (1,600 kilometres) in Davis Strait. On Christmas Day, the besieged men drank a toast to Lady Franklin and 'her adorable niece' Sophy Cracroft.

Fox was finally released in April 1858 after 250 days of severe battering from the winds and ice and exactly ten years after Crozier had abandoned *Erebus* and *Terror*. One of *Fox*'s officers said he did not believe that 'wood and iron could have stood such a pounding as we got'.

McClintock took *Fox* on the traditional route through Lancaster Sound, stopping at Beechey Island to inspect the 1845–46 camp of *Erebus* and *Terror* and the three gravestones. On the site, he erected a marble tablet sent by Lady Franklin and warmly dedicated to the memory of 'Franklin, Crozier and Fitzjames and all the gallant brother officers and faithful companions'.

Fox next turned south into Prince Regent Inlet. The party spent a second winter in the Bellot Strait, the narrow, ice-filled channel between Somerset Island and Boothia Peninsula where Crozier had been with Parry more than thirty years earlier.

On one sledging trip, McClintock encountered a large group of Inuit, most of whom carried relics from *Erebus* and *Terror*. Among the items were a silver medal, a few buttons and engraved cutlery. Some Inuit told of a ship crushed in the ice but reported that the men had escaped.

By the spring of 1859, McClintock was ready to send sledging parties in three directions for fresh clues as to the fate of the missing men. Captain Allen Young, who had paid the generous sum of £500 (approximately £40,000 today) to join the expedition, took his team northwest to Prince of Wales Island, while McClintock set off to explore the east side of King William Island and the mouth of the Great Fish River.

The task of examining the western shore of King William Island, the most promising area, fell to Lieutenant William Hobson, *Fox*'s highly regarded second officer, who had been to the Arctic in 1853–54. His father, Captain William Hobson, was born in Waterford and had been the first governor of New Zealand in 1841 after the territory became a separate British colony.

Captain Leopold McClintock and Lieutenant Henry Hobson leave Fox *on 2 April 1859 in search of the lost expedition.*

Hobson, a robust naval lieutenant of twenty-eight, was provisioned for eighty-four days. Sophy Cracroft said he possessed the 'merriest face in the world and was ready for anything'.

The parties set off on 2 April 1859, and McClintock soon met natives with a fascinating story to tell. According to the natives, two ships had been seen off the coast of King William Island. One had sunk, but the other had been forced ashore and still lay broken on a beach. The men were seen dragging their boats towards a 'large river'. One old woman said the men fell and died as they walked along. A year later, some bodies were found.

McClintock bought relics from the Inuit, including a knife and a telescope case. A little later, he bought pieces of silver plate bearing the initials of Crozier and Franklin.

McClintock moved south to the mouth of the Great Fish River, picking up scraps of information and noticing that Inuit had fashioned lumps of wood into tent poles and kayak paddles.

After skirting around the rugged Montreal Island in the estuary of the

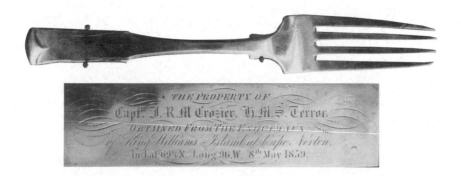

A silver fork belonging to Crozier which was found during McClintock's expedition. Inscription below reads:
The Property of Capt. F.R.M. Crozier HMS Terror
Obtained from the Esquimaux of King William Island
at Cape Norton Lat 69¼ N Long 96 W 8th May 1859

Great Fish River, McClintock began the return trip to *Fox*. Moving slowly along Simpson Strait, the party reached Cape Herschel on the southern shores of King William Island. In their path lay a skeleton, the bones bleached a ghostly white. McClintock said it looked as though the man had fallen asleep. Alongside the remains were a clothes brush and comb.

A few miles beyond Cape Herschel, McClintock made a startling discovery – a small cairn built by Lieutenant Hobson, who had stood on the spot only six days earlier. Inside was a brief note from Hobson with the news everyone had been seeking for over a decade.

Hobson's note revealed how his party had struck lucky exactly a month after leaving the ship. On 2 May, he had reached Cape Felix at the most northerly point of King William Island, where he found a cairn. Frustratingly, it had been looted and was empty. But all around was evidence that the men from *Erebus* and *Terror* had passed through the area. He found collapsed tents, discarded clothes and rusting tools. Hobson continued his search and found another empty cairn nearby. Days later, a third was uncovered, which contained an empty document canister and a broken pickaxe.

On 6 May, moving a few miles further down the coast, Hobson came upon the remains of another camp at Victory Point on the north-west coast of King William Island. The headland, which was discovered by James Ross in 1830, lies almost opposite where the ships were abandoned. The site was littered with debris left behind by the desperate men, who had discarded superfluous gear and possessions before embarking on the march south to the Great Fish River, just as the Inuit had indicated.

Among the flotsam and jetsam of the expedition, Hobson also found a cairn. His party dismantled the cairn of stones with a series of hefty blows from pickaxes. Inside, they found a metal container and a standard navy form supplied to all expedition ships. In the margins was the handwritten message from Des Voeux and Gore in 1847 giving the ships' position and signing off with 'All well'.

H.M.S.ships *Erebus and Terror*
{ Wintered in the Ice in

<u>28</u> of May 184<u>7</u> { Lat. 70° 5' N. Long. 98° 23' W.

Having wintered in 1846—7 at Beechey Island
in Lat 74° 43' 28" N. Long 91° 39' 15" W. after having
ascended Wellington Channel to Lat 77° and returned
by the West side of Cornwallis Island.

Commander.

Sir John Franklin commanding the Expedition.
all well

WHOEVER finds this paper is requested to forward it to the Secretary of the Admiralty, London, *with a note of the time and place at which it was found:* or, if more convenient, to deliver it for that purpose to the British Consul at the nearest Port.

QUINCONQUE trouvera ce papier est prié d'y marquer le tems et lieu où il l'aura trouvé, et de le faire parvenir au plutot au Secretaire de l'Amirauté Britannique à Londres.

CUALQUIERA que hallare este Papel, se le súplica de enviarlo al Secretario del Almirantazgo, en Londrés, con una nota del tiempo y del lugar en donde se halló.

EEN ieder die dit Papier mogt vinden, wordt hiermede versogt, om het zelve, ten spoedigste, te willen zenden aan den Heer Minister van de Marine der Nederlanden in 's Gravenhage, of wel aan den Secretaris den Britsche Admiraliteit, te London, en daar by te voegen eene Nota, inhoudende de tyd en de plaats alwaar dit Papier is gevonden geworden.

FINDEREN af dette Papiir ombedes, naar Leilighed gives, at sende samme til Admiralitets-Secretairen i London, ellér nærmeste Embedsmand i Danmark, Norge, eller Sverrig. Tiden og Stedet hvor dette er fundet önskes venskabeligt paategnet.

WER diesen Zettel findet, wird hierdurch ersucht denselben an den Secretair des Admiralitets in London einzusenden, mit gefälliger Angabe an welchen Ort und zu welcher Zeit er gefunden worden ist.

Party consisting of 2 Officers and 6 Men
left the Ships on Monday 24th. May 1847

Gm Gore Lieut
Chas F. Des Voeux Mate

[Marginal note, left side:] 25th April 1848. H.M.Ships Terror and Erebus were deserted on the 22nd April, 5 leagues N.N.W. of this, having been beset since 12th Septr 1846. The officers & Crews consisting of 105 souls under the command of Captain F.R.M. Crozier landed here — in Lat 69° 37' 42" Long 98° 41' 15". This paper was found by Lt Irving under the cairn supposed to have

[Marginal note, right side, top:] been deposited by the late Commander Gore in May 1847

[Marginal note, right side:] been deposited by the late Commander Gore in June 1847. and the total loss by deaths in the Expedition has been to this date 9 officers & 15 men.

[Marginal note, right side, lower:] and start on tomorrow 26th for Back's Fish River

[Signatures, right side:] James Fitzjames Captain H.M.S Erebus
F.R.M. Crozier Captain & Senior Officer
Sir John Franklin died on the 11 June 1847

Opposite: Crozier's last word. The brief note found by Lt Hobson from Fox *in 1859 which reveals Crozier's plan to reach Great Fish River. Details were scribbled around the margins of a printed naval document. Crozier's message was written upside down in the top right hand corner.*

Hobson decided to hurry back to *Fox* with his news. But only a few miles further south, he found another cairn. Inside was a container with another navy information sheet. The basic message was the same as the first. But around the margins of the note was significant new information written a year later which revealed Franklin's death, the abandonment of the ships and the march towards the Great Fish River.

The wording in the margin, which was the last written word of the expedition ever to be found, also contained Crozier's final message and said:

25th April 1848 HM Ships Terror and Erebus were deserted on 22nd April 5 leagues NNW of this having been beset since 12th Septr 1846. The officers & crew consisting of 105 souls – under the command of Captain F.R.M. Crozier landed here – in Lat 69° 37' 42" Long 98° 41'.
This paper was found by Lt Irving under the cairn supposed to have been built by Sir James Ross in 1831, 4 miles to the northward – where it had been deposited by the late Commander Gore in June 1847. Sir James Ross' pillar has not however been found and the paper has been transferred to this position which is that in which Sir J Ross' pillar was erected.
Sir John Franklin died on 11th June 1847 and the total loss by deaths in the Expedition has been to this date 9 officers and 15 men.
FRM Crozier   James Fitzjames.
Captain and Senior offr   Captain HMS 'Erebus'
And start on tomorrow 26th for Backs Fish River[6]

Hobson absorbed the full meaning of his momentous discovery and noticed that, although much of the writing came from the hand of Fitzjames, the crucial final words were written by Crozier. Hobson added: 'The brevity of the note and the weak, tremulous hand in which both that and his signature are written, incline me to the belief that he must have been in ill health at that early period.'[7]

Hobson also reported only small amounts of wildlife in the area and observed: 'There is not the slightest chance of a party subsisting by hunting on this shore.'

Hobson took the original note and left behind a copy before turning back to *Fox*, even though he was hampered by extremely poor weather and worsening scurvy. Hobson became so weak that he was carried on a sledge and was unable to stand by the time the group staggered back on-board *Fox*.

After a trek lasting seventy-four days, Hobson delivered the Victory Point document to McClintock. 'So sad a tale was never told in fewer words', McClintock wrote. The document, stained by rust from the tin canister was, he said, a 'sad and touching relic of our lost friends'. Modern historian Russell Potter described it as the 'most evocative document in the long history of Western exploration in Arctic regions'.

McClintock resumed his search on the coastline of King William Island. He came across a large boat, first discovered by Hobson, that contained two skeletons, a large amount of clothing and two loaded shotguns. More cutlery was found, including some inscribed with Crozier's initials. Strangely, the boat was pointed in the direction of Victory Point, as though the men had abandoned the march to the Great Fish River and were perhaps retracing their steps back to the ships.

Towards the end of May, McClintock reached the most westerly point of King William Island, which looks over the heavily iced waters of Victoria Strait that had claimed *Erebus* and *Terror*. He named it Cape Crozier, the second promontory in the world's coldest regions to be named after the man from Banbridge.

Fox was freed from Bellot Strait in August 1859 after a taxing two-year expedition that cost three lives and left many men, including Hobson, seriously incapacitated. *Fox* reached Portsmouth in late September with news of the expedition's discoveries and losses – fourteen years after *Erebus* and *Terror*, so full of hope and optimism, sailed from London.

However, Hobson's discovery and McClintock's popular book, *The Voyage of the Fox*, did not put an end to interest in the expedition or the lost men. Indeed, it triggered an obsessive fascination to uncover the truth, an unstoppable pursuit which has run into the twenty-first century.

CHAPTER 22

Last Man Standing?

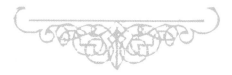

The fate of Francis Rawdon Moira Crozier in the Arctic wilderness is unknown and, in all probability, the precise date of his death will never be established.

The conventional belief, based mainly on Inuit testimonies, is that Crozier died after the terrible march to the Great Fish River in the summer of 1848. Others believe that he endured a fourth winter and lived until sometime in 1849. There is also the fascinating but far-fetched legend that he survived for years, wandering the Arctic wastelands for up to a decade in search of a route out of the frozen maze.

The Inuit, whose tradition of oral history has survived for thousands of years, knew Crozier from previous expeditions and understood his rank as an *esh-e-mu-tar-nar* (junior officer). But in recounting events of 1848 onwards, they correctly reported that Crozier had become *esh-e-mu-ta* (captain), which suggests the local people understood Crozier had assumed command from Franklin.

However, Inuit accounts of events are not entirely reliable. The stories handed down were a frustrating and confusing mixture of fact and fiction, often second- or third-hand accounts which, in turn, were interwoven with traditional Inuit folklore and supernatural myths. While some stories appear authentic, others were exaggerations, untruths or simply muddled versions, where it was impossible to separate reality from invention. It appears some may have told visitors what they expected to hear to please the listener.

Others mixed up the dates and the different expeditions – John Ross's 1829–33 voyage in *Victory* was often confused with the visit of *Erebus* and *Terror* fifteen years later – and some of the grains of truth were probably lost in translation. Woodman said it was a 'puzzle without the prospect of complete solution'. He also invoked the words of Lady Franklin, first written 150 years ago, to illustrate our helplessness in solving the mystery: 'What secrets may be hidden within those wrecked or stranded ships we know not,' Jane Franklin wrote in the 1850s; 'What may be buried in the graves of our unhappy countrymen or in caches not yet discovered we have yet to learn.'

Inuit names given to the white men have added to the confusion. Although Crozier was known as *Aglooka*, it has emerged that *Aglooka* was a common Inuit name given to white explorers. Loosely translated, it means 'one who takes long strides' and among those known as *Aglooka* to Inuit were Parry, James Ross and Rae. Woodman's book, *Unravelling the Franklin Mystery*, carries the interesting dedication: 'For *Aglooka*, whoever he was.'

The American adventurer Charles Francis Hall picked up a tale in the late 1860s that claimed Crozier had fought a running battle with 'Indians' (as Hall referred to the indigenous people) on King William Island. According to the story, Crozier, while out hunting, was supposedly attacked by an Indian and suffered an ugly gash across his forehead from a lance. Crozier shot and killed the Indian and had to fight off another attack the following day.

'It was after this fight that so many *kabloonas* [white men] froze and starved to death,' Hall recorded.[1] However, there were no known Indians on King William Island, and the incident may refer to a different band of Inuit or simply involve an entirely different expedition.

Another theory, pieced together by Woodman, is that Crozier survived

Crozier leading the escape from the Arctic wastes. He clutches a gun to repel a threatening bear and is surrounded by dead and dying colleagues. The painting from 1897 is called Starvation Cove *and the artist is Arctic explorer and painter Julius von Payer.*

the horrors of the 1848 march towards the mouth of the Great Fish River and somehow scrambled back to the abandoned *Erebus* and *Terror* with a handful of men. They were helped by visiting Inuit and some of the men – including perhaps Crozier – survived until 1849. According to these Inuit accounts, Crozier died on board one of the trapped ships in 1849 and was buried ashore in Erebus Bay, about 30 miles (48 kilometres) south of Victory Point, where the main party had first landed in 1848. If true, Crozier was fifty-three years old.

Other anecdotes report that Crozier's men were trying to reach Repulse Bay to the southeast on the edge of Hudson Bay, an area Crozier knew from his days with Parry was rich in wildlife. But this contradicts the brief note Crozier left at Victory Point, which cited the Great Fish River as the party's destination.

Another more fanciful theory is that Crozier and three others survived for years, wandering through the wilderness in search of food and rescue. The enticing possibility that Crozier had somehow managed to live for years only emerged from Hall in the late 1860s, two decades after leaving the ships. McClintock, however, had returned from the King William Island in 1859 convinced there were no survivors.

Following McClintock's visit, Hall spent years searching the high Arctic and interviewed some Inuit with first-hand knowledge of events. In 1865, he met a group who told him an astonishing tale that four white men – among them Crozier – had survived for years and might still be alive. Hall's diary recorded: 'Four souls of Sir John Franklin's expedition heard from – one of these F.R.M. Crozier! Three of these may yet be alive.'[2]

According to the Inuit, Crozier was the weakest of the four men because, as Hall noted, 'Crozier was the only man that would not eat any of the meat of the *koblunas* (white men), as the others all did.' The kindly Inuit fed the men seal meat, though one died shortly after.

After recovering, the three survivors used their guns to shoot birds and departed for the estuary of the Great Fish River, carrying a small boat. *Aglooka* (Crozier), the Inuit said, 'knew how to keep himself warm, how to live'. The men were never seen again.

Hall returned from the Arctic in September 1869 with the improbable suggestion that a few men might still be alive twenty-four years after the expedition had departed from England. One of them, according to Hall's account, was Crozier who would have been well over seventy years of age. Senior Arctic officers in London were consulted and the faint prospect of finding survivors was flatly dismissed. Sophy Cracroft, by now in her mid-fifties, dismissed the unlikely story as 'a fearful working up of the slumbering past'.[3]

Another story retrieved from Inuit folklore tells of Crozier and another man being seen alive in the years between 1852 and 1858, apparently the last survivors. The intriguing aspect of this tale, recounted a hundred years later by the Canadian writer and environmentalist Farley Mowat, is that Crozier and his companion were reportedly seen in the vicinity of Baker Lake.

Baker Lake lies over 350 miles (560 kilometres) due south of King William Island, hundreds of miles away from the Great Fish River, where Crozier supposedly led his party in 1848. If correct, the assumption must be that the two men were heading in the direction of the richer hunting grounds around Baker Lake and possibly the trading posts along the western shores of Hudson Bay.

The mystery deepened further in the twentieth century. In 1948, a cairn was discovered by Mowat on the nearby Kazan River which empties into Baker Lake. The cairn, said Mowat, was not typically Inuit and contained fragments of a wooden box that could not have been made by the Inuit. Subsequent research has failed to establish who built the mysterious cairn, but that did not prevent Mowat from concluding that 'the possibility remains that this mute monument was built by Crozier before he vanished utterly.'[4]

CHAPTER 23

A Fitting Memorial

The *Fox* expedition made Franklin a national hero and earned McClintock a knighthood, promotion to the rank of admiral and a £1,500 (about £85,000 today) reward from Parliament. While he was in the Arctic, McClintock's sister, Emily Anna McClintock, married George Crozier, the nephew of Francis Crozier.

Jane Franklin achieved near sainthood status and was fêted by the public as the 'weak and helpless woman' who did privately what the mighty Royal Navy, with limitless resources, had failed to achieve. She became the first woman to receive the Founder's Medal from the Royal Geographical Society.

The only known photograph of Jane Franklin (right in light bonnet) and Sophy Cracroft (to left of man in centre) taken by Carleton Watkins in Yosemite National Park, California, in 1861

The Victorian fondness for noble sacrifice was given full rein with the disaster. It also became a common assumption that Franklin had discovered the North West Passage, the man who 'forged the last link with his life'.

A statue in London's Waterloo Place, erected in 1866, proudly acclaims Franklin and his companions for having 'sacrificed their lives in completing the discovery of the North West Passage'. On the opposite side of the street stands a statue to Captain Robert Scott, the leader of another tragic polar expedition.

In fact, Franklin never saw the final passageway and it is not clear whether Gore and Des Voeux – who travelled to the south of King William Island in 1847 – ever managed to reach Simpson Strait. Even if Gore and Des Voeux did reach the channel, Franklin was almost certainly dead when they returned to the ships with news of the sighting.

It was Rae who found the crucial route to Simpson Strait, the open channel that passes on the east side of King William Island and which is now called Rae Strait. McClure made the first crossing of the region by ship and on foot, but Roald Amundsen was the first man to sail through the North West Passage.

However, it was Francis Crozier who, in leading his party to Simpson Strait in 1848, truly forged – with his life – the last link in the North West Passage.

Memorials to the lost expedition sprang up all over the country, the grandest being reserved for Westminster Abbey. Designed by Lady Franklin, it was embellished with full Victorian flourish in words composed by Tennyson. The epitaph reads:

Not here: The white North hath thy bones and thou,
Heroic Sailor Soul,
Art passing on thy happier voyage now
Toward no earthly pole.

Sir James Clark Ross, Crozier's best friend, late in life. He died in 1862, aged sixty-two.

But Jane Franklin did not live quite long enough to see the memorial in place. She died on 18 July 1875 at the age of eighty-three, less than two weeks before the unveiling ceremony performed by seventy-nine-year-old Sir George Back. Her funeral to Kensal Green Cemetery was a stately affair, with McClin-tock among the pall-bearers and Sophy Cracroft in full mourning. Crozier's nephew, Reverend Charles Crozier, was one of those in attendance.

Crozier's closest friend, James Clark Ross, had died more than a decade earlier, in 1862, doubtless aware that his reports of Peel Sound being non-negotiable had contributed to the rescuers spending almost ten years combing the wrong area.

Sophy Cracroft ended her life as she led it, sacrificing herself to the Franklins and fashioning the legend. She paid a heavy price for her selfless devotion, going blind in later life as she meticulously transcribed almost 2,000 letters and 200 private journals in Jane Franklin's tightly-packed and barely legible handwriting. Jane's proposed biography of her husband, an eighty-six-page manuscript, is written in Sophy's more accessible hand and can be found in public archives, unpublished to this day.

Sophy remained an enigmatic figure to the end of her life. Only one, slightly obscured photograph of her has ever been found. She died on 20 June 1892, aged seventy-seven. Sophy Cracroft, the 'sad flirt', never married.

No definitive account of her relationship with Crozier has ever been discovered and the truth may never be unearthed. But at the height of the search for *Erebus* and *Terror* in the 1850s, one of the ships sent in search of the expedition carried a letter from Sophy Cracroft to her uncle, John Franklin. She added a brief message to Crozier that, just possibly, hints at a slight change of feelings towards him. On the bottom of the letter she scribbled the words: 'Pray remember me very kindly to Captain Crozier.'[1] The letter was returned unopened.

However, Francis Crozier is not entirely forgotten. Several imposing memorials have been raised in his name and numerous parts of the globe have been named in his memory.

He was eligible for a single polar medal or clasp for his service on *Fury* (1821–23), *Hecla* (1824–25), *Hecla* (1827) and *Terror* (1845–48). Arctic Medals were first introduced in 1857 but the family never claimed the honour at the time and the medal was finally collected by a descendant, Rawdon Crozier, over a century later in 1988. However, Crozier received no recognition for the great voyage south between 1839 and 1843 because Antarctic Medals were only awarded from 1904 onwards.

The two most impressive memorials can be found in Crozier's birthplace of Banbridge: an imposing statue directly opposite Avonmore House where Crozier was born and a commemorative plaque in the nearby parish church.

The most striking feature of the memorial in the centre of Church Square, Banbridge is the 7-foot-6-inch (2-metre) statue of Crozier, which stands on a substantial plinth and pedestal. It is a measure of the respect and affection for Crozier that the people of Banbridge raised £700 (over £40,000 today) to erect

Arctic Medal, awarded posthumously to Crozier to commemorate four Arctic expeditions. Arctic Medals were first awarded in 1857, almost a decade after his death. The Crozier family collected the medal over a century later in the 1980s.

the memorial, which was unveiled in 1862.

The statue, which shows a dignified Crozier wearing his captain's uniform, was carved by the Dublin-born sculptor, Joseph Robinson Kirk, who had recently completed a statue of the third Marquis of Downshire. It was Kirk's better-known father, Thomas, who carved Nelson's Pillar in Dublin's O'Connell Street, which was subsequently destroyed by a bomb blast in 1966.

The 17-foot (5-metre) pedestal and plinth were designed by the eminent architect, William J. Barre, from Newry, County Armagh, who secured the commission in an open competition. Barre, who also designed Belfast's Ulster Hall, produced an elaborate Gothic edifice featuring *Erebus* and *Terror* in the ice and four oddly sized polar bears on guard at each corner. Originally, it was planned to fill the niches with scenes from Crozier's career, but the idea was abandoned because the proposers ran out of money.

However, Barre did manage to display Crozier's name on three sides of the structure and chisel two moving inscriptions. On the north side can be found the words:

To perpetuate the remembrance of talent, enterprise and worth as combined in the character and evidenced in the life of Captain Francis Rawdon Moira Crozier R.N., F.R.S. this monument has been erected by his friends who, as they valued him in life, regret him in death. He was second in command with Captain Sir John Franklin R.N., F.R.S. and Captain of H.M. Ship Terror in the polar expedition which left England on 22 May 1845.

On the south side, the inscription continues:

Altho' there remained no survivors of the expedition, enough has been ascertained to shew that to it is justly due the honour of the discovery of the long sought North West Passage, and that Captain Crozier, having survived his chief, perished with the remainder of the party after he had bravely led them to the coast of America; he was born at Banbridge September 1796, but the place or time of his death no man knoweth unto this day.

Appropriately enough, an explorer from a later age was instrumental in raising funds when the monument needed urgent restoration work in the late 1930s. Louis Bernacchi, who had distinguished himself on two ground-breaking Antarctic expeditions, responded to pleas for help from the Crozier family.

Bernacchi, a member of Borchgrevink's *Southern Cross* venture in 1898–1900 and Scott's *Discovery* expedition in 1901–04, sat on the Council of the Royal Geographical Society at the time and persuaded the organisation to contribute £5 towards the £100 bill for repairs, although the largest share of the bill was met by the Crozier family.

The simple marble tablet in the parish church was also carved by Joseph Kirk and shows *Terror* locked in the ice. The plaque was placed by the Crozier family with an inscription that reads:

Far from this spot in some unknown but not unhonoured resting place lies all that was mortal of Francis Rawdon Moira Crozier, Captain R.N., 5th son of the late George Crozier, Esq. He was born September 1796; entered the Royal Navy, June 1810 and served with distinction in several exploring voyages under Sir E. Parry and with Sir J. C. Ross in the Arctic and Antarctic regions. He left England, May 1845, in command of H.M.S. Terror, with Sir John Franklin with H.M.S. Erebus in the expedition for the discovery of the N West passage.

From the heroic service neither he nor any of his brave companions ever returned. His unbending integrity and truthfulness, combined with extreme amiability, won the esteem and love of all who knew him. The faith which influenced his life is now a source of truest consolation to his sorrowing friends.

Lasting memorials were also left in the territories visited by Crozier during three decades of polar exploration. His name has been attached to no fewer than eight points on the map, including three different Cape Croziers at both ends of the world.

Sir Leopold McClintock, whose party discovered Crozier's historic note in 1859, was among the last surviving links between nineteenth-century Arctic exploration and early twentieth-century voyages to Antarctica. The eighty-two-year old McClintock (right) is pictured on Discovery *in 1901 with Robert Scott and Ernest Shackleton (behind).*

The most famous Cape Crozier lies at the eastern side of Ross Island in the Antarctic, which was commemorated by Apsley Cherry-Garrard in *The Worst Journey in the World*. The second Cape Crozier can be found at the far western end of King William Island in the Arctic, near the spot where *Erebus* and *Terror* were abandoned in 1848. A third Cape Crozier is located at the western entrance of Mercy Bay on Banks Island, where Robert McClure's *Investigator* was abandoned prior to his completion of the first traverse of the North West Passage.

A Crozier Channel lies to the north of Banks Island between Eglington Island and Prince Patrick Island, and there is a Crozier Bay on the west coast of Prince of Wales Island. Crozier Strait runs between the islands of Cornwallis and Bathhurst, and the Crozier River was named by Parry near Fury and Hecla Strait. Overlooking Treurenberg Bay in Spitsbergen is Crozier Point, where Crozier remained in charge of *Hecla* during Parry's abortive attempt to reach the North Pole in 1827.

Many popular ballads were composed and sung about the fate of Franklin and Jane Franklin's anguished search for clues, most notably *Lady Franklin's Lament* which remains popular to this day. The song, which dates to around 1850, includes the familiar words:

> *We were homeward bound one night on the deep*
> *Swinging in my hammock I fell asleep*
> *I dreamed a dream and I thought it true*
> *Concerning Franklin and his gallant crew*

But another 150 years would pass before Crozier was commemorated in song when, in 2001, a group of eight Irish sailors and explorers saluted Crozier – and other Irish explorers – by navigating the North West Passage in the 49 ft (15 metres) *Northabout* under skipper, Jarlath Cunnane. Frank Nugent, the mountaineer and author with a gift for singing, chose the highly appropriate backdrop of the Arctic seaways to write his *Lament for Francis Crozier.* While *Northabout* was off the shores of King William Island, Nugent wrote *Lament For Francis Crozier,* which included the verse:

God rest Francis Crozier gentle Captain of Terror
In Terra Incognita you discovered new lands
With Ross and with Franklin your name lives forever
An explorer and sailor of great fame and renown.[2]

Perhaps the most significant memorial to Francis Rawdon Moira Crozier lies approximately 239,000 miles (382,400 kilometres) from Banbridge, on the surface of the moon.

Crozier's name has been given to a large crater that lies on the eastern face of the moon's near side, in the lunar sea of Mare Fecunditatis. The crater, about 14 miles (22 kilometres) wide, can be located at latitude 13° 5' south, longitude 50° 8' east. The significance lies in the company that Crozier is keeping a quarter of a million miles from where he performed so nobly.

Francis Crozier failed to receive full recognition for his outstanding abilities and achievements while he was alive. Even after his death, the remarkable record of six polar expeditions and almost forty years of dedicated service to the navy was shamefully undervalued by his superiors at the Admiralty and cruelly overlooked by history. Alone among the illustrious Arctic and Antarctic mariners and navigators of the age – Parry, Franklin, Back, Richardson and John and James Ross – Crozier was not awarded a knighthood for his prodigious efforts.

In 1851, the artist, Stephen Pearce, painted a revealing picture of the famous Arctic Council, showing a group of ten naval luminaries, including Parry, Richardson and Ross poring earnestly over charts at the Admiralty. On the wall, portraits of the dead Barrow, Franklin and even Fitzjames gaze hopefully down at the venerable gathering. Crozier, unaccountably, was not considered worthy of inclusion.

On the moon, however, Crozier is to be found among the select men who shaped the history of polar exploration. Crozier's name, at last, stands alongside the most celebrated polar explorers of any age: Cook, Parry, Ross, Nansen, Amundsen, Scott and Shackleton.

The imposing Crozier monument, which stands opposite his birthplace in Banbridge, was unveiled in 1862; the plague reads 'to perpetuate the remembrance of talent, enterprise and worth as combined in the character and evinced by the life of Captain Francis Rawdon Moira Crozier'.

CHAPTER 24

Lost and Found

The 1845 North West Passage expedition is a chapter of history which refuses to be laid to rest. The shocking evidence of the tragedy, first brought back from the Arctic by Rae and McClintock in the 1850s, did not satisfy the longing for an understanding of events and it was simply the opening phase in an enduring saga which has captured the public imagination for 170 years.

Interest has reached new peaks with the remarkable recent discovery of the navy ships, *Erebus* and *Terror*, above the Arctic Circle, and the anticipated slow drip-feed of information and analysis from the prolonged salvage operation will maintain the momentum for the foreseeable future. Marine archaeologists working on the ships, who have only a few weeks of access to the vessels every year because of the ice conditions, believe it will require at least ten years – possibly longer – to complete the extraction and examination of material recovered from the vessels. Crozier, Franklin and the other 127 men who perished in the late 1840s will not be permitted to lie undisturbed.

The first attempts to find out what happened to the expedition date back to 1848, three years after *Erebus* and *Terror* sailed down the River Thames on a wave of national optimism and enthusiasm. In the following years more than forty naval ships or private ventures travelled north in a vain attempt to locate the missing party.

Even the return of McClintock in 1859, carrying word of the expedition's sorry fate and Crozier's final message, did not dampen interest. On the contrary, it initiated the sustained programme of investigation which lasts to this day. In fact, more missions have been sent in search of the dead than were ever sent to rescue the living.

It is estimated that from 1860 onwards, well over fifty official and unofficial expeditions have travelled to the Arctic, plus an unquantifiable number of individuals or small informal parties who made private trips in search of evidence. The true number of investigations and investigators may never be known.[1]

Over the years, the quest for answers has attracted generations of explorers, historians, academics, scientists, writers, amateur enthusiasts and even a few eccentrics into the Arctic wastes. Some showed extraordinary dedication in the search for clues and some were simply obsessed. The search was also a cultural bonanza, encouraging dozens of historical books, novels, factual documentaries, a fictional TV series, various songs and plays.

The searchers came first by ships or by trekking overland with dogs and sledges, then by snowmobiles, seaplanes, helicopters and finally state-of-the-art research vessels equipped with remotely operated submersible vehicles and underwater cameras. The technology has advanced but the passion remained unmoved. As one expert observed, it is the not knowing which matters most.

The first serious attempt to unearth fresh clues after McClintock's return was made in 1860, fully fifteen years after the ships were last seen. Charles Francis Hall, probably the expedition's first true obsessive after Jane Franklin, travelled to the Arctic with high hopes, but came back empty handed.

But Hall, an endlessly optimistic character, went back in 1865 and made his most important discoveries. Hall picked up intriguing stories from local Inuit around King William Island, including accounts about a man called *Aglooka* – thought to be Crozier – who was in command of the white men. Hall also found many relics and the skeleton of an officer, who was presumed to be Le Vesconte. The body was shipped back to the UK but modern research suggests the skeleton is not Le Vesconte.

Hall was the first to hear Inuit accounts of how the ships had sunk nearly two decades earlier. A man named In-nook-poo-zhe-jook looked at an Admiralty chart and pointed to the location of a wreck near O'Reilly Island to the south of King William Island. One vessel, he was told, had sunk in shallow water and the masts were visible above the water. Hall also learned that Inuit went on board a ship and found a dead man.

Hall's own story ended in tragedy in 1871 when he was murdered during an attempt to reach the North Pole. By an unhappy coincidence, Hall left a final optimistic note in a metal tube which, like Crozier's message, lay unopened for years.

By 1878, exactly thirty years after Crozier led the escape bid, the American Geographical Society appointed Lieutenant Frederick Schwatka to search for the expedition's logbooks and other written records. Schwatka, a lawyer, doctor and serving army cavalry officer, went north with a small party which included Inuit guides and William H. Gilder, a New York journalist. Gilder's editor was the legendary James Gordon Bennett, who sent Henry Morton Stanley into deepest Africa to find Dr David Livingstone and hoped that another world exclusive story might emerge from the Arctic ice.

The expedition, the first Arctic venture sponsored by a newspaper, searched the coastline of King William Island and found graves, skeletons and various relics. Schwatka also returned with fresh reports of cannibalism by the desperate sailors. The remains of Lieutenant John Irving, one of Crozier's officers on *Terror*, were identified and returned to Britain for reburial in Dean Cemetery, Edinburgh.

Through interpreters, Schwatka was told that Inuit had seen a ship stuck fast in the ice off the coast of Grant Point, a headland on the Canadian mainland jutting out into Simpson Strait. It was much the same area as indicated to Hall a few years earlier.

Unsurprisingly, Schwatka found no trace of the expedition's records. Paper had little value to communities high above the tree line who, in the absence of the printed word, had developed their own rich tradition of oral storytelling and history. In this pre-literate society, the words, songs and chants of storytellers, poets and shamans meant as much to the Inuit as the complete works of Shakespeare to the literate. Eyewitnesses recalled how any documents found by inquisitive natives were simply tossed away.

Danish anthropologist, Knud Rasmussen, one of the outstanding Arctic explorers of the early twentieth century and the first to traverse the North West Passage by dog team, was among those who recognised the importance of Inuit accounts. In search of fresh clues, he interviewed communities around King William Island during his impressive Fifth Thule expedition in 1921–24 but, seventy years after the expedition went missing, he did not unearth any substantial new leads. At Starvation Cove, across the Simpson Strait, Rasmussen respectfully buried a few of the scattered bones he found.

The search for evidence continued over the following decades and from the early 1930s to the 1970s, the region attracted a long line of professional and amateur enthusiasts. These included official bodies such as the Canadian Geological Survey, Royal Canadian Mounted Police, the Canadian Department of Mines and Technical Surveys, and private aficionados such as William 'Paddy' Gibson, L.A. Learmouth, Paul Fennimore Cooper and Robert Cundy. However, most investigations returned with much the same information as brought back by Rae and McClintock in the 1850s.

The most illuminating development came in the early 1980s when Owen Beattie, an anthropologist, made the first expert examination of skeletal remains found in the region. Encouraged by his findings, Beattie was given permission to exhume the bodies of the three men – William Braine, John Hartnell and John Torrington – who died in 1846 during the expedition's first winter and were buried on Beechey Island.

The haunting sight of the well-preserved men, their eyes open and questioning, was electrifying. Scraps of clothing or old boots, broken pipes, spoons and rusty tins were important but intangible reminders of the Victorian tragedy. But high-quality colour photographs and TV footage of the faces staring back across the ages carried a more powerful message – these were real people like us.

One of the three corpses carried a special meaning for physics professor Brian Spenceley, a member of Beattie's team. Spenceley was a great-great nephew of John Hartnell, the able seaman from *Erebus* who died in January 1846. Spenceley had the rare privilege of looking into the wide-eyed face of a relative who had been dead for 140 years. Spenceley also recognised a striking resemblance to his grandmother.

Beattie, in collaboration with writer John Geiger, produced a memorable TV documentary and best-selling book, *Frozen in Time*, which gave fresh impetus to public interest in the expedition's fate.

However, the autopsies stopped short of confirming suspicions that lead poisoning was the cause of the overall disaster. A popular belief was that the men had ingested high levels of lead from the poor quality of soldering on the food tins. While the examinations showed that elevated levels of lead in the bodies had seriously debilitated the men, there was not enough evidence to show that lead poisoning alone had wiped out 129 men.

An important new discovery was made in the early 1990s when anthropologist Anne Keenleyside and archaeologist Margaret Bertulli examined over 400 bones or bone fragments recovered from the area. At least a quarter of the bones showed deep, clear-edged cuts likely to have been made by a blade, which supported Inuit accounts of cannibalism first given to Rae well over a century before.

Although researchers had begun looking for the wrecks of *Erebus* and *Terror* in the 1960s, the search gained new drive in the early 1990s with the emergence of David Woodman. Woodman, another passionate enthusiast, believed that Inuit testimonies held vital clues to the mystery and might even lead to at least one of the two most valued archaeological prizes – the wrecks of *Erebus* or *Terror*.

Woodman sensed that modern Inuit knew the location of the missing ships from the stories which had been passed down through generations. He studied the early accounts of Hall and Schwatka and made repeated trips to the region, emerging with a conviction that for 150 years archaeologists, historians and explorers had overlooked an obvious source of vital information.

By around 2006, there was renewed interest in the mystery of the missing expedition at Parks Canada, the country's official body responsible for sites of national historical and archaeological importance. Along with the Canadian Hydrographic Service, Parks Canada began to take a more proactive role, bringing a change to the dynamics of the investigation.

At much the same time, attitudes towards national sovereignty were hardening in Canada. Major geopolitical issues, such as who owned the Arctic and whether the North West Passage was an internal or international waterway, had become a highly combustible topic. Alarm grew in 2007 when Russia gave a theatrical display of ownership in the area by planting a titanium flag on the seabed at the North Pole. Unexpectedly, the wrecks of *Erebus* and *Terror* became unlikely symbols of authority as Canada asserted control.

The background was complex and tied into the country's history. In particular, the mysteries of 1845 Franklin expedition had taken root in the imagination of many Canadians and were familiar to many schoolchildren. Margaret Atwood, the acclaimed Canadian writer, once said that for Americans the name Franklin means Benjamin. 'But for Canadians it means disaster. Canadians are fond of good disaster, especially if it has ice, water or snow in it. You thought the national flag was about a leaf, didn't you? Look harder. It's where someone got axed in the snow.'[2]

Canada – the name comes from the Iroquois *Kanata* meaning settlement – gained largely self-governing dominion status from Britain in 1867, just nineteen years after Crozier abandoned his ships. The vast northern territories, which include today's Nunavut, were later ceded to Canada and for half a century all international claims to the region were firmly resisted.

The Second World War and the ensuing Cold War brought new challenges and provided a sharp reminder of the region's strategic importance. The most notable development was the Distant Early Warning (DEW) line, a chain of radar stations from Baffin Island to Alaska, administered by Canada and the US to monitor the movement of Soviet Union submarines and ballistic missiles. The designation of the North West Passage, itself a form of DEW, suddenly emerged as an important factor and, as global warming opened previously impassable sea routes, the significance of the passage grew rapidly.

By the end of 2019, seven passages linking the Atlantic and Pacific oceans were thought to be navigable through the same Arctic waterways which, for over three centuries, had routinely repulsed ships of all shapes and sizes. However, global warming has not lessened the dangers and since Amundsen's pioneering journey in 1903–06, only around 300 successful transits have been made through the North West Passage(s).[3]

In diplomatic terms, a further issue was that the ships were British Royal Navy vessels and the territory was under British control in 1845 when the expedition sailed. But this changed in the 1990s. In 1992, Canada declared the remains of *Erebus* and *Terror* a site of historic national importance – nearly two decades before the ships were even located – and in 1997 the British government surrendered 'custody and control' of the ships to Canada. In return, Britain was promised that key artefacts from the vessels, if found and recovered, would be made available for public display in the UK.

Against this backdrop of complex national sovereignty issues and renewed historic interest, Canada mobilised major national resources to the search. This included assistance from the navy, coastguard and defence establishments, while Woodman eagerly collaborated and passed on his insight into Inuit history.

One of the most influential contacts was local historian, Louie Kamookak, who had spent thirty years investigating the expedition in the region where it had gone missing. Kamookak was the last great individual Franklin hunter and recalled the memorable stories he first heard as a child. Fairly soon, he emerged as the link between oral Inuit history and modern research techniques and sophisticated equipment of Parks Canada and its partners.

For years, Inuit had pointed towards an area of sea locals called Ugjulik, which lies to the south of Simpson Strait and close to O'Reilly Island off the north-west coast of Adelaide Peninsula on the Canadian mainland. Hall and Schwatka were told the same stories 150 years before. The area is well over 100 miles (160 kilometres) to the south of Crozier's last reported position and had been partly investigated without success in 2010.

The underwater archaeological team, supported by the icebreaker *Sir Wilfrid Laurier*, was led first by Robert Grenier and later by Marc-André Bernier and Ryan Harris. It was painstaking work, slowly running side-scan and multi-beam sonar devices up and down, over miles and miles of grey, uninviting seas in bitterly cold conditions. Someone said it was like 'mowing the lawn'. Helped by further funding from the millionaire philanthropists Tim Macdonald and Jim Balsillie a new multi-agency Arctic Research Foundation was created and the specialist ship *Martin Bergmann* later joined the hunt.

Access to the area was limited because of the short ice-free season from August to mid-September and, by 2014, after six years of 'lawn mowing', no trace of the ships had been found. It was planned to switch attention northwards again towards the west of King William Island where Crozier had abandoned the vessels. However extremely poor ice conditions in Victoria Strait, which had trapped *Erebus* and *Terror* in 1847, prevented Parks Canada entering the area and, reluctantly, the search was resumed around Ugjulik.

The switch paid off and, in early September 2014, a shadow suddenly appeared on the sonar screen showing the rough outlines of a ship. Some on board were reportedly moved to tears.

Closer examination revealed Franklin's ship, *Erebus*, which was resting upright in about 35 feet (11 metres) of water and in remarkably good condition. Currents had carried the vessel approximately 130 miles (210 kilometres) south from where it had been left by Crozier 166 years year earlier. Shortly before his untimely death in 2018, Louie Kamookak told an interviewer: 'It was in the area where I expected.'

Early dives recovered many important artefacts from *Erebus*, including plates, bottles, navigational instruments, nails, belt knuckles, a shoe and the emblematic ship's bell. A few strands of hair were found in a brush and fresh clues will be extracted from analysis of the DNA.

While the Inuit were right about *Erebus*, the location of *Terror* was less clear. Once more, the survey was centred on the ship's last known position in Victoria Strait, where it was felt the ship had sunk.

A fortuitous moment in September 2016 changed everything when Sammy Kogvik, a native of Gjoa Haven, joined the research vessel, *Martin Bergmann*. The ship was travelling from Gjoa Haven along the south coast of King William Island to join the search area when Kogvik remarked that, during a hunting trip a few years earlier, he had seen a large piece of wood protruding through the ice in nearby Terror Bay. *Martin Bergmann* made an unscheduled turn and entered the sheltered and rarely visited bay which lies on the south west corner of King William Island.

Sonar images soon revealed the shape of a three-masted ship, standing upright in almost 80 feet (24 metres) of water. It was almost 50 miles (80 kilometres) from *Erebus*. While *Erebus* had drifted almost due south before sinking, *Terror* had taken a more circuitous route to the sea floor. Like *Erebus*, the path had initially taken the ship past the tip of King William Island before abruptly turning north again into Terror Bay, the last major inlet on the south western shore of the island.

The searchers were stunned to discover that *Terror* was largely intact and in better condition than *Erebus*. Marine archaeologists discovered that the

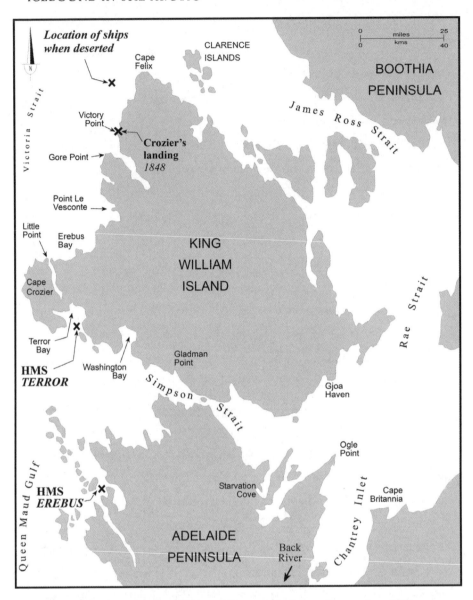

Locations of **Erebus**, *found in 2014, and* **Terror**, *which was discovered in 2016.*

hull had not been breached and there were other indications that the ship had sunk in the spring or summer when ice conditions were at their best. The propeller, which would have been withdrawn if the ship were encased in winter ice, remained in place. Skylights, which would have been closed in winter, were open.

Crozier's ship, Terror standing upright at a depth of 80 feet (24 metres) in Terror Bay, King William Island. The 102 (31 metre) foot-long vessel sank about 170 years ago and was discovered by Canadian-led search teams in 2016, whose sonar equipment captured this image.

Remotely operated vehicles (ROVs) with cameras were guided through skylights and hatches in an extraordinarily graphic tour of the sunken vessel. Small remote-controlled robots were also sent down and entered confined areas thought too dangerous for divers. The drones went eerily from room to room through about twenty compartments, entering the officers' mess, crew's quarters and Crozier's stateroom at the stern, containing his personal desk.

Dinner plates, glasses and bottles were stacked neatly on racks. Desks were in order, drawers closed tight, scientific instruments packed away in cases and beds made. Even the panes of glass in Crozier's cabin window were still intact. All was shipshape.

While the bacteria and worms typically found in warmer seas generally

Crozier's desk. The desk, which has been submerged in Arctic waters for 170 years, is where Crozier planned his escape. It may contain vital clues to the expedition's fate and even personal notes from Crozier.

destroy large portions of wooden vessels, the enveloping sediment, cold water and darkness found at a depth of 80 feet (24 metres) were ideal conditions for preserving the wrecks. Archaeologists were particularly excited by the prospect that organic material, such as paper and clothing, might be found in reasonably good condition, despite spending over a century and a half under water.

One intriguing possibility is that photographs, taken in the 1840s and believed lost, may also be recovered. The expedition carried a daguerreotype apparatus, the first commercially viable photographic process ever developed and the type which captured images of Crozier, Franklin and other officers in London in 1845. Images are displayed on a mirror-like silvered copper plate and there are reasonable hopes that modern techniques will allow at least some salvaged plates to reveal unforgettable pictures from the past.

Hopes of finding the ship's logbooks, charts, letters and other documents remain even stronger, particularly if they have been rolled up tightly or stored in tin containers. Early nineteenth-century paper was generally produced from linen and cotton fibres and was of higher quality and far stronger than most modern paper. Today's paper conservators sense that Crozier's logbooks and other documents from the 1840s stand a better chance of survival than modern documents from 2020 would, after even a short spell under water.

Researchers have an array of modern restoration techniques at their disposal, including freeze drying the paper, exposing the documents to ultraviolet light and X-ray, convective air-drying and vacuum drying under reduced atmospheric pressure. Multi-spectral imaging, which photographs documents in different wavelengths, can also be used to enhance text.

Analysts are also encouraged by earlier successes in restoring historic material, most notably precious documents damaged by floods in Florence in the 1960s. Significant conservation has been carried out at the Antarctic huts occupied by Scott and Shackleton a century ago, and paper and other organic material was successfully recovered from *Titanic* which lies at a depth of 12,500 feet (3.8 kilometres) beneath the Atlantic.[4]

Crozier's desk, sitting submerged and undisturbed in the centre of his stateroom for 170 years, is among the most poignant and compelling of all artefacts so far discovered by investigators. The humble desk, which has not moved because it is probably fixed to the floor, may be the ultimate discovery, particularly if it can provide answers to a myriad of questions which have occupied generations of investigators. It is also a forceful reminder of a personal tragedy.

Crozier, a methodical man accustomed to navy convention and routine, almost certainly kept the official records and logbooks up to date. Equally, the records would be stored safely, probably inside his desk or in a nearby cabinet and 3 feet (1 metre) of sediment, which has built up over the decades, provides an important layer of protection.

Crozier would have spent long spells at this desk during the final winter, studying the charts and maps, discussing his dwindling options with the remaining officers and drawing up plans for escape in the spring. He was often alone with his thoughts and unable to seek advice or guidance from hardened Arctic experts, such as Parry or Ross.

It is almost impossible to fully appreciate the enormous pressure bearing down on Crozier during that final winter of 1847–48. The few options – to navigate the Great Fish River, strike out for the cache of supplies at Fury Beach or hope the ice miraculously released the ships – offered precious little hope of survival and it is probable that scurvy or other illnesses were whittling down the numbers of those left alive. Outside it remained dark and bitterly cold, while inside Crozier contemplated the grave responsibility of holding the lives of over 100 men in his hands.

The other intriguing possibility is that, apart from official navy records, the desk may also contain a few personal letters written by Crozier before leaving the ship. Experience probably told Crozier that the chances of survival were remote and it is tempting to believe he felt the ships would eventually be found.

If so, the desk may hold messages written for posterity or private letters from Crozier to his family and his friend Ross or maybe a note to Jane Franklin expressing regrets at the death of her husband.

Or perhaps a personal letter to Sophy Cracroft.

Francis Crozier:
A Chronology

1796   *c.*17 September: born at Avonmore House, Banbridge, County Down, Ireland, the fifth son of George and Jane Crozier.

1810   12 June: enlisted in Royal Navy; joined *Hamadryad*.

1812   Served on *Briton*.

1814   May: first voyage around Cape Horn.

  September: visited Pitcairn Island.

1816   Served on *Meander* and *Queen Charlotte*.

1817   Obtained certificate as mate.

1818   Served on *Dotterel*.

1821   Volunteered as midshipman on *Fury* for Parry's second North West Passage expedition.

  8 May: *Fury* sailed from England.

  October: *Fury* and *Hecla* wintered at Winter Island, Melville Peninsula.

1822   7 July: *Fury* and *Hecla* released from Winter Island.

  July: Fury and Hecla Strait sighted.

  October: *Fury* and *Hecla* wintered at Igloolik.

1823   12 August: *Fury* and *Hecla* left Igloolik.

  14 November: *Fury* and *Hecla* arrived in London.

1824   Joined *Hecla* for Parry's expedition to North West Passage.

  19 May: *Fury* and *Hecla* left England.

  September: *Fury* and *Hecla* commenced winter at Port Bowen, Prince Regent Inlet.

1825 20 July: *Fury* and *Hecla* released from Port Bowen.

25 August: *Fury* abandoned and stored provisions at Fury Beach, Creswell Bay, Somerset Island.

October: *Hecla* returned to England.

1826 March: promoted to lieutenant.

1827 March: joined *Hecla* for Parry's North Pole expedition.

25 March: *Hecla* left England.

11 May: elected Fellow of Royal Astronomical Society.

20 June: *Hecla* anchored at Hecla Cove, West Spitsbergen.

July: Depot-laying journey to Little Table, Walden and Phipps Islands.

23 September: *Hecla* reached UK.

1831 26 April: joined *Stag*.

1835 23 December: joined *Cove*.

1836 6 January: *Cove* sailed from Hull.

April–August: *Cove* searched Davis Strait for missing whalers.

31 August: *Cove* returned to Hull.

1837 10 January: promoted to commander.

1839 Appointed commander of *Terror* for Antarctic expedition.

25 September: *Erebus* and *Terror* sailed for Antarctica.

1840 15 August: *Terror* reached Van Diemen's Land (Tasmania).

12 November: *Erebus* and *Terror* departed Van Diemen's Land.

1841 1 January: Crossed Antarctic Circle for first time.

15 August: promoted to captain.

1843 September: *Erebus* and *Terror* returned to England.

1845 March: appointed captain of *Terror* and second-in-command of North West Passage expedition.

19 May: *Erebus* and *Terror* sailed from London.

29–31 July: last sighting of *Erebus* and *Terror* in Baffin Bay.

October: *Erebus* and *Terror* winter on Beechey Island.

1846 July–August: *Erebus* and *Terror* left Beechey Island.

August: *Erebus* and *Terror* entered Peel Sound.

12 September: *Erebus* and *Terror* trapped in Victoria Strait.

1847 11 June: assumed command of expedition.

1848 22 April: *Erebus* and *Terror* abandoned.

26 April began march towards Great Fish River.

1848 onwards: Date unknown. Died in vicinity of King William Island.

References

Abbreviations

NMM   National Maritime Museum, London

PRONI Public Record Office North Ireland, Belfast

RGS   Royal Geographical Society

SPRI   Scott Polar Research Institute, Cambridge

Chapter 1: A Bond with History

1   Sir Walter Scott, *The Poetical Works of Sir Walter Scott* (Frederick Warne and Co., 1895), p. 600.

2   George Crozier and Jane Elliott Graham, the parents of Francis Crozier, had thirteen children: Rachel, Martha, Eliza, Jane, Sarah, William, George, Thomas, John, Charlotte, Francis Rawdon Moira, Margaret, Graham.

3   W.A. Maguire, *The Downshire Estates in Ireland 1801–1845* (Clarendon Press, 1972), p. 209.

Chapter 3: Seizing the Moment

1   Ann Parry, *Parry of the Arctic* (Chatto and Windus, 1963), p. 72.

2   John Barrow, *Voyages of Discovery and Research Within the Arctic Regions* (John Murray, 1846), p. 236.

3   Royal Society, 7 December 1843.

Chapter 4: A Promise

1   Pierre Berton, *The Arctic Grail* (Viking Penguin, 1988), p. 49.

2   William Edward Parry, *Journal of a Second Voyage for the Discovery of a North-West Passage in the years 1821–23* (John Murray, 1824).

3   David C. Woodman, *Unravelling the Franklin Mystery* (McGill-Queen's University Press, 1991), pp. 44, 195.

4   Ibid. p. 195.

Chapter 5: Fatal Errors

1   Pierre Berton, *The Arctic Grail*, op. cit. p. 56.

Chapter 6: Wreck of Fury

1   Sir Leopold McClintock, *The Voyage of the 'Fox' in Arctic Seas* (John Murray, 1859), p. 88.

2   Ann Parry, *Parry of the Arctic,* op. cit. p. 93.

Chapter 7: North Pole

1   Frank Nugent, *Seek the Frozen Lands* (The Collins Press, 2003), p. 35.

2   Ibid, p. 35.

Chapter 8: Arctic Rescue

1   Ernest S. Dodge, *The Polar Rosses* (Faber and Faber, 1973), p. 139.

2   *Cove* logbook, National Archive, London.

3   A.G.E. Jones, *Polar Portraits* (Caedmon of Whitby, 1992), p. 238.

4   James Clark Ross to Admiralty, 30 September 1836, RGS.

Chapter 9: South

1   Maureen Peters, *Jean Ingelow: Victorian Poetess* (Boydell Press, 1972), p. 103.

2   *Early Crozier Memorials*, published privately c. 1830, revised c. 1870, PRONI.

3   May Fluhmann, *Second in Command: A Biography of Captain Francis Crozier* (Government of Northwest Territories, 1976), p. 39.

4   M.J. Ross, *Ross in the Antarctic* (Caedmon of Whitby, 1982), p. 28.

5   May Fluhmann, *Second in Command*, op. cit. p. 41.

Chapter 10: Flirting with Love

1   Francis Crozier to Sarah Crozier, 31 January –8 February 1840, SPRI.

2   Frances Woodward, *Portrait of Jane: A Life of Lady Franklin* (Hodder & Stoughton, 1951), p. 228.

3   Alison Alexander, *The Ambitions of Jane Franklin* (Allen & Unwin, 2016) p. 165

4.   Woodward op cit p.365.

5   Frank Debenham, 'The *Erebus* and *Terror* at Hobart', *Polar Record*, no. 3 (1942).

6   Kathleen Fitzpatrick, *Sir John Franklin in Tasmania* (Melbourne University Press, 1949), p. 249.

Chapter 11: An Epic Voyage

1   Roald Amundsen, *The South Pole* (Hurst & Co., 1912), vol. 1, p. 12.

2   M.J. Ross, *Ross in the Antarctic*, op. cit. p. 93.

3   Apsley Cherry-Garrard, *The Worst Journey in the World* (Penguin, 1983), pp. 277–356.

4   Michael Smith, *Polar Crusader – Sir James Wordie* (Birlinn, 2004), p. 242.

5   James Clark Ross, *A Voyage of Discovery and Research in the Southern Antarctic Regions during the Years 1839–43* (John Murray, 1847), p. 322.

Chapter 12: Dangerous Waters

1   *Hobart Town Advertiser*, 7 May 1841.

2   Ernest S. Dodge, *The Polar Rosses*, op. cit. p. 203.

3   *Hobart Town Advertiser*, 4 June 1841.

4   M.J. Ross, *Ross in the Antarctic*, op. cit. p. 117.

5   Ibid. p. 164.

Chapter 13: Trembling Hands

1   M.J. Ross, *Ross in the Antarctic*, op. cit. p. 187.

2   Ibid. p. 206.

3   *Early Crozier Memorials*, op. cit.; Crozier family history, Banbridge Genealogy Services.

4   James Clark Ross, *A Voyage of Discovery and Research in the Southern Antarctic Regions during the Years 1839–43*, op. cit. p. 368.

5   Dr J.S. Crone, 'Distinguished Downshire Men – Captain Crozier', *Northern Whig*, 9 October 1906.

6   Ibid.

7   Ibid.

8   The watch can be found at the National Maritime Museum, London.

Chapter 14: 'I Am Not Equal to the Hardship'

1   M.J. Ross, *Ross in the Antarctic*, op. cit. p. 217.

2   Frank Debenham, '*Erebus* and *Terror* at Hobart', *Polar Record*, no. 3 (1942).

3   Francis Crozier to James Ross, 4 October 1844, SPRI.

4   Ibid.

5   May Fluhmann, *Second in Command*, op. cit. p. 73.

6   Richard Cyriax, *Sir John Franklin's Last Arctic Expedition* (Arctic Press, 1997), p. 19.

7   Sir Leopold McClintock, *The Voyage of the 'Fox' in Arctic Seas*, op. cit. p. xxxv.

8   Francis Crozier to James Ross, 30 December 1844, SPRI.

9   Francis Crozier to Charlotte Crozier, 19 February 1845, PRONI/SPRI.

10   Pierre Berton, *The Arctic Grail*, op. cit. p. 142.

11   Francis Crozier to James Ross, 30 December 1844, SPRI.

12   Francis Crozier to Charlotte Crozier, 19 February 1845, PRONI/SPRI.

Chapter 15: A Sense of Tragedy

1   May Fluhmann, *Second in Command*, op. cit. p. 82.

2   John Cyriax, *Sir John Franklin's Last Arctic Expedition*, op. cit. p. 47.

3   Pierre Berton, *The Arctic Grail*, op. cit. p. 149.

4   Hugh N. Wallace, *The Navy, the Company and Richard King* (McGill Queen's University Press, 1980), p. 57.

5   Frances Woodward, *Portrait of Jane*, op. cit. p. 253.

6   *Early Crozier Memorials*, op. cit.; Crozier family history, Banbridge Genealogy Services.

Chapter 16: North West Passage

1   Francis Crozier to James Ross, 9 July 1845, SPRI.

2   Ann Savours, *The Search for the North West Passage* (Chatham Publishing, 1999), p. 192.

3   Francis Crozier to John Henderson, 4 July 1845, NMM.

4   Pierre Berton, *The Arctic Grail*, op. cit. p. 146.

5   Richard Cyriax, *Sir John Franklin's Last Arctic Expedition*, op. cit. p. 58.

6   Frances Woodward, *Portrait of Jane*, op. cit. p. 252.

7   Pierre Berton, *The Arctic Grail*, op. cit. p. 146.

8   Francis Crozier to James Ross, 9 July 1845, SPRI.

9   Sir Leopold McClintock, *The Voyage of the 'Fox' in Arctic Seas*, op. cit. p. xlv.

10   Francis Crozier to Henderson, 4 July 1845, NMM.

11   Francis Crozier to James Ross, 9 July 1845, SPRI.

12   Francis Crozier to Henderson, 4 July 1845, NMM.

13   Ibid.

14   Francis Crozier to James Ross, 9 July 1845, SPRI.

Chapter 17: Ice

1   Anne Thwaite, *Emily Tennyson: The Poet's Wife* (Faber and Faber, 1996), p. 166.

2   May Fluhmann, *Second in Command*, op. cit. p. 106.

3   Sir Leopold McClintock, *The Voyage of the 'Fox' in Arctic Seas*, op. cit. p. 244.

Chapter 18: 'No Cause for Alarm'

1   Hugh N. Wallace, *The Navy, the Company and Richard King*, op. cit. p. 73.

2   Ernest S. Dodge, *The Polar Rosses*, op. cit. p. 226.

3   James Ross to Francis Crozier, 6 January 1848, SPRI.

4   Ann Ross to Francis Crozier, 6 January 1848, SPRI.

5   Hugh N. Wallace, *The Navy, the Company and Richard King*, op. cit. p. 75.

Chapter 19: Breakout

1   Sir Leopold McClintock, *The Voyage of the 'Fox' in Arctic Seas*, op. cit. p. 262.

Chapter 20: A Slow Execution

1   Sir Leopold McClintock, *The Voyage of the 'Fox'* p. 252.

2   David Woodman, *Unravelling the Franklin Mystery*, op. cit. p. 137.

3   Ibid. p. 124.

4   Roald Amundsen, *My Life As An Explorer* (Wm. Heinemann, 1927) p. 230.

5   Ibid. p. 61.

Chapter 21: Unsolved Mystery

1   Ralph Lloyd-Jones, 'The Paranormal Arctic: Lady Franklin, Sophia Cracroft and Captain and "Little Weesy" Coppin', *Polar Record*, no. 37 (2001).

2   Frances Woodward, *Portrait of Jane*, op. cit. p. 285.

3   Ann Savours, *The Search for the North West Passage*, op. cit. p. 273.

4   C. Stuart Houston, *Arctic Ordeal: The Journal of John Richardson*, 1820–22 (McGill-Queen's University Press, 1984), p. 150.

5   Ibid. p. 217.

6   Sir Leopold McClintock, *The Voyage of the 'Fox' in Arctic Seas*, op. cit. p. 246.

7   Lieutenant William Hobson, quoted by Douglas Stenton, Arctic, Vol 67, No 4

Chapter 22: Last Man Standing?

1   Chauncey Loomis, *Weird and Tragic Stories: The Story of Charles Francis Hall, Explorer* (Macmillan, 1971), p. 191.

2   Ibid, p. 190

3   Frances Woodward, *Portrait of Jane*, op. cit. p. 341.

4   Farley Mowat, *Ordeal by Ice* (Little Brown, 1960), p. 323.

Chapter 23: A Fitting Memorial

1   Frances Woodward, *Portrait of Jane*, op. cit. p. 273.

2   Frank Nugent, Author interview

Chapter 24: Lost and Found

1   Russell Potter, *Finding Franklin: The Untold Story of a 165-Year Search*, (McGill-Queens 2016) p. 221

2   Margaret Atwood, *Strange Things: The Malevolent North in Canadian Literature* (Virago, 2004).

3   R.K. Headland, *Transits of the North West Passage to the End of the 2019 Navigation Season* (Scott Polar Research Institute, 2020).

4   Guidance on paper restoration and conservation was obtained from: Harwell Restoration Company; National Archives of Ireland; Royal Museum's Greenwich; Victoria & Albert Museum.

Bibliography

Books

The volume of books written over the centuries about exploration of the Arctic and Antarctic regions is too vast to detail here. The list below shows those which were consulted and were most helpful to my research. It is by no means comprehensive and should be considered as a personal choice.

Alexander, Alison, *The Ambitions of Jane Franklin – Victorian Lady Adventurer* (Allen & Unwin, 2016).

Amundsen, Roald, *My Life As An Explorer* (Wm. Heinemann, 1927).

Amundsen, Roald, *The South Pole* (Hurst & Co., 1912).

Atwood, Margaret, *Strange Things: The Malevolent North in Canadian Literature* (Virago, 2004).

Barrow, John, *Autobiographical Memoir* (John Murray, 1847).

Barrow, John, *The Eventful History of the Mutiny and Piratical Seizure of HMS Bounty: Its Causes and Consequences* (John Murray 1831).

Barrow, John, *Voyages of Discovery and Research within the Arctic Regions: From the Year 1818 to the Present Time* (John Murray, 1846).

Battersby, William, *James Fitzjames – The Mystery Man of the Franklin Expedition* (The History Press, 2010).

Beattie, Owen and Geiger, John, *Frozen in Time: The Fate of the Franklin Expedition* (Grafton Books, 1989).

Berton, Pierre, *The Arctic Grail* (Viking Penguin, 1988).

Bryan, Rorke, *Ordeal By Ice – Ships of the Antarctic* (The Collins Press, 2011).

Bruce, William Speirs *Polar Exploration* (Williams and Norgate, 1911).

Burke's Landed Gentry.

Charlwood, Admiral Edward *Passages from the Life of a Naval Officer,* (Private 1869).

Cherry-Garrard, Apsley, *The Worst Journey in the World* (Penguin, 1983).

Clarke, R.S.J., *The Heart of Downe: Old Banbridge Families* (Ulster Historical Foundation Publications, 1989).

Cookman, Scott, *Ice Blink: The Tragic Fate of Sir John Franklin's Lost Expedition* (John Wiley, 2000).

Corner, George W., *Doctor Kane of the Arctic Seas* (Temple University Press, 1972).

Courtney, Nicholas, *Gale Force 10 – The Life and Legacy of Admiral Beaufort* (Headline Publishing, 2003).

Cunnane, Jarlath, *Northabout: Sailing the North East and North West Passages* (The Collins Press, 2006).

Cyriax, Richard J., *Sir John Franklin's Last Arctic Expedition* (Arctic Press, 1997).

Dodge, Ernest S., *The Polar Rosses* (Faber and Faber, 1973).

Eber, Dorothy Harley, *Encounters on the Passage: Inuit Meet the Explorers* (University of Toronto Press, 2008).

Edric, Robert, *The Broken Lands* (Jonathan Cape, 1992).

Fitzpatrick, Kathleen, *Sir John Franklin in Tasmania* (Melbourne University Press, 1949).

Fleming, Fergus, *Barrow's Boys* (Granta Books, 1998).

Fleming, Fergus, *Ninety Degrees North: The Quest for the North Pole* (Granta Books, 2001).

Fluhmann, May, *Second in Command: A Biography of Captain Francis Crozier* (Government of Northwest Territories, 1976).

Franklin, John, *Narrative of a Journey to the Shores of the Polar Seas in the Years 1819–22* (John Murray, 1823).

Franklin, John, *Narrative of Some passages in the History of Van Diemen's Land* (privately printed, 1845).

Friendly, Alfred, *Beaufort of the Admiralty: The Life of Sir Francis Beaufort 1774–1857 (*Random Press, 1977).

Geiger, John & Alanna Mitchell, *Franklin's Lost Ship: The Historic Discovery of HMS Erebus* (HarperCollins, 2017).

Gurney, Alan, *Below the Convergence* (Pimlico, 1998).

Hayes, J. Gordon, *The Conquest of the North Pole* (Thornton Butterworth, 1934).

Houston, C. Stuart, (Ed), *Arctic Ordeal: The Journal of John Richardson, 1820–22*
    (McGill-Queen's University Press, 1984).

Hutchinson, Gillian, *Sir John Franklin's Erebus and Terror Expedition – Lost and
    Found* (Bloomsbury, 2017).

Jones, A.G.E., *Polar Portraits* (Caedmon of Whitby, 1992).

Korn, Alfons, *The Victorian Visitors* (University of Hawaii Press, 1958).

Lambert, Andrew, *Franklin – Tragic Hero of Polar Navigation* (Faber and Faber, 2009).

Lambert, Richard S., *Franklin of the Arctic* (The Bodley Head, 1954).

Latta, Jeffrey Blair, *The Franklin Conspiracy* (Dundurn Press, 2001).

Linn, Richard, *A History of Banbridge* (Banbridge Chronicle Press, 1935).

Lloyd, C., *Mr Barrow of the Admiralty* (Collins, 1970).

Loomis, Chauncey, *Weird & Tragic Stories: The Story of Charles Francis Hall
Explorer* (Macmillan, 1971).

Lopez, Barry, *Arctic Dreams* (Picador, 1987).

Lyon, George F., *Private Journal During the recent Voyage of Discovery Under
    Captain Parry* (John Murray, 1824).

Maguire, W.A., *The Downshire Estates in Ireland 1801–1845* (Clarendon Press, 1972).

Markham, Sir Clements, *The Life of Sir Leopold McClintock* (John Murray, 1909).

McCannon, John, *A History of the Arctic: Nature, Exploration and Exploitation*
    (Reaktion Books, 2012).

McGoogan, Ken, *Ancient Mariner: The Amazing Adventures of Samuel Hearne*
    (Bantam Books, 2004).

McGoogan, Ken, *Fatal Passage: The Untold Story of John Rae* (Harper Collins, 2001).

McGoogan, Ken, *Lady Franklin's Revenge* (Bantam Press, 2006).

McClintock, Sir Leopold, *The Voyage of the 'Fox' in the Arctic Seas* (John Murray, 1859).

Mirsky, Jeanette, *To the Arctic* (Allan Wingate, 1949).

Mowat, Farley, *Ordeal by Ice* (Little Brown, 1960).

Murphy, David, *The Arctic Fox: Francis Leopold McClintock* (The Collins Press, 2004).

Nanton, Paul, *Arctic Breakthrough* (William Kimber, 1971).

Navy List (1810–54).

Neatby, Leslie H., *Search for Franklin* (Arthur Barker, 1970).

Nugent, Frank, *Seek the Frozen Lands* (The Collins Press, 2003).

Owen, Roderic, *The Fate of Franklin* (Hutchinson, 1978).

Palin, Michael, Erebus*: The Story of a Ship* (Hutchinson, 2018).

Parry, Ann, *Parry of the Arctic* (Chatto and Windus, 1963).

Parry, William Edward, *Journal of a Second Voyage for the Discovery of a North-West Passage in the Years 1821–23* (John Murray, 1824).

Parry, William Edward, *Journal of a Third Voyage for the Discovery of a North- West Passage in the Years 1824–25* (John Murray, 1826).

Parry, William Edward, *Narrative of an Attempt to Reach the North Pole in the Year 1827* (John Murray, 1828).

Peters, Maureen, *Jean Ingelow: Victorian Poetess* (Boydell Press, 1972).

Philbrick, Nathaniel, *Sea of Glory* (HarperCollins, 2004).

Potter, Russell, *Finding Franklin: The Untold Story of a 165-Year Search*, (McGill-Queens University Press, 2016).

Poulsom, Neville, *The White Ribbon: A Medallic Record of British Polar Exploration* (Seaby 1968).

Rawnsley, Willingham F., *The Life, Diaries and Correspondence of Lady Jane Franklin 1792–1875* (Erskine Macdonald, 1923).

Regard, Frederic, (Ed), *Arctic Exploration in the Nineteenth Century: Discovery the Northwest Passage* (Pickering & Chatto, 2013).

Richards, R.L., *Dr John Rae* (Caedmon of Whitby, 1985).

Riffenburg, Beau, *The Myth of the Explorer* (Belhaven Press, 1993).

Ross, James Clark, *A Voyage of Discovery and Research in the Southern Antarctic Regions during the Years 1839–43* (John Murray, 1847).

Ross, Sir John, *Narrative of a Second Voyage In Search of A North West Passage and of a Residence in the Arctic Regions 1829, 1830, 1831, 1833* (A.W. Webster, 1835).

Ross, M.J. *Polar Pioneers: John Ross and James Clark Ross* (McGill-University Press, 1994).

Ross, M.J., *Ross in the Antarctic* (Caedmon of Whitby, 1982).

Savours, Ann, *The Search for the North West Passage* (Chatham Publishing, 1999).

Scott, Sir Walter, *The Poetical Works of Sir Walter Scott* (Frederick Warne and Co., 1895).

Smith, Michael, *Polar Crusader – Sir James Wordie* (Birlinn, 2004).

Smith, Michael, *Shackleton – By Endurance We Conquer* (Collins, 2014).

Spufford, Francis, *I May Be Some Time* (Faber and Faber, 1996).

Stefansson, Vilhjalmur, *My Life With the Eskimo* (Harrap and Co., 1924).

Stefansson, Vilhjalmur, *The Friendly Arctic* (Macmillan and Co., 1921).

Stephens, G., *The Hutchins School 1846–1965* (Blubber Head Press, 1979).

Thomson, George M., *The North West Passage* (Secker and Warburg, 1975).

Traill, H.D., *The Life of Sir John Franklin* (John Murray, 1896).

Thwaite, Anne, *Emily Tennyson: The Poet's Wife* (Faber and Faber, 1996).

Vaughan, Richard, *The Arctic: A History* (Sutton Publishing, 1994).

Wallace, Hugh N., *The Navy, the Company and Richard King* (McGill-Queen's University Press, 1980).

Watson, Paul, *Ice Ghosts: The Epic Hunt for the Lost Franklin Expedition* (W.W. Norton & Company, 2018).

Woodman, David C., *Strangers Among Us* (McGill-Queen's University Press, 1995).

Woodman, David C., *Unravelling the Franklin Mystery* (McGill-Queen's University Press, 1991).

Woodward, Frances J., *Portrait of Jane: A Life of Lady Franklin* (Hodder & Stoughton, 1951).

Wright, Noel, *Quest for Franklin* (Heinemann, 1959).

Newspapers, Journals, Websites, etc

Arctic Book Review

Banbridge Chronicle

Banbridge Household Almanac

Bann Standard

Belfast Telegraph

Colonial Times

Dublin Evening Mail

East Anglian Daily Times

Equinox

Food Australia

Geographical Journal

The Guardian

Hobart Town Courier & Van Diemen's Land Gazette

Illustrated London News

Ireland's Own

Journal of the Craigavon Historical Society
Northern Whig
Polar Record
Royal Astronomical Society Monthly Notices
Scottish Geographical Magazine
Sunday News
The Times

Articles

Barrett, Cyril 'The Crozier Memorial' (publisher unknown, 1976).

Crone, Dr J.S., 'Distinguished Downshire Men – Captain Crozier', *Northern Whig*, (9 October 1906).

Crone, Dr J.S., 'Crozier, The Heroic Explorer', *The Household Almanac* (1907).

Cunningham, William, (Ed. Richard Campbell), 'The Journal of Sergeant William K Cunningham of HMS *Terror*' (The Hakluyt Society, 2009).

Debenham, Frank, '*Erebus* and *Terror* at Hobart', *Polar Record*, vol. 3 issue 23 (1942).

Headland, Robert, 'Transits of the Northwest Passage to the End of 2019' (Scott Polar Research Institute, March 2020).

Jones, A.G.E., 'Captain Robert Martin: A Peterhead Whaling Master in the 19th Century', *Scottish Geographical Magazine* (December 1969).

Jones, A.G.E., 'The Voyage of HMS *Cove*, 1835–36', *Polar Record*, no. 5, issue 40 (July 1950).

Keenleyside, Anne, Margaret Bertulli and Henry C Fricke, 'The Final Days of the Franklin Expedition: New Skeletal Evidence,' *Arctic*, vol. 50, no. 1 (March 1997).

Kerr, John, 'Crozier of Banbridge', *Journal of the Craigavon Historical Society*, vol. 5, no. 1 (date unknown).

Lloyd-Jones, Ralph, 'The Men Who Sailed With Franklin', *Polar Record*, vol. 41 issue 4 (2005).

Lloyd-Jones, Ralph, 'The Paranormal Arctic: Lady Franklin, Sophia Cracroft and Captain and "Little Weesy' Coppin", *Polar Record*, vol. 37 issue 200 (January 2001).

McCorristine, Shane, 'A Manuscript History of the Franklin Family by Sophia Cracroft', *Polar Record*, vol. 51, issue 1, pp. 72-90 (2015).

O'Farrell, Joe, 'Ships In The Ice', *Nimrod: The Journal of the Ernest Shackleton Summer School* (October 2011).

Rahmani, Geraldine, 'Francis Crozier', *Arctic*, no. 37 (1984).

Richards, Sir George, 'Death of Miss Cracroft', *Royal Geographical Society Proceedings*, no. 14 (1892).

Royal Astronomical Society, 'Francis Crozier Obituary', *Monthly Notices of Royal Astronomical Society*, vol. 15 (1854–55).

Rudd, Rev. Canon C.R.J., 'Moira: A Historical Handbook' (date and publisher unknown).

Stein, Glen M., 'Antarctic Fidelity Rewarded: Sergeant William Cunningham, Royal Marines', *Antarctic Circle* (2009).

Stenton, Douglas R, 'A Most Inhospitable Coast: The Report of Lieutenant William Hobson's 1859 Search for the Franklin Expedition on King William Island', *Arctic*, vol. 67 no. 4 (December 2014).

Stenton, Douglas R, Anne Keenleyside and Robert W Park, 'The Boat Place: New Skeletal Evidence from the 1845 Franklin Expedition', *Arctic*, vol. 68 no. 1 (March 2015).

Archives

Archives Office of Tasmania

Banbridge Genealogy Services, Banbridge (BGS)

Banbridge Library, Banbridge (BLB)

Bank of England, London

Berkshire Record Office (BRO)

British Library, London (BL)

National Archive, London (NA)

National Maritime Museum, London (NMM)

Public Record Office North Ireland, Belfast (PRONI)

Royal Astronomical Society, London (RAS)

Royal Naval Museum, Portsmouth (RNM)

Royal Society, London (RS)

Scott Polar Research Institute, Cambridge (SPRI)

Unpublished diaries, journals, letters, etc.

Banbridge Urban District Council, pamphlet, January 1939, re. Crozier Memorial (RGS).

Bernacchi, Louis, letter to Royal Geographical Society, 29 November 1938, re. Crozier Memorial (RGS).

HM *Cove* 1835–36: log, ADM 51/3586; master's log, ADM 52/3994; muster roll, ADM 37/8947 (NA).

Cracroft, Sophia, journal, autumn 1843–June 1844; notes of letters 1844–56 (SPRI); will, J 121/1270 (NA).

Crozier Family, *Early Crozier Memorials* (published privately, *c.* 1830, revised *c.* 1870, PRONI); Crozier family history (BGS).

Crozier, Charlotte, note on birth of Francis Crozier (RSG).

Crozier, Francis Rawdon Moira: family history, D/2714/5A (PRONI); letters to Admiralty re. piloting, c. 1843 (RGS); letters to Charlotte Crozier, Sarah Crozier, Thomas Crozier, 1 October 1836 (RGS); letter to Thomas Crozier 14 July 1841 (RGS); letters to Sir John Franklin, Sir James Clark Ross (SPRI); letters to Charlotte Crozier, 19 February 1845, 3 June 1845 (PRONI); letter to John Henderson, 4 July 1845 (NMM); letter to Lord Minto, 16 August 1841 (RGS); certificate of Admiralty examination, 22 January 1816 (RGS); log of HMS *Hecla* November 1826–September 1827, ADM 55/69 (NA); last will and testament, 11/2198 (NA).

Crozier, Graham, letter to James Clark Ross, 1856 (SPRI).

Crozier, Commander Louis, letters re. Crozier Memorial, 1938 (RGS).

Crozier, Major Sir Thomas, letters to Louis Bernacchi, November–December, 1938 re: Crozier Memorial (RGS).

Franklin, Lady Jane, correspondence with James Clark Ross, 1840–45 (SPRI); letter to Admiralty, 24 February 1854 (RGS).

Gardiner, Captain Allen, letter re. Captain Crozier (BRO).

HMS *Hecla*, log, 1826–27 (NA).

McLaren, Allan, journal of Allan McLaren on HMS *Hecla*, February 1824–October 1825 (NA).

National Maritime Museum, re: Francis R.M. Crozier, watch, E1874 (NMM).

Nugent, Frank, Lament for Francis Crozier

Ross, Anne, letter to Francis Crozier, 6 January 1848 (SPRI).

Ross, Sir James Clark, letters to Admiralty re: Francis Crozier, 30 September 1836 (RGS); letter to Francis Crozier, 1848 (SPRI).

Royal Astronomical Society, letters to Francis R.M. Crozier, 1840; papers re. Francis R.M. Crozier proposal for fellowship, 1826–27 (RAS).

Royal Geographical Society, letter to Louis Bernacchi, 30 November 1938 re:

Crozier Memorial; letter to Banbridge Urban District Council, 13 December 1938 (RGS).

Royal Society, papers re. Francis R.M. Crozier, fellowship, EC/1843/24 (RS); fellowship election papers, 8 December 1843 (RGS).

HMS *Stag*, log and muster roll, 1831, ADM 32/439 (NA).

HMS *Terror*, log and meteorological record kept by Captain Francis Crozier, 1840 and 1843, MSS 77 and MSS 78 (RNM).

Index